a Gift to wo

a wonderful son:

[illegible]

# General Anders and the soldiers of the The Second Polish Corps

By
Harvey Sarner

Published by Brunswick Press
1997
Cathedral City, CA

Library of Congress catalog card number 97-094609
ISBN 1-888521-13-9

First Edition
1997

Published by Brunswick Press
P.O. Box 2244, Cathedral City, CA 92235

Printed in the United States by
McNaughton & Gunn, Inc., Saline, MI.

Dedicated

To the memory of

Jan Romanowski

Soldier - Engineer - Friend

# INTRODUCTION

This book is about General Wladyslaw Anders and the soldiers of the Polish Army which was formed under his command in the Soviet Union in 1941, evacuated to the Middle East in 1942 and, as the Second Polish Corps fought with distinction in Italy in 1944-1945. It is the story of hundreds of thousands of men and women, who after being deported from Poland struggled to find and fight their way home. They went through the glaciers and taigas of Siberia, up the Steppes of Kazakhhstan, past the marshes of Iran, across the deserts of Iraq and Palestine and finally through the mountains and canyons of Italy's Apennine Peninsula.

This is the true story of an Army in Exile, which having set out on its path dressed in rags and armed with wooden rifles, achieved numerous feats of valor. The greatest of which was to capture the seemingly impregnable fortress of Monte Cassino which was defended by crack German troops. Their story is profoundly tragic because for most of these men and women the hope of returning to their homeland, the hope which helped them survive six arduous years of war, did not materialize. This sad denouement epitomizes the fate of Poland during the Second World War.

I first heard about General Anders and his soldiers when a Polish-American physician told me that she had learned Hebrew when she was with the Polish Army in Palestine during the Second World War. I could hardly believe my ears. The Polish Army in Palestine!! Subsequently, I read about this subject and ended up studying it for ten years, during which I made over a hundred visits to several dozen libraries and archives in the United States, Poland, the USSR, Israel, England, and France and conducted over 180 interviews with the army's former officers and soldiers.

This is not, of course the first book on the subject. It is, however, much more comprehensive than any other existing account since I was able to unearth information missed by earlier researchers or not available to them. I was able to get more than 100 documents declassified at the National Archives in Washington, D.C.

Some of the veterans and others who previously had been reticent to speak up were now willing to share their stories. This was due to a feeling that time was running out as much as the fact that the Soviet yoke finally was taken off Poland's neck. Some still feared Soviet retaliation on their families in Poland if they would talk about their experiences in the USSR 50 years ago.

Barbara Tuchman, in one of her lesser known books, "Writing History" argues that oral testimony should never be included as history unless confirmed by documentary evidence. Having said that, I will now explain why I have not followed what is otherwise sound advice.

Its easy to succumb to the temptation of quoting recognized authorities and get information from secondary sources rather than to do primary research. A quote from a written document made by one historian and uncritically repeated by another soon acquires the authority of "common knowledge". The best example I encountered of this is book by a Jewish chaplain in the Polish Army, Leon Rozen, which is taken as gospel on conditions for Jews soldiers while the army was in the Soviet Union. Until I called attention to him, no one ever took the trouble of interviewing another Jewish chaplain, who was in Anders' Army from the beginning until almost the last day, compared to Rozen who was in the army for a relatively short period. Rabbi Rosengarten tells an entirely different story including the fact that Rozen was expelled from the Polish Army without objection from other Jewish Chaplains. But Rozen's comments were written and Rosengarten's were not!

Another example that demonstrates that oral testimony is at least as valuable as written testimony involves the little known fact that Menachem Begin first came to Palestine as a soldier in Anders' Polish Army. Begin refused to desert on grounds that a deserter could not lead the Irgun. He was released from the army with an honorable discharge. The British were upset about Anders' cooperating with Jewish interests so a document was put in the Polish Army files indicating Begin was given an extended leave but did not return, which according to the document made him a deserter. I showed the document to Merek Kahan, another Irgun leader, who immediately characterized the document as false. He laughed as he confessed that he was the author of the forged document. These two examples prove that oral testimony is as good, if not better, at times than documentation.

This is not to suggest that oral testimony is always accurate and valuable. Far from it. Some of the interviews were entirely worthless and some were of limited value. Some had little or no information and wasted time by telling the obvious. Others tried to pass off something they read as a personal experience. The most difficult were those who were confused between what happened and what they would have liked to have happened.

I learned not to ignore oral testimony just because it sounds fantastic. When Ludwig Lubienski told me about 400 Polish airmen who escaped from internment in Romania disguised as Hasidic Jews, I dismissed the story as incredible. I couldn't imagine 400 Polish airmen dressed in black gabardine, growing beards and changing the color and style of their hair. To my amazement, when I told this story to Keith Sword, he said this incident was recorded in an interview he had with Sir Robin Hankey in 1952. In 1939-1940 Lubienski and Hankey were close to the scene, the former being interned in Romania as secretary to the Polish Foreign Minister and the latter as the first Secretary of the British Embassy in Warsaw which evacuated with the Polish government to Romania. When confirmed by two such respected and well informed individuals the story must be accepted, although I still have some doubts.

Apart from predictable and obvious ethnic loyalties, I encountered others which were not expected or which were much stronger than anticipated. One was loyalty to the army. A significant number of interviewees would not tolerate any question or suggestion which was even implicitly critical of the army or its officers. Such attitudes result in the fabrication of history. For example, no previous history mentions that the failure of the Polish army's first assault on Monte Cassino was caused in part by the conduct of a senior officer who failed to launch a diversionary attack.

Most surprising was the continued intensity of the animosity between the pro-Pilsudski and anti-Pilsudski factions which largely corresponded to the anti and pro-Sikorski split. It was not appreciated at first that 50 years later the answers to my questions were affected by the interviewee's affiliation with one or the other faction. But the greatest loyalty of a few were to political parties, some of which had not been viable for two generations.

A word about relying on translators. Translations were needed for almost a dozen languages, including Polish, Russian, German, Hebrew and Yiddish. Being monolingual there was a need to rely heavily on translators, who, in addition to literal translations, were sometimes required to make decisions as to which sentences or paragraphs were worthy of translation. The potential bias of translators was an important consideration. Two controls were instituted.

First, a translator was asked to translate at least one document that had been previously translated, for the purpose of comparison. The second control was to reject a translator who showed bias. In two instances the bias was not immediately recognized. In those instances the sensitive documents were translated again. Most, but not all, of the many translators did so in good faith and made an effort to control their own bias.

I relied very heavily on what could be called impeccable witnesses. In addition to the usual problems associated with all witnesses, there is a special problem with the impeccable witness. He is not infallible and may have a lapse of memory, a personal ax to grind, or a prejudice. His good material could lead into the trap of accepting everything he says as being unimpeachable. After finding this rare witness, there is the tendency to accept everything as gospel, and therein is the trap. Three examples will suffice.

Rabbi Rosengarten was as close to being an impeccable witness as anyone interviewed. We talked about Koltubanka and he agreed with a historian who claimed there were no photos taken at Koltubanka. At a subsequent interview I produced some photos which he identified as having been taken at Koltubanka. After the passage of "only" 50 years, he had forgotten the photos. He is still an excellent witness and would be the first to agree that no witness is infallible.

Another example. A two-volume work on the life of Jabotinsky and the Revisionist movement fails to mention the name of Merek Kahan with whom the author was at odds, so this otherwise excellent source fails to mention Kahan.

The third example is more complex, but probably occurs more often. In this case, the individual interviewed proved to be an excellent witness and source of good information, but one piece of information turned out to be false. He said that live ammunition had been distributed to the Polish soldiers being inspected by General Sikorski in 1943, when he visited the Middle East. In a dozen interviews with people who should have known, it was said that live ammunition was not issued. Later, this otherwise impeccable source explained that at the time of the interview, he wanted to make a complicated political point and to do so he elected to contrive the ammunition story. He was going to use me for his own purposes. He was not the only one.

Two more problems were encountered relating to almost all witnesses, which include oral and written reports. There is the addition of second hand information when the witness strays from his own experience and starts to provide information gained from his reading or from what others told him. There is also the obvious, the halo complex, striving not only to present one's self in the best light but doing the same for one's group or organization.

In collecting information we are always faced with the witness being tempted to make the story more interesting. This is the major reason why witnesses were not be paid for their testimony, i.e. they would then be tempted to make their story more interesting to justify the compensation. In retrospect, it was a mistake to conduct some interviews in very nice restaurants. I would cringe each time a guest-interviewee asked at the end of the meal, "Was it worth it?", i.e. did they provide enough information to justify the expense? The implication was that, if necessary they would provide more information to justify the expense, even if they had to fabricate it.

For his doctorate, a historian reinterviewed witnesses asking the same questions five years after the initial interview. He noted that at the second interview, the witnesses moved themselves closer to the center of the events and their roles had grown in importance. The same tendency was noted when I interviewed some witnesses a second time.

Another problem was the tendency to generalize from one's own experience. For example, a soldier who wrote of his experiences providing much good information, described the manner in which the Polish Army moved from the USSR to Iran in 1942. The vast majority went by train to a Soviet port on the Caspian Sea, and then by ship to Palavi in Iran. This witness was one of the small minority who traveled the over land route by truck. Writing from his own experience, he tells that the route from the USSR to Iran was over land, and only a few went by ship. An understandable but significant error.

A critic may complain that this book about Anders' Army gives a disproportionate amount of attention to Jewish issues. There are two reasons for this. First, Jewish issues were of major concern to the Polish Government in Exile and to Anders' Army and second, they are naturally of interest to a Jewish writer.

Poles and Jews lived together in Poland for 900 years, each group smugly convinced of its superiority over the other. The degree of mutual insensitivity was amazing. The Poles seemed insensitive of the emotional impact of what they said to Jews and Jews seemed insensitive to the fact that three million non-Jewish Poles, including 1,500 Roman Catholic clergy were killed in the Second World War.

An interview with one Jewish woman, who said she hated the Poles, demonstrates the complexity of the Polish Jewish relationship. She was asked to give an example of an event which justified her hatred. She was in a Nazi slave labor factory where Jewish women repaired army coats and where their food rations were below the subsistence level. The women survived because a Polish foreman surreptitiously provided them with food. The Germans caught the Pole and the Jewish women were forced to witness his execution. Thus, asked for a reason why she hated Poles, the woman narrated a story of a Pole who forfeited his life to help Jews. When I pointed out the contradiction, she cried, "I know, I know, its so confusing".

In the preface to "Witness," the historian Rafael Scharf writes,

> "In their understandable resentment of the misfortunes that engulfed them, Jews were often not sufficiently sensitive to the Polish situation and the agonizing choices facing their neighbors. Only by comparison with the terminal tragedy of the Jews does the fate of the Polish people appear tolerable. By any other standards, their sacrifices, their suffering and their losses during the war, mark them out as the great victims of their history and geography."

To which I add, the Poles see themselves as fellow victims, but the tragedy of the Jews makes it difficult for some Jews to see most Poles as anything other than gentile villains. A Rabbi disappointed me when he said, "Jews lost 90% and the Poles lost only 10%; their losses aren't comparable, and I have no room in my heart for their suffering." But, a Jewish philosopher said, "If we lose our humanity, then we Jews have suffered two holocausts, the holocaust of the body, which was inflicted upon us, and the holocaust of the soul, which we risk inflicting on ourselves."

The Poles have been notoriously weak in public relations in telling their story to the Western world. To often their story has been written as a comparison to Jewish history and has been offensive to Jews. Instead of a comparison between Jewish and Polish suffering the approach should be along the following line; The Jews have suffered like no others and their tragedy is unequaled in history, but for the moment we are considering another tragedy, that of the Polish people who also suffered. And then there should be little or no further reference to Jews in telling the Polish story.

A word of explanation is needed here about the terms "Pole" and "Jew". Especially, an American might wonder, Weren't the Polish Jews also Poles? Both groups were citizens of Poland, but a distinction is made between "citizenship" and "nationality", a distinction foreign to Americans. Hence, the use of the term "Pole"or "Jew" (or "Ukrainian or Byelorussian) indicates a person's "nationality" and presupposes Polish citizenship unless otherwise stated, very much like Americans using the term Polish-American which denotes American citizenship with a Polish background. It's reminiscent of the comment of an Israeli who said when he lived in Poland he was a "Jew", and he didn't become a "Pole" until he arrived in Israel.

Another term that needs comment is "of Jewish origin" which may seem to imply conversion, but is also used in polite Polish society to avoid using of the word "Jew" which is so often used as a pejorative.

"Palestine" is used in referring to events that occurred prior to the founding of the Jewish State, and "Israel" is used thereafter. "USSR" is used interchangeably with "Russia", even though we appreciate that Russia was one of the Soviet Republics. We conform in this common error otherwise it could be exact but confusing. Reference is made to the "Soviet Union" as it existed in the years covered in this book and the subsequent dissolution of the USSR is ignored.

The most significant source of documentation was the Public Record Office in Kew Gardens, England. The organization of information at "Kew" is second to none. The problem however is that many files with titles suggesting significant information, are still closed. In contrast the files of the United States National Archives in Washington, D.C. and Maryland, were treasure troves, often providing information that is still classified and is unavailable at Kew. The problem with the National Archives is poor organization caused in part by changing methods of identifying documents and the fact that some files had no more identification than "Poland". The interest in wartime Polish affairs is greater in London than in Washington, D.C., which may explain why much of the information available in the National Archives has not been seen by historians.

When using material from interviews, I sometimes give the name of the source, more often the source is merely identified as a soldier. In some cases this is because the witness wouldn't talk unless I agreed not to identify the source.

Special effort has been made to accurately report statements, especially those attributed to named individuals. If anyone is misquoted, the error was made in good faith and an apology is offered.

Although not within the scope of the purpose of this book, after making more than 100 references to OSS reports I am compelled to make some comment about the American intelligence community, especially the OSS. The intelligence reports have limited value as it seems anyone who wanted to make a point or spread propaganda fed "information" to an OSS agent who would classify and then distribute it as an intelligence report.

Acknowledgments: A list of the persons interviewed follows and everyone is thanked for their contributions. But there is one person who has had the patience to stick with this project almost from the very beginning. Of course I am referring to the late Jan Romanowski, aide to General Anders. Without his help it would have been another two years of labor to produce this book and for this I am grateful. Others, who went above and beyond, were the late Ely Tavin (Director of the Jabotinsky Institute in Tel Aviv) Mrs. Renata Anders, widow of General Wladyslaw Anders, Ludwig Lubienski and members of the Polish-Jewish veterans' organization in London.

We acknowledge with thanks the editing services of Wojciech Kwiryn Siewierski and Lori Sarner.

Harvey Sarner
Palm Springs, CA

## LT. GENERAL WLADYSLAW ANDERS
## 1892-1970

Wladyslaw Anders was born August 11, 1892, in the Village of Blonie, 60 miles west of Warsaw, in what was then a part of the Russian Empire. At the time of his birth Poland did not exist as an Independent country, having been divided between Russia, Prussia and Austria at the end of the 18th century. His father held a degree in agriculture science and earned his living as an administrator of country estates.

Wladyslaw attended a technical high school in Warsaw and later went to the Polytechnic in Riga, capital of present day Latvia, which at that time was under Russian rule. After graduation Anders continued his education at the Russian Military School for reserve officers and was commissioned as an officer in the Russian Army on the eve of the First World War.

Mobilized during the First World War, he served in the Russian Cavalry and was wounded several times. In 1917, when as a result of the February Revolution Poles were allowed to form a separate Polish Corps in the Russian Army he switched to that Corps and was given command of the 1st squadron of the 1st Krechowiecki Lancers Regiment. Soon he was promoted to Chief of Staff of the 1st Infantry Division. When Poland miraculously regained independence in November, 1918, Anders joined the newly created Polish Army. At the dawn of Poland's independence he fought against the Red Army in the Polish-Soviet War of 1919-1920 and received the highest Polish military decoration -the Silver Cross of the Virtuti Militari. After Poland's victory in the war against the Bolsheviks he was sent to the French staff academy, Ecole Superieur de Guerre, and upon graduation returned to Poland where he served on the general staff under General Rozwadowski.

Although sympathetic to the objectives and motives of Marshal Pilsudski, Anders would not break his oath to the legitimate government when the Marshal launched a coup d'etat in May 1926. He led the defense of the Presidential Palace and smuggled the President and his ministers to safety. When as a result of the coup, Marshal Pilsudski took power in Poland, he respected Anders' loyalty to the previous regime and welcomed him as an officer loyal to the new government. In 1931 Anders impressed Pilsudski during the war games and was given command of a cavalry brigade. His commanding general wrote an evaluation of Anders rating him very highly and describing him as qualified for the highest military posts. Three years later Anders was promoted to the rank of general.

From an early age Anders had a great love for horses and riding. He was a first class rider and led the Polish equestrian team in the Olympics in Nice where the team won four cups, including the Nations Cup. Because of his fascination for horses and his life style of a gallant bon vivant he was often described as a typical Russian or Polish cavalry officer.

Anders' three brothers all followed a military career. During the Second World War, two of them became German prisoners of war and the third served in the Second Polish Corps. Anders was raised a Protestant (Evangelical Church) but kept his vow to enter the Roman Catholic Church if he survived imprisonment in Russia and regained the use of his legs. He was twice married and was survived by his second wife Renata Anders. He had a son and two daughters. He died on the night of May 11-12, 1970, the anniversary of the Polish Army's first attack on the German positions at Monte Cassino.

Anders never returned to Poland after being captured by the Russians in 1939. As an outspoken anti-communist, he could not return to Soviet dominated Poland after the war and spent his post-war years in exile in Great Britain, working on behalf of various charities and welfare organizations. He did not live to see an independent Poland.

# PROLOGUE

In the ninth decade of this century a saga ended that had begun five decades earlier in central Europe. Little notice was taken by those not directly involved with the withdrawal of Russian troops from Poland in 1989, just as scant notice was taken of the Russian invasion of Poland five decades earlier.

Without getting into the relative horrors and bestiality of the German and Russian invaders the fact is the invaders from the east occupied Poland ten times the numbers of years as did the Germans. This is not the story of life in occupied Poland; it's just the opposite. It's the story of Polish soldiers and civilians, gentiles and Jews, gentry and peasantry forcibly taken from their homes in 1939 and the fortunate few who were able to return half a century later.

Their saga began on September 17, 1939, when the Russians from the east invaded Poland which was barely able to contain German invaders from the opposite direction. The result was that more than a million and one-half Polish citizens were deported to the wastelands of the USSR, less than ten percent of whom were destined to ever see their homeland again.

The German invasion of Russia in 1941 saved the lives of some deportees who became soldiers again, brothers in arms with the Soviets they had learned to hate and despise. For some, such as those murdered in Katyn Forest, the amnesty came too late. Nowhere else was a stronger hatred for communism generated than among the Poles who now had to tolerate their Russian allies in order to concentrate efforts to slay the German beast.

One man arose to become both the leader and the symbol of the independent Polish army and community contained in the USSR. Lt. General Wladyslaw Anders was this man. Anders led a portion of the surviving but devastated Poles to the middle-east, to glory on the battlefields of Italy and to exile in England. There was no room in post war occupied Poland for this band of committed anti-communists

Now known as the heroes of Monte Casino and revered as patriots, the men of Anders' Army are welcome in their homeland now that the hated Russians have departed. For most of the exiles the change in circumstances again has come too late. But their name and glory will be long remembered as the soldiers of the Second Polish Corps.

## TABLE OF CONTENTS

**Chapter Six – 193**
**On to Bologna**



**Chapter Seven – 216**
**In Political Limbo**



**Chapter Eight – 254**
**Unwanted Heroes**

# CHAPTER ONE

# SEPTEMBER: DEFEAT AND CAPTIVITY

## The September Campaign

On September 1, 1939, the Second World War began with the German Army crossing the Polish border. No one could have envisioned the death and carnage that would erupt. Over 30 million soldiers and civilians would die in a war that started with a contrived border incident. When the war finally ended six years later neither Poland nor Europe was the same. This would be a total war, pitting against each other not only soldiers on the front lines but whole societies with their propaganda machines. Civilians would become legitimate targets and would be killed in greater numbers than soldiers.

No one expected that Poland alone could successfully resist the Germans. Polish defense preparations were not helped when a general mobilization order was revoked by pressure from the British and French who didn't want to provoke the Germans. The mobilization order was reimposed 24 hours later but the revocation had created chaos and delays.[1] Seventeen days after the

Germans invaded Poland from the west, the Soviets invaded from the East. They were acting in accordance with the secret protocol of the Ribbentrop-Molotov Pact that divided Poland between the USSR and Nazi Germany. In the confusion some Polish soldiers were under the impression that the Red Army was intervening against the Wehrmacht. Poland was doomed. On September 18, the day after Soviet troops had crossed the Polish border, the Commander-in-Chief, Marshal Smigly-Rydz and the Polish Government crossed the border to Romania.[2] Retreating Polish units trying to make their way into Hungary and Romania found themselves being fired upon by German and Soviet troops as well as some Ukrainian irregulars.[3]

According to the Soviets, Poland had ceased to exist as a state and therefore the Soviet Union had the right to fill the vacuum and occupy the eastern half of Poland in order to protect Ukrainian and Byelorussian minorities. To legitimize their occupation, the Soviets conducted "elections" in which candidates advocating incorporating the area into the Soviet Union were elected almost unanimously.[4] This Soviet action found support in rather odd quarters. In the Sunday Express the venerable Lloyd George applauded the Soviet annexation of the eastern half of Poland as an act liberating the Soviet peoples from Polish occupation.[5]

The Polish nation and its armed forces deserved better leadership than they had in the September campaign. According to military experts, the Polish High Command used poor judgment, in 1939. Zealously patriotic, they tried to defend every mile of Polish land when it would have been better to withdraw, consolidate forces and shorten the line of defense.[6] Blame for the collapse of the Polish Army falls on its leadership, especially Marshal Smigly-Rydz. His critics would say that he turned out to be "too small" for his job.

In spite of poor leadership and the overwhelming strength of the Germans and Soviets, the Polish Army generally fought well, as it took Hitler thirty five days to finish the Polish campaign. In comparison, it took him only twenty one days to force the French Army to capitulate in May-June, 1940.[7] Polish persistence to resist was in a large extent due to the devotion and heroism of its young officers. The Polish Army never capitulated to the Germans. Those units that were not totally destroyed tried to follow the Polish Government to Romania and Hungary, hoping to continue fighting the Germans on the Western front. According to the Hague Convention the Romanian Government was obligated to intern Polish officers and soldiers, which contradicted prewar Polish-Romanian agreements. In practice the Romanians were concerned about the great expense involved in maintaining the internees and permitted many Polish soldiers to escape to France and the Balkans, enabling tens of thousands of Polish soldiers to join the newly formed Polish Army in France or the Independent Carpathian Brigade in the Middle East.

One of the few generals to prove themselves on the field of battle was Wladyslaw Anders, who began the September campaign as commander of a cavalry brigade on the border with East Prussia protecting northern approaches to Warsaw. On the fourth day of the war the Polish Northern front collapsed and Anders was put in charge of a group of several large units withdrawing towards the capital. Faced by constant air attacks and pursued by mechanized German troops, Anders skillfully managed to extricate his units from a difficult situation and bring them to Warsaw. He was ordered to take up a position defending Warsaw from the south to prevent the Germans from completely encircling Warsaw in the southeast. When this last task proved impossible his cavalry group was ordered to join the reserves of the high command in Southeastern Poland.

When he learnt of the Soviet attack on the morning of September 17, Anders decided to try to go south and reach the Romanian or Hungarian border between the advancing German and Soviet armies. He hoped the Soviet troops might let them pass without a fight, but the Soviets attacked, and heavy fighting occurred. Surrounded by an overwhelming Soviet force, and out of ammunition, Anders split his unit into small groups hoping they could sneak through to the border. The group led by Anders again ran into Soviet troops, and during the close range fighting that followed, Anders was seriously wounded and later captured.[8]

Anders' cavalry group was one of the very last Polish units to be destroyed.[9] The general proved to be a skillful and resourceful commander in the most difficult of circumstances. Several times he managed to extricate his units from extremely dangerous situations and even his harshest critics agree that he was a capable general, in 1939. Anders himself had nothing to be ashamed of for his conduct in the September campaign of 1939 and could bear no blame for the Polish Army's defeat.

The reaction of Jews to the Soviet invasion is of great interest because it had grave consequences for Polish-Jewish relations during the war and afterwards. Jewish soldiers were fighting side by side with other Polish soldiers against German and Soviet invaders, and Jewish civilians were digging trenches side by side with Polish civilians. Even sworn anti-Semites were moved by the display of Jewish loyalty.

However, relations between Poles and Polish Jews were not enhanced when some Jews welcomed the invading Red Army. For some the new regime meant an opportunity to "get even" for discrimination and humiliation, while others simply saw it as a chance to better their lives. Jan Karski, clearly not an anti-Semite, claimed that some Jews cooperated with the Russians by identifying the Polish officers who would then be arrested. To understand how gravely such actions affected Polish-Jewish relations one has to realize that the majority of the captured Polish officers were later executed by the Soviets at Katyn and other places.

The British Foreign Office also saw Jews as the main collaborators with the Soviet Union, in 1939-40. Frank Savery, who was on the British Embassy staff in Warsaw in

1939 attempting to explain Polish attitudes towards the Jews wrote that "we must not forget that in September last the Jewish population in the provinces occupied by the USSR, notably in Eastern Galicia, with the exception of the wealthy Jews who had much property to lose, sided in the main with the Russian invaders" and that "the Jews in those parts of Poland are still the main support of the Bolshevik regime."[10] Savery's comments reflected the attitude of the Foreign Office which can only be called anti-Semitic.

Some Poles could understand and accept the reasons for Jews being easily misled into welcoming the Russians, what they couldn't accept, however, was the fact that some "fingered" Polish officers who, after being captured by the Soviets, tried to pass as regular soldiers in order to be able to stay with their men or to avoid being categorized as "class enemies."

Jews had good reasons for welcoming the Soviets as there were Ukrainians and others who started robbing and killing them as soon as Polish authority collapsed. The Soviets were also clearly preferable to the Germans who had already started rounding up and killing Jews. In Przemysl 600 prominent Jewish citizens were executed.[11]

## Prisoners of the Soviets

Soon after completing the annexation of the eastern part of the Polish state the Soviet authorities began to deport Polish citizens into remote parts of the USSR, especially Siberia, Northern Russia and Kazakhstan. This was not a new or unknown phenomenon for Poles and other nations of the region, as exile to Siberia had also been a traditional tool of Russian penal policy under the tsars. The Soviet state used deportations for implementing its ethnic and class policies. This time, the scale and brutality of their actions were incomparably greater than under the tsars. After the amnesty General Anders organized a collection of statements from former prisoners about their experiences in Soviet prisons and camps and created a special Documents Bureau to head this operation, which was kept secret from the Soviets. The Director of the Bureau went one step further by not disclosing the information even to the Polish Government fearing that a change of government might result in disclosing the information to the Soviets.[12]

The most common estimate is that one and a half million Polish citizens were deported to the USSR between autumn, 1939, and June, 1941. The figure of one and a half million includes both ethnic Poles and minorities, and soldiers as well as civilians. Those deported can be divided into three categories. First were captured military personnel who were put in POW camps. Second were people accused of criminal behavior by the Soviet authorities who were sent to hard labor camps or prisons. Their crimes were mostly political, the usual being "anti-Soviet behavior or propaganda." Third were those who might be called "improper" deportees. This was the largest group, comprising over a million men, women and children, deported from Eastern Poland and scattered over Siberia, Kazakhstan and Uzbekistan.

According to a recent study there were four major waves of deportations affecting the civilian population. The first began on February 10, 1940, when 220,000 men, women and children were sent to Arkhangelsk region. It affected mostly lower civil servants and settlers with families. In the second wave 320,000 people, mostly women and children, were transported to Kazakhstan on April 13, 1940. This wave included well-off peasants, military families, families of landowners and families of higher civil servants. In June and July of 1940, the authorities deported 240,000 people, mostly refugees from German-occupied Poland. In the last and fourth wave, which occurred just before the German attack on Russia, 300,000 people, mostly members of the intelligentsia, skilled workers, and railway employees were deported. These statistics, which account for a million people, do not include soldiers taken as prisoners of war or people who were arrested and sent to prisons or labor camps.[13]

s never announced their reasons for formal charges were made against he deportees were usually permitted ovable property, and for those who of this privilege it often meant the and death as they had something to ing. Most deportees were sent to rers and they were not allowed to ch they were sent. The death rate very high. An official report from at between 22% and 28% of the etween September, 1941, and

ble statistics as to how many Polish the USSR. Estimates vary from September of 1940, the Red Army at during the September campaign d 190,000 POWs, including over ng to recently declassified Soviet mber of POWs in Soviet hands amounted to 226,391.[16]

The Soviet Union never signed the Geneva Convention, and therefore the Polish prisoners could not benefit from its provisions. The Soviets distinguished between prisoners of war and criminals, but had their own definition of "criminals." Polish soldiers, who would qualify for POW treatment under the Geneva Convention, were considered criminals by the Soviets for committing such crimes as hiding one's rank, illegal crossing of the border, refusal to answer questions or to confess.[17] It would later turn out to be very important whether one had been put in the POW or the "criminal" category because under the Amnesty agreement with the Polish Government Stalin agreed to release all prisoners except "criminals."[18]

Soldiers and officers, with some exceptions, were placed by the Soviets in separate POW camps. Some officers did not reveal their rank and thus found themselves in camps for lower ranks. By mid-November, 1941, most privates and NCOs were released from the camps. About 14,000 were put to road construction in labor camps near Lvov, while 10,400 were "contracted out" by the NKVD to the Ministry of Metallurgy and sent to work in steel plants. All officers, including those from the reserve and those already retired, were retained in captivity, since the Soviets clearly considered them to be potential leaders. All policemen and gendarmes were also kept in captivity. The prisoners in these categories were put into three special camps: 4,700 in Kozelsk, 3,900 in Starobelsk and 5,900 (policemen) in Ostashkov. Altogether, the Soviets kept about 9,500 officers and 6,000 police personnel (including about 250 officers) in these camps.[19]

The Soviets subjected these prisoners to very close surveillance. Beria reported to Stalin in November, 1940, that he had infiltrated the Polish prisoners by placing NKVD agents in the prisons and labor camps. It seems Stalin took a personal interest in the attitudes of Polish POWs, judging by the large number of surveillance reports which he received. The Poles knew of this infiltration and realized it was necessary to be constantly on their guard.[20]

No figures are available of those who were sent to prisons and hard labor camps. Their situation was by far the worst. The prisoners were degraded and humiliated; prison trousers were loose fitting and without belts, which meant the prisoner was always using one hand to keep his pants from falling down. The Kharkov prison had cells in which the prisoner could only stand up. The prisoner excreted standing up and had to stand in his own filth. During interrogation prisoners were routinely beaten and kicked and it was not unusual for the interrogator to put a loaded gun to the prisoner's head. There were more refined tortures like being forced to sit for hours on the very edge of the seat. One Polish prisoner had a small section of his hair shaved, and he was tapped on this spot at two minute intervals by Russian soldiers working in relays. Prisoners were often strapped on their back to a bench and made to look directly into a glaring light with eyes propped open with little sticks. The water torture with water dripping on the victim's head was also used. Interrogators would also put out cigarettes on prisoners' hands.

Conditions in the forced labor camps were also extremely harsh. Most of the camps were located in the part of the USSR east of the Ural Mountains known as Siberia. In the bleakness of Siberia, escape was virtually impossible for in addition to Soviet soldiers, escaped prisoners would have to face the snow and cold of Siberia. Even against these odds, there were attempts and even some successful escapes.[21]

The rule in Soviet labor camps was that prisoners who did not or could not work would have their food rations, already meager, cut even further, regardless of the reason for not working. Such prisoners had to rely on friends or relations willing to share their rations for survival. The Soviets delighted in assigning the most menial jobs to Polish professionals and white collar workers who were unaccustomed to hard physical labor.[22] The mortality rate in the camps was high, especially in the first months, as prisoners died from the exhaustive trip to Siberia.[23]

Prisoners were mostly put to work on construction projects or in mines. For example, Pincus Rosengarten, who would later become a Jewish chaplain in Anders' Army, was sent east to build a railroad. Particularly lethal were the camps at Kolyma where gold was mined. The death rate there was about 30% per year and most survivors were crippled by frost bite. Of the ten thousand Poles sent to Kolyma fewer than two hundred managed to survive.[24] Polish prisoners also worked in uranium mines, with few living to tell their story.

One should add that a small group of Poles, mostly Communists, but also a handful of officers who had personal grievances against the army, voluntarily went to the USSR. Apart from these Poles, tens of thousands of Jews voluntarily went to the USSR, to flee the Nazi killing machine.[25]

Anders himself, after being captured in September, 1939, was at first kept in hospitals but was shifted from one town to another. In December he was transferred to Lviv (Polish Lwow) and locked in a cellar in what was a make-shift NKVD prison. He was interrogated by the NKVD and told he had been arrested for "serious offenses against the Soviet Union" and only if he signed a declaration about his readiness to join the Red Army would he be able to save himself. When he refused to sign he was sent to "Brigidki" prison where he was put in a solitary, unheated cell without windows. Since the temperature outside reached -30 degrees celsius, Anders suffered serious frostbite. This failed to break his will and he still refused to sign the declaration.[26]

In February of 1940, he was transported to the central NKVD prison in Moscow, the notorious Lubianka, where living conditions were somewhat more bearable. After a period of harsh interrogation, during which he was routinely hit in the face and had his chair kicked out from under him, he was moved again, this time to Butyrki prison. In Butyrki he was placed in solitary confinement with a bright light shining on his face day and night. He was again returned to Lubianka in September, 1940, and held there until the amnesty.[27]

## Soviet Plans for a "Polish" Army in the USSR and the "Villa of Happiness"

According to V.S. Parsadanova, a Russian official specializing in Polish-Soviet relations, the Soviet authorities attempted to organize a Polish unit in the Red Army roughly a year before Nazi Germany broke its treaty with the Soviet Union.[28] She claims that an offer was made to General Anders to head this unit. This is indirectly confirmed by Anders who mentions in his autobiography that, in October of 1939, he was invited to join a Polish puppet government under the Soviets and to accept the post of an army commander in the Red Army. Pressure to join the Red Army continued until his February, 1940, transfer to the central NKVD prison Lubianka in Moscow.[29] According to his memoirs the matter was not raised while he was interrogated in Moscow. According to Parsadanova in September-October, 1940, about a dozen Polish officers agreed to join a Polish unit under Soviet auspices but its formation was delayed for lack of an appropriate Polish general to lead it.[30]

Parsadanova's statements are confirmed by a memo that the head of the Soviet security services, the notorious Lavrenti Beria, sent to Stalin on November 2, 1940. Beria recommended formation of a Polish Division to be led by those Polish colonels who had "correct" political opinions and who were "sincere." Beria also thought that Generals Januszajtis and Boruta-Spiechowicz should be used since their names would attract certain circles of former Polish soldiers. The recruitment of Polish soldiers for these units would be conducted by the NKVD and after checking the "attitude" of each soldier the NKVD would send them to division headquarters for appropriate training. Organization and preparation of the Polish Division was to be carried out by the General Staff of the Red Army. The division would contain a special section for the NKVD to insure proper control over the Poles."[31]

The Politburo took six months before it gave a go-ahead to Beria's proposals. It was only on June 2, 1941, three weeks before the Germans attacked the Soviet Union, that a conversion of one of the existing Red Army rifle divisions into a Polish Division was ordered. The conversion was supposed to have been completed by July 1, 1941, by replacing soldiers currently in that division with Polish or Polish speaking personnel.[32]

Attempts to form a Polish military unit suggest that Stalin anticipated a conflict with Nazi Germany since he had no other reason for arming the Poles. However, he obviously had to move very cautiously since he did not want to give Hitler any justification for breaking their non-aggression treaty. An important difference between Polish military units contemplated by the Soviet leadership before June 22, 1941, and those formed under Anders after the Nazi invasion of the USSR was that the former were to be a part of the Red Army, while the latter constituted a separate Polish Army which was subordinate to the sovereign Polish Government in London. What Professor Parsadanova did not mention when talking about plans to use Polish POWs, in 1940, was the fate of the 8,500 Polish officers who had been in three special camps, Kozelsk, Starobelsk and Ostashkov and had not been heard of since the spring of 1940.

A handful of Polish officers managed to get out of these camps, when after intensive interrogation they were brought to Moscow, as potential candidates for the so called "Villa of Happiness" (sometimes called the "Villa of Delight"). The "Villa" was a political indoctrination center created by the Soviets to encourage Polish officers to join the Soviet cause. It was located in Malakhovka, about 30 miles from Moscow, and was a combination of resort hotel and school. The "students" were given better rations and enjoyed better living conditions than prison or labor camp inmates. They were treated as guests rather than as prisoners. The conditions at the Villa were even described as "luxurious." Therefore, later it was not difficult to determine which officers had been at the Villa since their faces reflected their experience. Anyone who looked healthy must have been at the Villa.

The program at the Villa was started with seven senior Polish officers from the camp at Griazovets and twenty one from the Kozielsk camp. Both groups were brought to Moscow in October, 1940, and put in Butyrki prison. They were subjected to intensive interrogation but were well treated. One of the original group of seven was rejected as unwilling to cooperate while the remaining six were transferred to Lubianka prison for further questioning and then sent to the "Villa." Approximately seventy five Polish officers ultimately accepted the Soviet invitation to go to the "Villa."[33] It's not clear who selected them from among other Polish POWs, but the final decision was likely to have been taken by Beria. They were obviously picked because they were deemed willing to cooperate with the Soviet authorities, but rank, popularity and ability were also likely to have been a factor in their selection. The officers invited were chosen from "the most flexible element from among Polish prisoners."[34] Raczynski estimated that among the seventy five who went to the Villa there were fifteen to twenty senior officers holding the rank of Colonel or General.

Those enrolled at the Villa were required to sign a statement obligating them to inform the NKVD of anything they learned that might be of interest to the Soviet authorities. This however was not unique. Officers who were not at the Villa were also given such statements to sign, even after the 1941 amnesty.

Only thirteen officers completed the course of instruction at the Villa. When the Germans invaded Russia they were given Soviet passports and money and placed in apartments in Moscow. Colonel Zygmunt Berling, on behalf of the group, offered to join the Red Army. They were, however, told to join Anders' Army. After reporting to the Polish Military Mission they were sent to various units for active duty.[35]

Soon after his release from prison in August of 1941, Anders was visited by two senior officers from that group (Colonels Zygmunt Berling and Kazimierz Dudzinski), and was very suspicious of them, as they kept stressing a need to cooperate with the Russians. He had already heard of the "Villa" and knew that Berling and some of his compatriots had applied for service in the Red Army even before the Germans attacked the USSR. After the evacuation of the army from the USSR officers who had been to the Villa were put into the "Second Group," which means removed from active service.

## Lt. Col. Zygmunt Berling

Lt. Col Berling was driven by ambition and when Anders failed to promote him from Lt. Colonel to Colonel it became clear that he would never be promoted to general in Anders' Army. Berling's ambition drove him to the alternative, becoming a general in the Red Army. When he was called a "communist" the word was used as a pejorative rather than than description of his philosophy.

Rosengarten called Berling a socialist. General Rudnicki called him an opportunist and a troublemaker and Alexander Werth described him as, "an ugly, burly man with cropped hair, and looking older than his age."

Berling was known to be in favor with the Soviets even before he went to the Villa. In May, 1941, he attended the May Day festivities and was "at liberty" prior to the German invasion of the Soviet Union, suggesting Berling's collaboration started at an early date.

## General Sikorski Takes Command

While Anders and hundreds of thousands of Polish officers, soldiers and civilians were being taken prisoner by the Soviets, important political changes were taking place in the West. After the fall of Poland a new Polish Government in exile was formed in France by General Wladyslaw Sikorski. His main qualifications were his good contacts with the French and his freedom from any responsibility for the September, 1939, disaster. In fact, the Western Allies vetoed an earlier attempt to form a government in exile made up of supporters of the prewar Pilsudski regime.

In May of 1926, when Marshal Joseph Pilsudski, the foremost leader of the Polish independence movement before the First World War, staged a coup d'etat against the legitimately elected parliamentary cabinet, Sikorski repudiated his action. He was removed from active service in the army and became a determined political foe of

Pilsudski and his supporters, who continued to rule Poland after the Marshal's death, in 1935. Because of his opposition to the regime, Sikorski was refused readmission into active service at the outbreak of the war.

In October of 1939, Sikorski, with support from the French and the British, prevailed upon the President of Poland to appoint him simultaneously to three most important posts--that of Prime Minister, Minister of War, and Commander-in-Chief of all Polish Armed Forces. In September of 1942, he relinquished the Ministry of War to his old friend General Marian Kukiel. Sikorski purged the Pilsudskites from the new government and the army which was being formed in France. A rare exception was made in the case of Poland's Ambassador to Great Britain, Edward Raczynski who was left in his post in spite of being a "Pilsudskite" because of his good relations with the British.

The new Polish Prime Minister and Commander-in-Chief was respected as a general, but most people found him pompous and difficult to work with. A British diplomat, Sir Frank Roberts, remembered that it took him a long time to get to know Sikorski but once he did he liked him.[36] Sikorski had a reputation for pettiness. He was also not very popular with the officer corps.

The following story might help to explain why Sikorski was not popular among some of the officers. In November, 1939, Sikorski met with 750 Polish officers in France. He reported briefly on French-Polish relations and then told the audience that the French had agreed to permit Polish officers to wear prewar style square-shaped hats. Sikorski talked about hats but said nothing about the organization of the new army or the military agreement with France. What was worse he introduced the leader of the Peasant Party, Stanislaw Mikolajczyk, who told them that the Polish soldiers had lost all respect for their officers. Perhaps this was true in the case of some senior officers but not for most junior officers. The audience, composed primarily of junior officers, felt Sikorski and Mikolajczyk were trying to blame them for the September defeat. The officers particularly resented hearing such accusations from a civilian.

On the other hand Roberts described Sikorski as the only Pole who could deal with the Russians. Roberts claimed that Stalin considered all Poles puppets of the British, with Sikorski being the only exception.

When France capitulated in June, 1940, tens of thousands of Polish soldiers were evacuated to Britain. Surprisingly, they were not received warmly. Churchill asked Sikorski why he was bringing his soldiers to Britain. One can wonder what Churchill expected Sikorski to do? Of course Churchill's problem was that he had two million men in uniform but only 750,000 rifles.[37]

When the Polish Government reached England, President Wladyslaw Raczkiewicz dismissed Sikorski as Prime Minister after the Polish National Council (the governing body of the Polish Government in exile) adopted a motion of "no confidence." This was partly a reaction to Sikorski's authoritarian personality and partly because the Council blamed Sikorski for delaying, out of loyalty to the French, the evacuation to Great Britain. The delay resulted in a loss of three quarters of the newly formed Polish Army. In the end however, the Vice-President, General Kazimierz Sosnkowski, prevailed upon President Raczkiewicz to retract Sikorski's dismissal. It is ironic that it was Sosnkowski who convinced the President to reinstate Sikorski in 1940, since Sosnkowski was a leading Pilsudskite, and he would himself resign, in 1941, in order to demonstrate disapproval of Sikorski's policies.

Footnotes:

1. T. Rawskki, "Poland Did Not Cease Existence in September," Contemporary Poland, 6 (1989), p. 15.
2. J. Feldman, Z. Wojciechowski, "Poland and Germany: The Last Ten Years," in Poland's Place in Europe (ed.) Z. Wojciechowski (Poznan, 1947), p. 40; General Anders (London, Instytut Polski i Muzeum im. Gen. Sikorskiego, 1989), p. 189.
3. W. Anders, An Army in Exile (London: Macmillan, 1949), p. 10-12.
4. J. Rothschild, Return to Diversity: a Political History of East Central Europe since World War II (New York: Oxford UP, 1993), p. 28.
5. K. Sword, "British Reactions to the Soviet Occupation of Eastern Poland in September of 1939," Slavonic and East European Review, v. LXIX/1 (January 1991), p. 93.
6. J.L. Ready, The forgotten axis: Germany's partners and foreign volunteers in World War II (Jefferson, N.C.: McFarland & Co., 1987), p. 10, 18.
7. R. H. Kennedy, The German Campaign in Poland, 1939 (Washington: Dept. of the Army, 1956), p. 120.
8. W. Anders, An Army in Exile, p. 8-12.
9. S. Zaloga, The Polish Campaign, 1939 (New York: Hippocrene Books, 1985), p. 155, 165.
10. Public Records Office, Kew (England), Foreign Office collection FO 371/24481.
11. J. Gross, Revolution From Abroad: the Soviet Conquest of Poland's Western Ukraine and Western Byelorussia (Princeton, N.J., Princeton UP, 1988), p. 32-33.
12. K. Zamorski, Telling the Truth in Secret (London: Poets and Painters Press, 1994), p. 15.
13. J. Slusarczyk, Stosunki polsko-radzieckie 1939-1945 (Warsaw, 1991), p. 71. Some Polish officers and statesmen claimed that Jews constituted at least 35%, and perhaps as high as 50% of those deported. Interview with Z. Siemaszko. If however the deportations affected mainly military officers, civil servants, governmental officials and others holding jobs from which Jews had traditionally been excluded, then the high percentages of Jews among those deported is probably exaggerated.See HI Anders Boxes 80-87.
14. A report by Mr. Dobkin to the World Jewish Congress (September 24, 1942), Jewish Agency Archive, New York [further cited as JAA].

15. Z. Siemaszko - 196 000, a lecture in the London School of East European and Slavonic Studies (November 23, 1988); J. Gross - 250,000, Jews in eastern Poland and the USSR, 1939-46, N. Davies, A. Polonsky (eds.) (Houndmills, Basingstoke, Hampshire: Macmillan, 1991), p. 9.; Sikorski's estimate was 300,000 Sovetsko-angliiskie otnosheniia vo vremia Velikoi Otechestvennoi voiny 1941-1945 (Moscow, 1983), v. I, p. 515.
16. V. Abarinov, Katynskii Labirynt (Moscow, 1991), p. 14.
17. Numerous examples see HI, Ms collection (11), l. 3-10, (734), l. 1-2, (452), l. 1-2, (151), l. 1-4, (335), (198), l. 1-6, (335), l. 1-2, (275), l. 1-4.
18. FO 371/34564.
19. Soviet documents published in Voenno-Istoricheskii Zhurnal 6 (1990), p. 52-53 and in Katyn: dokumenty zbrodni v. I (Warsaw, 1995), p. 269, also a table in ibid., p. 481.
20. Beria's order about the organization of networks of informants in the POW camps publ. in Voenno-Istoricheskii Zhurnal 6 (1990), p. 50-51 and Beria's report to Stalin (November 2, 1940), publ. in Novaia i Noveishaia Istoriia 2 (1993), p. 60-61.
21. For a story of a successful escape see, S. Rawicz, The Long Walk (London, Constable, 1956), passim.
22. S. Mikolajczyk, The Rape of Poland: Pattern of Soviet Aggression (New York, Whittlesey House, 1948), p. 26.
23. Numerous stories from survivors of labor camps can be found in, HI Anders, box 81 and HI Ambasada USSR, boxes 46-49.
24. W. Anders, An Army in Exile, p. 71-73.
25. A lecture by Z. Siemaszko (an officer in Anders' Army) at the London University School of East European and Slavonic Studies (November 23, 1988).
26. W. Anders, An Army in Exile, p. 20-24.
27. Ibid., p. 25-44.
28. Interview with V.S. Parsadanova, Senior Archivist, Ministry of Defense (July 1993, Moscow).
29. W. Anders, An Army in Exile, p. 17, 18, 22-23.
30. She names Imach (Communist), Wicherkiewicz, Berling, Okulicki, Gorczynski, Tyszynski, Dudzinski, Zawadzki (Communist), Szumigalski, Tomala, and Siewierski.
31. Beria's report to Stalin (November 2, 1940), publ. in Novaia i Noveishaia Istoriia 2 (1993), p. 60-62.

32. A resolution of the Politburo of the Central Committee of the All-Union Communist Party (June 4, 1941) in ibid., p. 62.
33. A lengthy account about the creation of the "Villa of Delight" appears in FO 371/71610. There are minor differences between this account and other reports but they agree as to the overall purpose and objective behind the "Villa," according to Bartoszewski, about 50 Polish officers agreed to cooperate with the Russians, S.W. Slowes, The Road to Katyn: a Soldier's Story (Oxford, U.K.; Cambridge, Mass.: Blackwell Publishers, 1992), p. XVI.
34. J. Garlinski, Poland in the Second World War (New York: Hippocrene Books, 1985), p. 157.
35. They included Gorczynski, Tyszynski, Dudzinski, Rozen-Zawadski, Imach, Siewierski, Tomala, Szumigalski, and Szczypiorski, "Materialy o powstaniu i poczatkowym rozwoju polskich oddzialow wojskowych pod dowodztwem Berlinga 1939-1944," Hoover Institution, Polish Embassy in the USSR files, box 16, folder 302; Garlinski, op.cit., p. 157.
36. While still in the USSR, Anders received from London a long list of names of officials and officers who were not to be used in forming his army. This "black list" was prepared by the Bureau of Information run by Kot or Stronski at that time. The names listed were of officials of the previous government, including General Tokarzewski-Karaszewicz. Captain Lubienski and Col.Okulicki, the later being Anders' Chief of Staff. Col.Okulicki gave the list to Romanowski to put in a special safe so that no one else would see it.
37. J. Retinger, Memoirs of an Eminence Grise (Brighton: Sussex UP, 1972), p. 91.

# CHAPTER TWO

# UNEASY ALLIANCE

## Soviet-Polish Agreements of July-August 1941

Operation Barbarossa turned Europe upside down. Blinded by his military successes and acting contrary to the advice of his generals, Hitler attacked the Soviet Union on June 22, 1941. The lines were now rejoined. The Great Patriotic War (the Russian name for World War II) had begun and Britain, the Soviet Union and Poland were now allied. The day after the German attack, in a radio speech addressed to Poles in the USSR, Sikorski called upon the Soviet Union to begin cooperating with the Polish Government in the struggle against Germany. The Polish-Soviet alliance was formalized on July 30, 1941, by an Agreement signed by General Sikorski and the Soviet Ambassador in London, Ivan Maisky. Sikorski signed the Agreement without the advance approval of the Polish President.

The "Sikorski-Maisky Agreement" nullified the 1939 Soviet-German Agreement and restored diplomatic relations between Poland and the Soviet Union. It also provided for the formation of a Polish Army in the USSR. In a special Protocol to the Agreement the Soviet Government promised to grant amnesty to Poles being held in Soviet prisons and labor camps. Although these documents were full of ambiguities and unresolved issues, they at least made it clear that Polish soldiers and civilians captured or arrested in 1939-40, and deported to the USSR, were granted amnesty and were to be released.[1]

The Sikorski-Maisky Agreement is best remembered for what it doesn't include, namely the clarification of Polish-Soviet borders. The crucial issue of whether the areas of Poland taken by the Soviets in 1939 were to be returned to Poland, was not addressed. Subsequently, Sikorski was heavily criticized for not insisting on settling the border issue before signing the Agreement. Sikorski's response was that the most important and immediate objective was to get Poles out of prisons and labor camps where they were dying with each passing day. On August 3, 1941, Sikorski wrote to Anders: "Some Poles did not understand that, at a moment when the issue is the liberation of hundreds of thousands of fellow countrymen, this, above all, must decide the argument."[2]

Sikorski's critics argued (and still argue) that because the Soviet Union was at its weakest, and anxious to conclude an agreement, Sikorski should have taken advantage of this opportunity. They assume that at that time the Soviets would have accepted Poland's territorial demands and would not later disavow them. Even if the Polish Government had gained border concessions after prolonged negotiations, additional Poles would have died during the delay while all "gains" would have been lost when the Soviets unilaterally severed diplomatic relations, in 1943.

Sikorski tried to enlist the aid of the British on border issues by asking them to present a statement to the Soviets calling for a return to prewar borders and signing a protocol guaranteeing the integrity of the Polish territory. The British declined. Sikorski pointed out that he didn't have the authority to negotiate away any Polish lands. In the end it was agreed that the Agreement between Poland and the USSR would not address the border issue.[3] The British Minister of Foreign Affairs, Anthony Eden, praised Sikorski for his statesmanship in getting the Agreement finalized and wrote, "Our part was only patient diplomacy tinged with anxiety for what the future might hold for the Poles as the weaker partner."[4]

If the Polish-Soviet Agreement was welcomed by the British Government its reception among the Polish exile community in Great Britain was predominantly unfavorable. According to the counselor at the British Embassy to the Polish Government in Exile, Frank Savery, 80% of the Poles in London were against the Sikorski-Maisky Agreement. It also aroused some anti-British sentiment among Poles who felt that Churchill played on Sikorski's well known vanity to get him to sign the Agreement.[5] The National Democrats, the Socialists, and the Pilsudskites were all united in their criticism of Sikorski for having signed. General Sosnkowski, the deputy Commander-in-Chief, resigned in protest, followed by a number of other officials. The Polish Ambassador to Britain, Count Edward Raczynski, who supported signing the Agreement acknowledged that it definitely increased anti-Sikorski sentiment. General Anders, on the other hand, was definitely in accord with Sikorski's decision. Reacting to Sosnkowski's resignation he said, "If Sosnkowski does not like this agreement he should get out, because he is either stupid or in bad faith."[6]

After the borders question the next important issue was formation of a Polish Army in the USSR and the preservation of its autonomy versus the Soviets. The Sikorski-Maisky Agreement stipulated merely that a Polish Army, under a commander appointed by the Polish Government but subordinated operationally to the Soviet High Command, would be formed in the USSR. The details were to be dealt with in a subsequent military agreement.

Reportedly, on the day the Sikorski-Maisky Agreement was signed Sikorski informed Maisky that the commander of the Polish Army in Russia would be General Anders. Anders and Sikorski had a good relation going back to the 1920s when they both remained loyal to the legitimate government when Marshal Pilsudski staged a coup d'etat in May of 1926. Sikorski liked Anders and during the coup appointed him Commander of the Warsaw garrison. After Pilsudski's victory they went their separate ways. Anders remained in the army and was promoted by Pilsudski while Sikorski was forced to retire and became actively involved in political opposition against the Pilsudski regime. Therefore, it is not surprising that Sikorski would hesitate and consider another candidate, General Stanislaw Haller, for the post. Joseph Retinger, a close political adviser and confidante of Sikorski, claims that a few days after signing the Agreement, Sikorski told him that he wanted Haller to head the army in Russia, and that he would appoint Anders only if Haller was not available.[7] There is also a memo written by Sikorski, naming Haller commander of the Polish Army in Russia, and listing Anders as one of eight officers who were to assist him.[8] By August 4, Sikorski had finally made up his mind and formally advised the British and the Soviets of his choice of Anders.[9]

The Soviets had no difficulty with the appointment of Anders.[10] Both sides agreed that Anders would be the best candidate for the job. On August 4, 1941, Anders was brought directly from his cell in Lubianka to a meeting with the dreaded NKVD chief Beria and his deputy Merkulov, and told that he was a free man, and was appointed, with full agreement of the Soviet Government, to the post of commander of the Polish Army in the USSR. He was installed in a comfortable hotel flat but was kept away from the Polish military mission for a few days, probably to allow signs of his imprisonment to wear off.[11] The head of the mission, General Szyszko-Bohusz, who met Anders four days after his release, noted that "he was much slimmer than in the past" and "he dragged one foot and supported himself with a cane" but "his gaze and voice showed energy."[12]

Szyszko-Bohusz brought Anders a letter from General Sikorski, offering him command of the Polish Army in the Soviet Union. Sikorski wrote Anders that he believed that "the Agreement with Russia is adequate - we keep all the territory from 1939 and we have the support of Great Britain and USA in the subject of our western frontiers." We now know that this was not accurate. Anders accepted the post and asked Sikorski to quickly send him the official nomination so that he could start working.[13] Anders must have been under considerable personal strain: his wife's son had been killed in the September Campaign and he had no information about his wife, son, or daughter.[14]

On August 14, 1941, a Polish-Soviet military agreement was signed for the Polish side by General Szyszko-Bohusz and for the Soviets by General A. Vasilevski stipulating that a Polish Army was to be formed in the USSR as soon as possible that would be part of the Armed Forces of the Republic of Poland and would return to Poland after the war. In the meantime, the army would be subordinated to the High Command of the Soviet Army with its commander appointed by the Polish Government but subject to Soviet approval. Polish units were to be moved to the front only after achieving full readiness. What the agreement left unclear was who was to decide when the army was "fully ready." An important provision stated that Polish units would not be used in groups smaller than a division. Another stated that while on Soviet territory soldiers of the Polish Army were subject to Soviet laws and decrees. "For crimes against the state, soldiers of the Polish Army on the territory of the USSR will be answerable to the military courts of the USSR."[15]

The Polish-Soviet Military Agreement provided that the Soviets would equip and arm the Polish force[16] and that credits were to be granted to the Polish Government, from which the Poles would pay for food, transportation, arms, uniforms, ammunition, etc. During the first two weeks the Poles had already used ten million rubles. In November, 1941, the Russians offered Poles credits in the amount of 65 million rubles to cover expenses up to January 1, 1942. These credits were to be repaid within ten years after the end of the war with payment to be made in dollars, gold, or goods.[17]

The signing of the Military Agreement was followed by protocol conferences on August 16th and 19th, attended by Anders and Szyszko-Bohusz. During these conferences the Polish and Soviet military representatives worked out details for the organization of Polish military units. Special recruiting commissions were to be set up consisting of representatives from the Polish Army and from local Soviet military committees. Since the Soviets claimed there were only twenty thousand Polish soldiers available, Anders suggested at first that the Polish forces should be organized into two (smaller) "light" infantry divisions and requested that Polish citizens serving in the Red Army be permitted to transfer to the Polish Army. At the second meeting the Soviets agreed to the formation of two full (larger) divisions of 10,000 men each, for which they promised to provide weapons. They also agreed that Poles serving in the Red Army would be allowed to transfer to the Polish Army. The Soviet side set October 1, 1941, as the date when the Polish Divisions should be ready for battle. This deadline, only six weeks from the date of the conference was clearly unrealistic.[18]

Sikorski was not happy with the military protocols and instructed General Szyszko-Bohusz to try to modify them. He particularly did not like the provision which permitted the Soviets to use separate Polish Divisions, preferring to have them used as a single Corps under Polish command. Sikorski was willing to accept the Soviet veto over his choice for Commander of Polish Forces in the USSR, but would not accept a provision that gave the Soviets the right of approval on all personnel issues.[19]

## The Amnesty and the Great Trek South[20]

For all its faults and ambiguities, the Sikorski-Maisky Agreement was clear on one important point--Polish military personnel captured by the Soviets, and Polish civilians arrested and deported for real or imagined crimes against the Soviet Union, were to be granted immediate amnesty.[21] On August 12, 1941, the Politburo of the Communist Party, the top decision making body in the Soviet Union, formally resolved to free all Polish POWs, internees and prisoners. The amnesty included those already sentenced to prison or labor camps and those still under investigation and it was also to apply to Polish citizens deported from Western Byelorussian and Ukraine to "special" (forced) settlements.

The liberated Poles were to be allowed to choose a place to live (except for border areas, so-called "closed" regions and major cities). The NKVD was to provide them with temporary documents, to be later replaced by Polish passports issued by the Polish Embassy. Financial assistance, charged to the Polish Government, was to be extended to needy Poles pursuant to an agreement that the Commissariats of Foreign Affairs reached with the Polish Government. Amnestied Poles were to be helped in finding jobs and accommodations by Soviet and Communist Party organizations. The decision was passed on to Beria for implementation.[22] On August 13th, the Soviet Government newspaper Izvestia printed an announcement that "according to the decree of the Presidium of the Supreme Soviet of the USSR from August 12, 1941, an amnesty was granted to the Polish citizens, imprisoned on the territory of the USSR."[23] According to an August 16, 1941, decree of the Committee of State Defense, the Polish military personnel, upon their release, were to be paid lump cash sums ranging from five hundred rubles for NCOs and lower ranks to ten thousand rubles for generals. Anders was to receive twenty five thousand.[24] Civilians were to get free railroad travel to a destination of their choice and a subsistence allowance of five rubles per day while en route.[25]

Imagine this if you can. The gates of prisons and labor camps are thrown open and hundreds of thousands of men, women and children walk through these gates with a single objective - to find the Polish Army and to come under its protection. They start trekking in Siberia, from above the Arctic Circle, or from the Altai mountains heading southwest. Imagine, if you can, people walking for four months to find an army that may or may not exist. Imagine getting on a train without a ticket and without knowing its destination, with the hope that it will go in a southwesterly direction. Imagine people building rafts and spending days on them just because the river was flowing southward. Imagine elderly people and children taking turns on a horse-drawn cart, going in the direction where somebody had said the Polish Army could be found. In small groups but sometimes alone, as many as one million Poles started traveling, mostly on foot, in that direction. The Great Trek South had begun, racing to get to the south before the start of winter.[26]

The trek across the Soviet Union to find the Polish Army wasn't limited to soldiers and potential soldiers. Civilians unfit for military service, and women and children also headed for towns where the army was recruiting, in hope of finding protection and compassion in addition to food, clothing and a warm place to sleep. They yearned for a bit of Poland, a place where they would not be strangers in an alien land, a place where their fellow Poles would look after them and help them escape their misery.

Few ex-prisoners knew exactly or even approximately where the Polish Army was, but everyone somehow knew it was "south." Very few had a map and few had any idea of where in the south they were headed. Some prisoners were released with nothing more than the clothes on their back, others had meager possessions. Some had small amounts of food and money. The majority had nothing and none had sufficient food, clothing and money for the journey southward. Very few were paid the allowance or given the free railway travel promised by the Soviets. The trekkers lived mostly on raw potatoes and unboiled water. Even those who had some money or something to trade for food couldn't do so legally, as an official identification card was needed showing they were workers eligible to buy food.

Poles congregated at railroad stations waiting for trains, sleeping on station floors, afraid to give up their place in case a train arrived. It was not unusual for people to spend two weeks living in a train station hoping to find a train going south. They waited without knowing whether a train would ever arrive and where it would be going. Trains in remote parts of the USSR didn't operate on schedule. When trains did arrive at the stations, they were immediately boarded but they didn't necessarily move. There was no possibility of providing medical assistance to those who needed it, and many died for lack of medical care. For some the trek was too hard, and they became exhausted to the point where their lives could not be saved. Thousands died during this long trek and many more died once they reached their destination. The dead and dying were taken off the trains and placed in rows on station platforms. A witness wrote, "I was on hand when a train load of 2,000 came into Kuibyshev. There were sixteen corpses in the cars, men and women who had died of hunger on the way."[27]

The trekkers had no scheduled place to sleep so they slept in fields and railroad stations. No one arranged for food, water and shelter along the way. No one told them that high altitudes in parts of the south would bring temperatures as low as in Siberia. No one told them there were disease epidemics in the south worse than anything they had experienced in the north.

The granting of amnesty on August 12th, didn't mean that all prison and labor camp doors were immediately opened. The amnesty was not implemented immediately and consistently. Most imprisoned Poles were released months after the amnesty decree had been issued. When Poles were detained after the amnesty, they were told that problems of transportation and money were caused by a lack of interest or obstruction by the Polish Government.

A woman, who as a young girl was deported with her family to Siberia, wrote of how they learned about the amnesty. In early September, a month after the amnesty, all Poles in the area were called together and a NKVD representative gave everyone a piece of paper stating that they were free to go anywhere except to large cities. They could leave the collective farm, but most didn't have any money to go any where. Slowes wrote that the prisoners were not released from his camp until September 2, 1941.[28] In some cases the local authorities ignored the amnesty and numerous inmates were never told about it. A Pole who was still a prisoner in the spring of 1942, learned about the amnesty only by overhearing a conversation in which it was mentioned. A soldier told of being moved from a labor camp in Siberia to a collective farm in the south, in early 1942. He wasn't released until the middle of 1942. Some weren't freed because they knew too much or their labor was badly needed. A number of inmates were immediately rearrested after being released. Some civilians and soldiers who the Russians were supposedly sending south to enter the army were instead sent to labor camps in Turkestan where most died.

There were many reasons why the implementation of the amnesty was delayed, starting with the sheer size of the country and the difficulty of communicating with remote areas in which many labor camps were located. Secondly, it was difficult for the authorities to release all prisoners without creating congestion on the railway. Another major reason was the NKVD's attempt to interrogate prisoners for a last time before their release. A non-commissioned officer reported that he wasn't released until December 1, 1941, and was interrogated until the last day but was not tortured after August 1st. It was not unusual for officers to be held for a two week period during which, while being treated decently, they would be interrogated and asked to sign a statement obligating them to collaborate with the Soviet Government. Jan Romanowski, a future aide de camp of General Anders, said he didn't sign but was sure there were some who did, he specifically mentioned Captain Klimkowski and Colonel Berling.

On October 1, 1941, Beria reported to Stalin and Molotov that out of a total of 391,575 Polish citizens held in prisons, POW and labor camps as well as in places of deportation, the NKVD released 50,295 from prisons and labor camps, 26,297 from POW camps and 265,248 from deportation places.[29] It seems that most prisoners were freed during the period September 1, 1941, to October 15, 1941.

The Polish trek to the south was quite unique, unlike other treks, or mass movements of people in history. The latter consisted of large members of people moving as a group under identifiable leadership, with a predictable course and objective. The Poles moved in small groups or as individuals, did not have leadership and were unsure of their destination. Harold Macmillan, in an introduction to Anders' memoirs called the Polish trek "epic" and compared it to the march of the Greeks under Xenophon. Macmillan wrote, "After incredible adventures they walked (like the Greeks in Xenophon's anabasis) all the way eastward until they finally reached Persia and Palestine." At the end of their trek, the Greeks reached the sea and their homeland, while for Poles the trek ended in disillusionment and despair. Perhaps a better word than "trek" would be "roam," because many released Poles had no idea where to go and simply "roamed." There were reported instances where groups of amnestied Poles would meet other groups on the road, heading in the opposite direction.

Many trekkers became aware of the magnitude of deportations and of the extent to which Polish citizens were spread over the USSR only after talking to other trekkers whom they met waiting at the train stations. The first topic of discussion was always finding the army. The second, family members who hadn't survived. In spite of the hardships, morale was high, and the Poles felt indebted to Sikorski for forcing the Soviets to release them. They also felt indebted to the British. But most of all they wanted to find the Polish Army and get out of the USSR.

The Soviet authorities strictly controlled internal travel. It was easier for a Pole with "Polish nationality" stamped on his Soviet passport to travel to find the Polish Army than for Polish citizens who were not ethnic Poles. Poles coming from the north out of labor camps had no money so some worked for a time on farms and in textile factories to get money to continue their journey. Local Soviet officials in need of labor often created obstacles preventing the Poles from continuing their trek.[30] When they stopped in towns where they didn't get sufficient help in finding accommodations and places to work, they sent telegrams to the Polish Embassy asking for immediate assistance, which was not available.

Some of the experiences are full of pathos and tragedy. One group had heard there was a railroad in a certain city and made it their objective. After walking for two weeks and finding the railroad they were allowed on the empty trains which took them within one mile from the place where they had started. One family had enough money to buy a horse and cart but had no idea how to drive the horse. They enlisted the help of a peasant in exchange for letting his family share the cart. After two weeks the peasant's family took over the cart completely and the owners had to walk behind the cart. The roles were reversed again when they reached a railway station: now it was the peasant who kissed the owner's feet when told he could keep the horse and cart.

A man, his wife and their young son lived in forced exile in a place called Tesovaya and didn't hear of the amnesty until September 8, 1941. They were paid laborers and couldn't leave the camp until they received their earnings on October 14. Their meager possessions consisted of some worthless bundles, four kilograms of bread, several kilograms of potatoes and three hundred rubles. After joining a large group of Polish refugees heading south, they traveled for two months, mostly in box cars, paying a fare of forty five rubles each. During the trip they lived, by the most part, on stolen beets, managing to get a few morsels of bread once a week. They traveled in the eastern and southern parts of the USSR searching for the Polish Army. On December 18, 1941, railroad and NKVD officials kicked them off the train at a little stop-over place called Tiantiaksai, in Kirgizia. From there they went by camel and cart to search for a place where they could get work so that they could subsist on a small daily wage. They did not find the Polish Army until February, 1942. A Polish Jew named Bevin walked for twenty two days until he found a recruiting station where he could join the Polish Army. A father and two sons in forced exile were brought to a prison in Akmolinsk in April, 1941. In January, 1942, the father left his sons to look for the Polish Army. He walked one week to find a train station and it was six more weeks before he found the army.

The trekkers suffered from extreme exhaustion, dysentery, frostbite, and many lost their teeth. Their feet were wrapped in rags. Open sores became infected owing to a lack of vitamins. Measles, bronchitis and pneumonia were epidemic among the children. About 3% percent of the trekkers had boots or shoes, the others wore rags tied around their feet. The horrid plight of the Polish refugees who came after the amnesty can be attributed to several causes. First, there a food shortage and famine in Turkestan. Second, local agencies of the Soviet Government usually failed to pay the Poles money allowances or to help them get jobs and accommodations. The few Polish citizens who reached the Polish Embassy offices received some money. In the middle of October, the Polish Embassy received large quantities of food and clothing from Britain and the West, yet this met the needs of only a small fraction of the trekkers. Third, Poles as aliens were barred from the better jobs. Fourth, most available jobs were on collective farms but most of the Poles, and especially the Polish Jews, were not accustomed to farm work. Fifth, these jobs did not pay a living wage and the ways of getting supplemental income were closed to people who were not Soviet citizens.

After arriving in the south the trekkers found they had accomplished very little in the short term. They had come under the "protection" of the Polish Army but the food shortages and cold weather differed little from conditions in the north. Those that reached their objective in the winter of 1941-42, found themselves in a cold mountainous area living in mud huts or summer tents without adequate food or clothing. It was estimated that three hundred and fifty civilian refugees died daily during that long winter. What they found in the south was not what they had hoped for.

At the same time, Poles in the far north, not having received instructions, were still traveling to the southern regions of the Urals and Central Asia. Because of calamities caused by the arrival of ex-prisoners in Central Asia, the Soviets, with concurrence of the Polish Army, had to send back those who had reached the region. The shortages there were so acute that allowing more people into the area would have resulted in more deaths from hunger and disease. The hard facts were that further sharing of existing rations would result in everyone dying of starvation.

Confusion was rampant. In the autumn of 1941, more than 100,000 Polish citizens arrived in Uzbekistan and there was utter chaos when the Soviets collected trekkers and began sending them back to camps in the north. Some trekkers lived in train stations waiting for trains that would never come. Many died of hunger and exposure. On September 27, 1941, Beria wrote to Stalin that it was "absolutely necessary" to get the Polish Embassy to agree that the released Poles should not leave the places where they had been living and should accept employment there. Those wishing to change their location should be recommended to settle temporarily in Uzbekistan and those unfit for military service should also be directed towards Uzbekistan and provided with immediate material assistance. If no additional Polish units were to be authorized Poles who had been recruited in excess of the agreed number should also be sent to the Uzbek region. The local authorities in Uzbekistan were to assist the Poles while the cost of resettling them was to be covered by the Polish Government from funds loaned them by the Soviet Government.[31]

On November 8th, 21,500 Poles were sent to Southern Kirgiziia. On November 19th, the Soviets decided to move 45,000 Polish civilians from Uzbekistan to South Kazakhstan, Dzhambul and Semipalatinsk and allocated 10 million rubles to help the most needy. All transports of Poles going to the south were halted and they were put on trains heading north. Some were never seen again. Despite all Soviet attempts to stop it the uncontrolled movement of Polish citizens in Siberia, Kazakhstan and Central Asia continued. Finally, in February, 1942, the Soviet Government, trying to control the situation, instructed local authorities to stop all unauthorized movement of Polish citizens from their place of residence.[32]

The people of Turkestan were friendly to the Poles although their own conditions were difficult. A typhoid epidemic left people dying on the streets. It was estimated that more than 5,000 Poles died in an epidemic in Uzbekistan. Those who survived the ordeal of the trek south and lived to tell their stories were nearly unanimous in their praise of the Soviet people who shared their meager food with them. The trekkers had to live by their wits and by handouts from peasants. Survivors of the trek may be vehemently anti-Communist but still speak with affection of the Russian peasants on whose handouts they relied for survival. I often heard the comment: "I hate the Communist Government but I love the Russian people."

In the spring of 1942, the Polish Embassy received information about Poles who had worked on farms during the past winter. They were often mercilessly exploited-getting for their labor only 800-1,000 calories per day, when the norm was 3,500 calories. The Soviets wanted all Poles to accept Soviet citizenship and some said they were Communists just to obtain Soviet papers. In March, 1943, the Soviets declared that all Poles in the Soviet Union were now Soviet citizens and any Pole not accepting citizenship would be sentenced to two years in a labor camp. The Great Trek had ended.

Not all ex-prisoners headed south. The amnesty didn't require that everyone join the newly formed Polish Army; there were alternatives. Poles could stay in work camps where they had a place to sleep and sufficient food to stay alive. Leaving the camps involved the enormous risk of being left without shelter and food. As bad as conditions were in the camps there was at least some food. Another possibility was to live and work in the Soviet Union. A few preferred the security of the labor camp and some sought employment in small towns and villages. They did it for a variety of reasons. Some were fearful of coming under Polish jurisdiction (criminals or collaborators?) while others appreciated the risks of an arduous walk south. An overwhelming majority however desired to find the Polish Army either to join it or to come under its protection. The same conclusion was reached by the NKVD.[33]

## The Organization of the Army

Immediately after signing the military protocols in Moscow, the Polish military mission, joined by a few released officers, set down to work on the organization of the army. In spite of difficult conditions, members of the mission were mostly optimistic about their task. A principal reason for that positive attitude was the personality of the commander, General Anders, who radiated energy and inspired confidence. He seemed to be able to win everyone's trust. On August 14, 1941, Joseph Retinger, a close adviser to Sikorski and a savvy political operator wrote to Sikorski from Moscow "I like Anders who is manifestly sincere and honest, and is devoted to you."[34] Anders also seemed an excellent choice from the point of view of establishing good relations with the Soviets. A former tsarist officer, he spoke perfect Russian, was an engaging conversationalist and at the same time had a reputation for straight talking, a trait which won him a grudging respect among Soviet officials. He managed to establish a reasonably good relation with Stalin, certainly not an easy man to deal with. Stalin demonstratively showed Anders to be in his favor by showering him with gifts: a car, a diamond cigarette case, an ancient airplane, and two beautiful horses. The most unusual gift was a Jewish violinist who was under a death sentence and whom Anders "requisitioned" in order to save his life.

On September 28, General Bohusz-Szyszko, in a letter to Retinger, gave a characteristic of Anders which is worth quoting at length:

> "Of the greatest importance is the personality of General Anders, who has the complete trust equally of Soviets and Poles. Without exaggeration, I can say that he is a central character not only for us but for the Soviets as well. They consider him as someone who could play an extremely important role for them, so they take good care of him. Without exaggeration, I can also say that here no one else can accomplish anything. For example, all the problems with the transfer of our civilian population did not begin to move until Anders came back from Buzuluk to Moscow. What the Polish Embassy could not accomplish in two weeks he did in half a day; and even got the Russians to follow through on their promises. This was not a fault of our Embassy but a manifestation that Soviet authorities trust only Anders, want to talk only with him and accept almost without objection his demands. Towards everybody else they are reserved and mistrustful...He [Anders] is a type of soldier who carries out each order with loyalty and best understanding...General Anders is absolutely loyal, lacking any personal ambitions, full of energy and dashing. He is directed only by the Polish cause..."[35]

It would be difficult to think about a more glowing recommendation. Unfortunately the letter also demonstrated that there was suspicion about Anders' loyalty and malicious gossip was being spread in London about him being influenced by Communism. As Anders began to function as commander of Polish forces in Russia this was still just a tiny and distant cloud.

For the first few days Anders' headquarters was in the Polish Embassy in Moscow. At the time Moscow was under threat from the fast approaching Wehrmacht and both the Soviet Government and the foreign embassies were moving eastward. On August 22, 1941, Anders was officially notified of the localities assigned for stationing the Polish Army. The army headquarters would be in Buzuluk, the 5th Infantry Division would be in Tatishchevo, with the 6th Division and the reserve regiment in Totskoe.

These are not the best places for forming an army. Buzuluk and Totskoe are located in Orenburg province, where the Central Asian Steppe flows into the East European Plain. Winter temperatures in the region fall to -52 degrees centigrade and soldiers were literally freezing to death in their tents. Tatishchevo was in the Siaratov region, on the other, western side of the Volga river, some 300 miles from Buzuluk and it took from four to eleven days to get there from headquarters. When the first soldiers arrived in Tatishchevo nothing was there: no food, no equipment, no telephone links and the nearest railway station was miles away.

Totskoe, about 25 miles from Buzuluk, was designated the location for a recruiting office which opened on September 2, 1941.[36] Later, similar offices were set up in other localities where the army was stationed and where there were POW camps. A majority of those joining were in very bad physical condition. Anders remembered that a group of officers arriving at Tatishchevo were in such an appalling state that sixty three died within a month.[37]

By September 19, 1941, Anders had already 26,400 soldiers organized into two divisions and reserve units. A week later there were already 14,647 soldiers in excess of the agreed number and Beria reported to Stalin that Poles were asking for permission to form additional units. By the first week of November the army expanded, without Soviet authorization, to 44,000 soldiers. On November 11, 1941, the Soviet liaison officer, Colonel Volkovyskii, instructed Anders to reduce the army to 30,000 and send the surplus personnel to Tashkent where they would be put to work as laborers. Anders threatened to resign rather than carry out this order.[38]

Apart from difficulties with getting food rations from the Soviets, the army also suffered from a shortage of arms and other equipment. It had 40 rifles per 10,000 soldiers and most men had to train with wooden rifles. A few days after the second protocol conference during which the Soviets promised to arm two Polish Divisions, Anders was notified that they had only enough supplies to equip a single division.[39] The Soviets did in fact provide arms for the 5th Division. But even the 5th Division's armament wasn't complete--it lacked anti-tank weapons and artillery. In order to speed up training, equipment delivered by the Soviets for the 5th Division was distributed by Anders among all Polish units.

As of November 25, 1941, the Polish Army in the USSR consisted of 40,961 soldiers including 1,965 officers and 11,919 NCOs: 14,703 in the 5th Division, 12,480 in the 6th Division, 8,764 in the reserve regiment, 508 in the Army Headquarters, 3,466 in the construction unit at Koltubanka 3,466 and 1,040 soldiers not yet assigned to any unit.[40] General Panfilov asked Stalin to approve October 1, 1941, as the date on which the two Polish Divisions should achieve battle readiness. This was a totally unrealistic date: the Soviets apparently didn't appreciate the poor health and physical condition of the newly released prisoners. Anders was notified about this date and did not protest because, he says, "I knew it was a waste of time to make any objections."[41]

When the date came the units were far from being ready. Many soldiers (from 40% to 75%) still had no shoes and few had weapons.[42] In December, 1941, the Soviets requested that each battalion, as it became ready, be sent to the front. Anders refused fearing that his soldiers, not fully trained and equipped, would suffer heavy casualties. He also suspected that Stalin was not very concerned about Polish losses. Sikorski told Panfilov that the Polish Army would not be ready to fight before June 15, 1942, which he justified by the delays in getting weapons from the United States and England. Panfilov reported to Stalin that when he asked Sikorski in which direction the Polish Army should move, Sikorski responded, "in the southern direction" and only later caught himself and said "in the direction of the Front."[43]

In November, 1941, the size of the Polish Army issue was raised by Kot during his talks with Stalin before Sikorski's visit to Moscow planned for December.[44] Stalin reiterated that he had agreed only to the formation of an army of no more than 30,000, consisting of two divisions with a reserve regiment. One division was to be equipped by the British and Americans, and one by the Soviets. Kot protested, arguing that the size of the Polish Army should be limited only by the number of Polish soldiers that could be recruited. In his view the number of eligible Poles reached 150,000. Stalin however refused to yield. He told Kot that he didn't care if the Poles formed five, six or seven divisions, but he could neither feed nor arm them. However when Kot complained about Panfilov's order to reduce the existing army to 30,000, Stalin replied that Panfilov had no authority to issue such an order.[45]

In spite of apparent Soviet unwillingness to approve an expansion of the army above the ceiling agreed upon in August, Sikorski still talked about a 100,000 strong Polish Army in the USSR. He wanted a big army so the Allies would treat Poland as an important Ally and would be represented on the Supreme War Council.[46]

On December 3, 1941, a top level meeting was held in the Kremlin to consider a number of delicate issues. From the Polish perspective this was one of the most important meetings of the war. The Soviet side was represented by Stalin, Molotov and General Panfilov, the Polish side by General Sikorski, Ambassador Kot and General Anders.[47]

Sikorski came right to the point by charging that a great number of Poles, including many prominent people, had not yet been released from Soviet prisons and labor camps. Stalin maintained that they had all been released and, when pressed to explain their absence, said they must have escaped to Manchuria. He assured Sikorski that "the Soviet Government has not the slightest reason to retain even one Pole." He claimed he had released "even Sosnkowski's agents who attack us and murder our people."

When Anders complained that Jews were released first, with able-bodied Poles being released last, after Ukrainians and physically weak Poles, Stalin declared that camp commandants delaying the release of Polish prisoners "should be put on trial."

At one point Stalin mentioned that Churchill and Roosevelt's Special Envoy, Avrell Harriman, had requested that the Polish Army be evacuated to the Middle East. Stalin for the moment seemed to be saying that two or three divisions may leave or, if the Poles prefer to stay in the USSR, he would provide the means for seven Polish Divisions. Anders confronted Panfilov with the fact that the food supply was cut from 44,000 to 30,000 rations and the higher number of rations had not been restored in spite of earlier promises by Stalin. Anders listed all other shortages suffered by the Poles in addition to food, i.e. medicine, medical care, soap, tools, lumber, etc. Stalin severely chastised Panfilov for not seeing that his orders were carried out, but this surely was a charade. Stalin said he had authorized the increase in food rations two and a half weeks earlier. The Poles did not believe him.

Romanowski's notes indicate that in December, 1941, there were attempts to gain Soviet approval for 150,000 Polish troops, but the Soviets insisted the army be limited to 30,000. His notes show that Stalin promised he would release all the Poles and would approve an army of 150,000. Romanowski says he wrote in his notes at that point, "I am curious whether the Soviets will keep this promise." They didn't.

When Stalin commented about Poles being the best soldiers and not wanting minorities, Sikorski immediately saw the broader and political implications of Stalin's statement. Stalin referred to the 1940 elections and said the minorities were now Soviet citizens.[48] This is the point where Anders is quoted as saying "a great number of Jews do not want to serve in the army." This doesn't make sense as the Polish Army had a disproportionally high number of Jews and Jews were being rejected for enlistment and even expelled to lower their number. Stalin then made his often quoted statement that "Jews are poor warriors." A response was made from the Polish side that Jews were poor soldiers and black-marketeers. Kot attributed this comment to Anders but it is generally agreed that the comment was made by Sikorski.[49]

Anders is reported to have said that two hundred Jews deserted from Buzuluk and fifty more deserted from the 5th Division a day before weapons were distributed. Even Anders' supporters can't explain why he made these two statements which he knew were not true. The Polish Jews were fighting to get into the army at this point, so the statements don't make sense. It is Romanowski's guess that some Jewish and other soldiers went searching for their families.

By the end of the meeting it was decided to create a mixed Polish-Soviet commission as soon as possible to work out details of the agreements reached at the meeting. It was agreed that Anders would represent the Polish side. As the Poles were leaving, Stalin asked Anders to stay a few minutes longer. It must have been exasperating to Sikorski to hear Stalin invite his subordinate to a private discussion. The short conversation was about cooperation with Panfilov, and Stalin commented to Anders, "I am very sorry that I did not meet you before." Anders' response was "It was not my fault that I was not called to you, Mr. President."[50]

As a direct result of the December 3, 1941, meeting Stalin and Sikorski signed a Declaration of Friendship and Mutual Assistance, but like all previous agreements, this document didn't settle border issues. During their talks in Moscow in December, 1941, Sikorski called for restoration of the prewar boundaries, to which Stalin answered that he would like "to have some alterations in those frontiers, they'll be very slight alterations."[51] On the basis of this exchange, some of Sikorski's critics, most notably the British, said that if Sikorski and the Polish Government in Exile had been malleable, the Poles could have avoided Soviet domination after the war. They argue that if Sikorski had agreed to the small alterations Stalin wanted, Poland could have kept the remainder. Sikorski and his supporters claimed he lacked authority to negotiate the transfer of any land to the Soviets.

Stalin raised the issue of borders again during a banquet. Sikorski refused to be drawn into the discussion, explaining that it wasn't the proper time and place, and that he had no authority to discuss border changes, since under Polish law only the Polish Parliament could do this. Sikorski was later criticized for not being willing even to listen to what Stalin wanted to say about the border issue.[52]

A practical result of the December talks was that Stalin, on December 25th, authorized the Poles to proceed with the organization of six divisions with reserves, with a total strength of 96,000 soldiers and promised to provide them with food rations.[53]

After this productive meeting with Stalin, Sikorski sent Anders a list of political and military instructions[54] which opened with a pointed reminder that it was he, Sikorski, who was the Commander-in-Chief and that Anders was subordinated to him. Sikorski instructed Anders not to use all available soldiers to form a maximum number of combat units. Instead, one third should be kept in a reserve pool. This was Sikorski's favorite idea, which, however, was ignored by Anders. Sikorski also advised Anders that, with Moscow's consent, twenty five thousand soldiers should be evacuated from the USSR, apart from those who had already been sent to England. He put Lieutenant-Colonel Tuskiewicz in charge of this operation and ordered that minorities should constitute no more than five percent.of these evacuees. The last point suggests that Anders is not to be blamed for the relatively low number of minorities among the evacuees.

In May, 1942, General Sikorski gave Anders another set of instructions which again began by reminding him of the proper relationship between a subordinate and a superior. Sikorski acknowledged there were differences of opinion on the organization and use of Polish forces and stressed that Anders must follow directions from his superior. Sikorski made it clear he did not want Anders to take risks that could result in the loss of the entire Polish Army. He wanted the army spread around so that it could not be destroyed in a single major battle.[55] Sikorski's intention was to husband forces, so that a Polish Army would be available when the Allies liberated Poland from the Germans. This was, however, inconsistent with his other instruction that the Polish Army should engage the enemy as a single unit.

At the start of 1942, Anders' Army (on paper) consisted of six divisions, only one of which, the 5th, was equipped to fight. In February, 1942, the army was moved further south, where climatic conditions were better, but where contagious diseases were endemic. Army units were scattered all over South Central Asia. Anders' headquarters was now in Iangi Iul, near Tashkent, were most units were located. Other parts of the army were based in Samarkand,

Shakhrisabz (Uzbekistan), Margilan (Tajikistan), Frunze, Dzhalal-Abad (Kirgizia), Ashkhabad (Turkmenia), Alma-Ata, Chimkent, Lugovoi and Merke (Kazakhstan).

Since women also streamed into the area where the army was being formed, General Anders created a British style Women's Army Corps. According to Mrs. Anders her husband placed the creation of the ATS high on his list of achievements. Officially it bore the British name "Auxiliary Territorial Service" (ATS), but Polish soldiers referred to it as "PSK," a Polish language acronym for Auxiliary Women's Service. When the women arrived at Polish Army camps they were in very poor physical condition, ill, hungry, infested with insects, bare footed and in rags. The first Polish ATS unit was formed in Buzuluk, in September, 1941, and subsequently similar units were formed at all bases. Polish women chosen to be officers were trained in British ATS camps. The commanding officer of the ATS in the USSR, was Mrs. Piechowska, later replaced by Mrs. Bronislawa Wyslouchowa who had been imprisoned in the USSR for underground activity, and was beaten and tortured during interrogations. Lieutenant Colonel Maria Lesniak who was named Commander of all Polish ATS and served in London, was described in a newspaper article as having left a Soviet prison only two months earlier, but at present enjoying "the full confidence of the Soviet authorities."[56]

The Polish ATS played the same role as the British ATS and generally followed the British Army model. Its purpose was to relieve men for combat by caring for orphans, doing clerical work, processing signals and working as cooks, drivers and nurses' aides.

The patriotism of the ATS was exceedingly high. In personal interviews, former ATS members boasted of taking an oath not to dance or wear civilian clothing until the war ended. Symbolic self-sacrifice was not unusual among Polish soldiers but in the case of women these oaths also were self-protective. In October, 1941, while Anders' Army was still in the initial phase of its organization, the ATS numbered 1,500 women[57] but it grew to 3,000 by the first evacuation in March-April of 1942.

Anders was strongly committed to education, seeing it as an important method of uplifting the Polish people. Although the education of children was the first priority, Anders was adamant that his soldiers, including officers, should continue to learn. Classes were held at all army locations and at all levels. When Anders learnt that an illiterate sergeant had harassed a soldier who was teaching other soldiers to read he stripped him of his rank.[58] There was no shortage of teachers or students, but virtually no books. Special cadet schools were organized for boys of high school age who could become officer-cadets one year after graduation.

By February of 1942, relations between Anders and the Soviets worsened over Anders' refusal to send the 5th Division to the front. This division consisted mainly of personnel of the 1939 Polish Army and its soldiers and officers had declared their willingness to advance to the Front. On February 2, 1942, Soviet and Polish commanders met in Tashkent to discuss the mode of employment of Polish troops at the front. Maneuvers, carried out at the end of February, 1942, demonstrated that the division was ready for battle. The division had British uniforms and small arms but it still did not have the necessary heavy weapons. The Soviets said that its full armament would be completed once it arrived at the front. Anders demurred saying the soldiers needed to train with the new weapons before going to battle. He was against sending individual units to the front before the entire Polish Army was ready and, in his opinion, it would not become ready before June 1, 1942.[59]

When the Soviet liaison officer, Zhukov, pointed out that the British used single Polish units in North Africa and at Narvik in Norway, Anders answered that this was not the same thing because those soldiers had not gone through prisons and POW camps.[60] He referred to Stalin's promises to wait until the entire Polish Army was ready before committing it to battle so that the first battle would have a positive result for the Poles. Anders, in turn agreed to take steps to shorten the training period.

Anders' cautious assessment of the state of battle readiness of his troops was probably right. Zhukov himself, after inspecting the army, was very critical of the officers, who, in his opinion, were not very knowledgeable and did not know how to plan for battle and had not mastered their new weapons, e.g. machine guns and mortars. As an example of their lack of expertise he cited an accident with a land mine which exploded in the middle of an infantry unit wounding eighteen men. In his report to Stalin, Zhukov said the artillery men were receiving good training but did not know how to cooperate with the infantry. He complimented junior officers and soldiers on their ability to endure physical strain and on their military discipline, but pointed out that they did not know even how to use shovels for digging trenches. The commanders didn't know how to use sappers in battle and needed additional training.[61]

Anders was adamant about not letting Stalin use Polish soldiers as cannon fodder. According to a British journalist who visited Anders' Army the Polish soldiers were anxious to get into battle, and Anders had a difficult task convincing them they were still too sick to go into immediate combat.[62] The wisdom of Anders' caution was confirmed at the battle of Lenino (near Orsha) where the Soviet sponsored Polish Division under Berling suffered tremendous losses after having been put into battle before the soldiers recovered from malnutrition and illness and before receiving adequate training.

The decision to refuse the Soviet request to send the 5th Division into action was not taken by Anders on his own. He consulted Sikorski, who agreed with him about not splitting the Force.[63] Sikorski wanted the whole Polish Army, acting as an independent unit, to be given an independent military task which it could successfully accomplish on its own, thereby demonstrating its willingness and ability to defeat the Germans. He gave as an example the protection of various oil fields. Sikorski was very specific about use of Polish troops when he wrote, "the troops (Polish) may be used in a way enabling them to fulfill single-handed a task which would be important from the point of view of the whole war." In the same order Sikorski pointed out that he did not want Polish troops to be used until they have "attained full combat readiness."[64]

After Anders refused to send the 5th Division to the front he was advised that from March 1, the food allotments would be decreased to 26,000 rations. Anders personally went to Moscow and told Panfilov to arrange a meeting with Stalin to discuss the question of supplies, hoping to solve all supply problems. Anders told Panfilov that the British were prepared to deliver 10,000 rifles and several hundred machine guns but if his army continued getting only the 30,000 rations it was presently allotted, the surplus soldiers would have to be evacuated to Iran. Anders was counting on deliveries of small arms from the Soviets, on financial help from the British and supplies of equipment and uniforms from the Americans. He also asked for Red Army weapon instructors.[65] He also asked for thirty three uniforms for the higher commanding ranks and for 1,000 second hand uniforms for privates whose uniforms had worn out. Moreover he wanted permission to issue identity cards printed both in Polish and Russian.[66]

On March, 14, 1942, Beria reported to Stalin that the personnel strength of the Polish Army was as follows: 3,090 officers, 16,202 NCOs, and 40,708 soldiers for a total of 60,000. Two divisions (5th and 6th) were up to strength with respectively over 12,000 and 14,000 in the ranks. One division (7th) was at half strength with over 7,000 soldiers and the remaining three divisions were in skeletal form numbering from seventeen to twenty eight hundred soldiers. Moreover there were over ten thousand soldiers in reserve. Thus while the original plan was to create six divisions, only two were operational by March of 1942. Only the 5th

Division was near fully armed, while the 6th received only a few arms. However, Anders redistributed some of the arms of the 5th Division to other units.[67]

On March 18, 1942, Stalin received General Anders who complained about another decision i.e. that starting March 21, 1942, the Polish Army of 70,000 soldiers would be receiving only 40,000 rations. Stalin said the United States and Great Britain promised to supply 200,000 tons of wheat per month but presently only a total of 60,000 tons had been provided forcing them to limit rations for the Polish Army and stop formation of new units in the Red Army. Eventually Stalin agreed to continue supplying Anders with seventy thousand rations until the end of March and with forty four thousand afterwards. Soldiers above the 44,000 would be evacuated to Iran. In the Soviet Union three Polish Divisions would be formed: the Soviets would arm two divisions and the British one. The part of the Polish Army in Iran, after reorganization and training, would be sent to the Soviet-German front where it would be supplied by the Soviets.[68]

At another meeting with the Soviets on March 28, 1942,while the first evacuation was taking place, Anders agreed to recall recruiting officers working outside the designated recruiting areas. It was also agreed that all volunteers for the Polish Army must go through the recruiting centers at their places of residence and only afterwards would they be sent to the Guzar station.[69]

Two weeks before Anders' meeting with Stalin, Beria reported that Anders intended to draft all eligible Polish citizens living in the USSR. If this recruitment were to take place it would again exceed the agreed upon ceiling of 44,000 and again raise the question of evacuation of surplus soldiers to Iran. Beria proposed to tell Anders that at first he would be allowed to draft only the number necessary to complete existing units up to the agreed ceiling of 44,000 and calling up the remaining Polish citizens would be allowed only when the Polish Army went to the front.[70]

By May 1, 1942, after the first evacuation, the numerical strength of the Polish Army in the USSR reached 40,668 officers and soldiers.[71] In June, Raczynski advised the Soviets that it was possible to increase this number to 123,000 soldiers. According to his calculations there were at the time 44,000 soldiers in the USSR, 30,000 in Iran plus an expected 49,000 new recruits in the USSR.[72]

From the beginning Poles and Soviets pursued different objectives. While Sikorski wanted a substantial Polish Army of three hundred thousand in the Soviet Union, Stalin wanted the Polish presence to be more symbolic than real. From the day the Sikorski-Maisky Agreement was signed there was a conflict over the size of the Polish Army. There was no provision in this Agreement or in the Military Agreement restricting the numerical strength of the army. On the other hand, arming and clothing three hundred thousand Poles would have required Stalin to take uniforms and weapons from Red Army Divisions. The Red Army was not limited by available manpower but it was limited by available food, equipment and supplies. The Soviets manipulated the formation of General Anders' Army in various ways. The number of food rations supplied by the Soviets was the crucial instrument allowing them to control its size, even though the Polish command tried to divide the allocated food between a larger number of soldiers than had been authorized.

It is, of course, true that a food shortage in the Soviet Union forced Stalin to limit food supplies for civilians. Although the rations given to Polish soldiers and civilians, were meager, there is no indication that they differed from the quantities made available to Soviet civilians. Politics aside, food supplies were a major problem.[73]

A major stumbling block in the Polish-Soviet alliance was the mysterious absence of thousands of officers interned in Kozelsk, Starobelsk and Ostashkov POW camps who had not been heard from since the spring of 1940. At the first protocol conference, Anders asked Panfilov for a list of Polish officers held in the camps and for the location of the camps. He was told that officers were kept in three camps, Griazovets (Vologda region), Suzdal and Iuzhev (Ivanovo-Voznesensk region), and Starobelsk camp. At the second protocol conference, Zhukov gave Anders a list of the names of 1,658 Polish Army officers. At first, little attention was given to the fact that the Polish soldiers reporting for duty were almost exclusively from the lower ranks. A few sergeants showed up, but the number of officers was very small. When Anders first mentioned this to the Soviets he was informed that this was only temporary and that work camps and prisons for officers were further away than the others and thus more travel time was required.[74] On September 28, 1941, Molotov stated, in a memo to the Polish Government in London, that all Polish prisoners had been released from prison and labor camps. "I believe it impossible that your people are still in camps," declared the Soviet Foreign Minister. Only later it would become apparent that he was, in a sense, telling the truth. In October, the newly appointed Polish Ambassador to the USSR, Professor Stanislaw Kot, complained that there were still Poles in labor and prison camps who had been neither released nor advised they were entitled to participate in the amnesty. He specifically demanded an explanation of the fate of 7,500 officers who had been taken prisoner by the Soviets, in 1939 who had not turned up after the amnesty.[75] On November 14, 1941, approximately three months after the amnesty, Ambassador Kot again raised the issue of missing officers during his talk with Stalin, who assured him that all Polish officers had been freed.[76] At the end of October Sikorski personally pleaded with the Soviets to release all Polish officers from POW camps.[77] All these entreaties were in vain.

The mysterious issue of missing officers from the POW camps in Kozelsk, Starobelsk and Ostashkovo naturally stirred up emotions and caused uneasiness in Anders' staff. Anders assigned his most respected officer, Captain Joseph Czapski to head a search for the missing officers. Czapski traveled all over the USSR and talked to the top NKVD leadership but his efforts were unsuccessful and the mystery persisted.[78]

In the meantime the situation with the officers in the army was paradoxical. On one hand there was a shortage of junior officers, and on the other, there was a surplus of senior and retired officers. At the same time, there was also a surplus of officers in Great Britain. Nevertheless, relatively few were transferred from Britain to Polish forces in the USSR. Their reluctance to leave England for the USSR is understandable and there was much less opposition to going to Iraq, where approximately a hundred officers joined the Anders' forces. To remedy the shortage of junior officers Anders organized cadet schools.

The problem of the surplus officers remained. Salaries for Polish soldiers and officers were paid by the British through funds allocated for the Polish Army and were paid according to the function held and not according to rank. The Poles paid according to rank. In cases of lower ranking officers holding higher posts, the Polish Army used the difference to pay "surplus" officers. Some of the "excess" officers were employed by doubling the number of officers assigned to certain roles by the Tables of Organization. Sikorski wanted some 700 older officers retired. Because most of these officers spoke little or no English and would have a difficult time in the work market as civilians, a majority preferred staying in uniform at half pay, even if they had no official duties.[79] In the first half of 1942, General Sikorski did place 200 aged officers on the retirement list.[80] Sosnkowski suggested that 110 surplus Polish officers with ranks of major and lieutenant colonel be attached to the American Army. Nothing came of this suggestion.[81]

With very few exceptions Anders took all officers wanting to get out of the USSR, but once in the Middle East, he purged those suspected of collaborating with the Soviets and those too old for their posts. The purged officers were placed in the so-called "Second Group" and were left in Palestine at half pay for the duration of the war.

Another issue that contributed to the deterioration of Polish-Soviet relations was the Soviet refusal to allow Polish citizens who had been drafted into the Red Army to transfer into Anders' Army.[82] Between September of 1939, and June, 1941, the Soviets took four intakes of draftees from the territories taken from Poland.[83] On February 3, 1940, the Polish Government protested against the drafting of its citizens. Only after the Amnesty did the Soviets stop drafting Poles and this lasted until Anders' Army left the USSR, in the second half of 1942. They continued however to draft "former Polish citizens" who were not Polish by nationality. By November, 1942, there were 100,000 Polish Jews serving in Soviet labor battalions.[84] According to American intelligence reports, at the end of 1942 there were at least 60,00 former Polish soldiers serving in Russian labor battalions and another 80,000 Polish soldiers who the Soviets wouldn't release because they were "minorities," i.e. Jews, Ukrainians and White Russians. Americans estimated there were as many as 250,000 Polish soldiers whom Stalin should release, including 8300 Polish officers who had been deported to Franz-Joseph Island, above the Arctic Circle.

Kot protested the drafting of Polish citizens of Ukrainian, Byelorussian and Jewish origin, but the Soviets maintained they were now Soviet citizens. In November of 1941, Kot protested against this in a note to the Soviet Ministry of Foreign Affairs, but the Soviets did not budge.[85]

In January, 1942, Anders asked that all Polish citizens in the Red Army, including those in labor or construction detachments, be discharged and sent to the Polish Army. Some Poles did not wait for official discharge and deserted from the Red Army[86] causing the Soviets to complain that Polish officers were encouraging such desertions.[87] Soviet policy seemed not very consistent on this point. While some Polish Jews were executed for deserting the Red Army to join Anders' Army, in at least one case seven Jewish doctors, who had been drafted into the Red Army in June of 1942, were later released and allowed to join the Polish Army.[88]

Like any other army, the Polish Army in the USSR had its share of problems with crime and misbehavior. Discipline was a special problem for Anders' Army because it was difficult to punish soldiers who had only recently been released from prisons or labor camps where they had suffered so many deprivations. The NKVD, which from the very beginning closely monitored Anders' men and women, had a very low opinion of their moral qualities. Beria reported that they were stealing bread from each other, selling their uniforms, getting drunk and stealing from the Soviets. Beria was hardly an impartial witness and his testimony should not be uncritically accepted.[89] However, it is true that the Polish military prosecutor reported five hundred cases of theft, embezzlement and desertion.

In an attempt to persuade two soldiers to report to him about discipline in the army, Kot said that "soldiers behave badly in headquarters. Soldiers shouldn't get drunk, but the officers are getting drunk with women from the headquarters and have complete orgies. We are receiving complaints daily and remember the command is weak."[90]

Zhukov, the Soviet liaison officer to Anders, reported that the "outrages" were mostly committed by soldiers in the 5th and 7th Divisions. In Dzhalal-Abad Polish soldiers took over buildings and equipment and destroyed hundreds of fruit trees. They also allegedly stole wood and glass, and twenty wagons of straw from a railroad station. During the first two weeks seven Polish soldiers were arrested in Dzhalal-Abad for stealing from local civilians. Zhukov demanded punishment for the guilty, replacement of losses and prevention of such incidents in the future, and ordered the NKVD and the police to arrest any Polish soldier disturbing public order and to charge him before a Soviet military court. The Soviets gave Anders a list of "outrages" committed by Polish soldiers. Anders gave them his assurance that he would take very strong measures against any soldiers guilty of transgressions.[91]

Anders' problem was complicated by the fact that the Polish Army didn't have a permanent home base and therefore no prison facilities. The choice was often between resorting to capital punishment or letting the culprits escape unpunished or with minor punishment. As a consequence, an unspecified number of Polish soldiers in the USSR were executed by the Polish Army for criminal acts. Romanowski recounts a case in which Anders approved the execution of two Polish soldiers for robbing Embassy storehouses. Romanowski, who served on the court-martial that sentenced the two soldiers to death, later called their execution a "big mistake." The judges had expected Anders to commute the sentences and were disappointed when he approved the verdict. Anders, who wasn't in the habit of explaining or justifying his actions to subordinates made a rare exception in this case. He explained that although the soldiers had not killed anyone, they were armed, and could have killed a guard and added that shortly before this incident the Soviets had executed two Red Army soldiers for stealing a cow. Anders knew that the awful conditions in which his soldiers were living was undermining their morale and he was afraid of losing control over the troops and therefore he resorted to such harsh measures.

What must have contributed to the worsening of relations from the Polish side were the numerous demonstrations of hostility towards the Soviet Union by both officers and men which did not escape the attention of the Soviet authorities. From the very beginning the NKVD subjected the Polish Army personnel to close surveillance. No Polish patriot liked to consider the possibility, but NKVD reports demonstrate that a small number of Polish officers and soldiers did report to the NKVD.[92] General Anders and others knew their conversations were being monitored but they probably did not appreciate the full extent of the surveillance. Beria boasted to Stalin that he had a contact in Anders' most intimate circle. Veterans of Anders'

Army did a lot of speculating about who was spying for the Soviets. Soviet documents make it clear that Anders' favorite aide-de-camp, Captain Jerzy Klimkowski, was reporting to a NKVD Major. At one point, when Anders relationship with the Soviet authorities was tenuous, Klimkowski even volunteered to arrest his Commander-in-Chief on behalf of the NKVD.[93]

According to Beria's reports, very few Poles showed ideological sympathies for the Soviets. A larger group cooperated with them as they would cooperate with anyone fighting the Nazis.[94] There also were opportunists without strong convictions who, motivated by ambition, did the Soviets' bidding for personal gain. That this small group included Berling and Klimkowski, was an opinion often expressed.

Beria prepared lists of names of officers known to be hostile to the USSR.[95] Those officers included Pilsudskites, Nationalists, and other anti-Soviet elements who thought that after defeating Germany the army should turn against the Soviets. Outwardly, they professed loyalty to the Soviet-Polish alliance, but regarded it merely as a necessity for the revival of Poland and that "sooner or later the Polish people should settle its scores with the USSR." They could not forget the experience of Soviet prisons and camps and believed the Polish Army "should accumulate its strength and fight only on the Polish territory."[96] The anti-Soviet officers were supported by Poles released from labor camps or exile who constantly called attention to other Poles still remaining in Soviet prisons and labor camps and made other complaints. Anti-Soviet sentiments were also stimulated by the difficult material conditions in which the army had to live.[97]

Beria also reported to Stalin that initially Anders and a group of senior officers had demonstrated a positive attitude towards the USSR and had supported honest cooperation. General Boruta-Spiechowicz even declared that in case of an outbreak of anti-Soviet disorders in the USSR he would come to the defense of the Soviet Government. But his attitude began to change because of the bad conditions in which the Polish civilians had to live. Boruta-Spiechowicz felt the Soviet Government was responsible for the care of amnestied Poles because it was responsible for their deportation and consequent suffering. He declared that "I carry within me anti-Soviet feelings but I gave my word to General Anders not to do anything against the Soviets, and I shall keep it."[98]

Beria also noted that some Polish officers showed a pro-British attitude, but delays in the delivery of British arms as well as Red Army successes and British defeats in the Middle East weakened such attitudes. Some officers were even identified as anti-British by talking about Poland being sold out by Great Britain.[99]

Some officers didn't limit themselves to propaganda and established political groups. In the 6th Division a conspiratorial group was formed by the commander, General Michal Tokarzewski-Karaszewicz which included Major Domon and Colonels Koc and Lis. The group discussed the possibility of replacing Sikorski as Prime Minister and Commander-in-Chief with General Tokarzewski-Karaszewicz. The commander of the 16th Regiment of the 6th Division, Lt. Colonel Szafranski formed a battalion called "The Lvov Children," consisting of inhabitants of Lvov. Colonel Jerzy Grobicki formed an illegal organization composed of Nationalist and anti-Soviet elements in the 5th Division. A group headed by Colonel Krogulski thought the Sikorski Government was not sufficiently tough in its negotiations with the Soviets and conducted Nationalist propaganda to defend the concept of 1939 borders. Taking advantage of its good relations with Colonel Okulicki it tried to place its members in important positions. Some Polish officers allegedly argued that Poland could be restored only with German assistance.

According to Beria the "anti-Soviet elements" sent anonymous letters to Berling and Dudzinski, threatening them with death sentences for their pro-Soviet stance. Other pro-Soviet individuals, like Captain Rosen-Zawadzki and NCO Szczypiorski, were warned that they "will be taken care of" when the Polish forces reach the front. Beria also detected anti-Soviet sentiments in the army's cultural and educational activities: a puppet theater show attacked writer Boy-Zelenski and Wanda Wasilewska for their collaboration with a Soviet Polish-language journal. At the same performance "a piece was shown which tendentiously depicted the stay of Polish citizens in concentration camps." The army propaganda bureau and many priests conducted their propaganda campaign in a way that was "indirectly to the advantage of the anti-Soviet side." He cited Captain Dzieduszycki who praised an institution in fascist Italy and said that the Jewish problem in Poland should be resolved by the emigration of the Jewish population.[100]

Beria conceded however that Anders and the army command was concerned about anti-Soviet attitudes among the officers and attempted to struggle against them. He also admitted that the majority of soldiers expressed hostility towards Germany.[101] In December, 1941, the Soviets officially informed Anders about the anti-Soviet attitudes and statements in his army.[102]

In response to that, on January 30, 1942, Sikorski issued a secret order forbidding the Poles from making anti-Soviet statements and instructed Anders to fight against any demonstration of anti-Soviet attitudes in the army.[103] On his part, Anders, after the Soviet notification regarding anti-Soviet attitudes in the army, called an officers meeting in which he explained that "All anti-Soviet conversations, reminiscences about prisons and camps give [the Soviets] a basis to treat us with mistrust, at the time when we - our government and I personally, are permeated by a sincere desire of liberating the Motherland together with the Red Army. No other state would do for us what the Soviet state have done... As long as I command the army, I will mercilessly shoot and punish even more severely than it is done by the Soviet Government, those who with their twaddle will dare to disturb our relations with the Soviet Government."

Anders issued two orders regarding punishment of those engaging in anti-Soviet agitation, and instructed the army's Chief Prosecutor to charge the guilty before a court. At the same time as Anders was saying that, he found it difficult to completely liquidate the anti-Soviet elements and knew he had to maneuver cautiously because of the Poles in England who suspected him of ties with the NKVD.

The situation of the army was further complicated by the presence of tens of thousands of civilian refugees, for whom Anders felt responsible. The issue of refugees, their living conditions and their status, also contributed to a worsening of relations between the army and the Soviets.

## Religion

While the army was being formed in the USSR, local Soviet authorities were instructed by the Kremlin to take into account the spiritual needs of the Poles. Kot complained that although the Soviets were accommodating the religious needs of the soldiers, religious freedom was being denied civilians as no priests or churches were made available to them.

At the inception of army, Roman Catholic and Jewish chaplains were appointed. Bishop Gawlina[104] came from England to Russia to be Chief of Chaplains and served in that capacity until after the dissolution of the Second Polish Corps.

The first Orthodox Cleric in the army was Bishop Sawa who joined Anders' Army, in the second half of 1943. Although most Ukrainians were Orthodox there were some who were Roman Catholics and there were some Poles who were Orthodox.[105] The Protestant chaplains came later.[106]

## The Relief Effort and the Conflict Between Kot and Anders

The Polish Army attracted not only able bodied men, eligible for draft, but also tens of thousands of civilians including women and children expecting to find protection, food, clothing and shelter. They were in for an unpleasant surprise. The army itself suffered from food and equipment shortages. The Polish soldiers' rations were less than half of those in the British Army. In spite of that, in order to feed the civilians, each soldier gave up one daily ration a week (an officer two rations a week). Other supplies were meager as well. In October, 1941, only one in four soldiers in Anders' Army had shoes.[107] There was precious little to give to civilians.

Soviet promises of employment for Polish civilians went largely unfulfilled. There was severe unemployment in the regions of the USSR to which the Poles were arriving due to the huge influx of refugees and the dislocation of industry. The Soviets gave preference to Soviet citizens who were also the only ones eligible for the more remunerative jobs. At first, Poles were able to survive by selling their meager belongings, but the sale of clothing was regarded as profiteering and treated as illegal, including even the sale of items obtained from the relief programs.

After the amnesty the Polish Government instituted a world-wide relief program to provide food, clothing and medicine to former prisoners in the Soviet Union. Survival of the Polish soldiers and civilians depended in large part on relief programs run by religious, ethnic and charitable organizations. From the very beginning, however, the relief program ran into a series of difficulties. The first problems began at the source, in the United States, where aid programs were troubled by corruption and profiteering. A big scandal arose when the contents of some parcels were totally worthless.[108] This was because relief agencies did not, in most instances, prepare the parcels themselves but purchased them commercially, usually for nine dollars per parcel (in addition the Soviets levied a 100% import duty).

Both Polish and Jewish organizations fell victim to fraudulent businessmen. For example, when the parcels from Detroit, paid for by Polish agencies were opened by the starving Poles, it turned out that they contained nothing but rags. Parcels paid for by Jewish agencies in Philadelphia were sent out without being inspected and contained nothing but tea, broken buttons, shoe laces, bits of broken soap and knitted shorts.[109]

The delivery of relief aid was also delayed by a jurisdictional dispute between Anders and Kot, the Polish Ambassador to Moscow. When civilians began flocking to the area where the army was stationed, Anders could not remain indifferent to their fate, many of whom had relatives in the ranks. He immediately tried to organize help for them and sent military teams to all areas with Polish refugee colonies. Polish Army representatives were sent to railroad stations to guide ex-prisoners to the right trains. Reception centers were set up by the army in the north at Kirov and in the south at Tashkent, Samarkand and Alma-Ata.

Anders' attempts to organize relief for civilians were obstructed by the Polish Ambassador in Moscow Stanislaw Kot. Professor Kot's position was that he, as Ambassador, was responsible for all civilian matters, including the relief program, and that Anders was transgressing his prerogatives. Kot wanted to make relief distribution an exclusive preserve of his delegates so that everyone would know that relief had come from the Embassy and not from the army. Anders' response was that only the army had the ability and facilities to distribute relief and that the needy couldn't wait until Kot got organized. Relief supplies were stored in a warehouse in Buzuluk but the army was not authorized to distribute it; even medical supplies were withheld until they could be distributed by the Embassy staff. In the meantime, the sick had to go without medicine.[110]

As Ambassador, Kot had responsibility for the civilians and Anders had responsibility for the soldiers but it was clear to everyone that Anders felt Kot was not doing his job adequately, so the general began to assume the responsibility for civilians as well. Anders' rationale was that he could not be expected to build an effective Polish Army when his soldiers were worried about the welfare of their families. Many of the soldiers who flocked to the Polish Army camps brought their families with them because leaving them behind would, in many cases, mean death from starvation or disease.

Kot launched his own relief effort. He organized relief agencies under the Embassy's jurisdiction and eventually took entire control over the administration and distribution of relief. The Polish Embassy managed to open 304 local relief offices scattered throughout the USSR, wherever there were large groups of Polish citizens.[111] The offices distributed food, opened and ran schools, kindergartens and medical shelters reaching about 300,000 Polish citizens. The administration of relief was far from perfect. Distribution of aid was uneven and some parcels were sent to people who did not qualify for relief and some were sold instead of being distributed.[112]

The most serious obstacle to relief efforts was the obstructionist attitude of the Soviet authorities, which was surprising in view of the purely humanitarian nature of the relief program. From the very beginning the Soviets created delays in shipping and distribution of relief items. For example, in October, 1941, the Polish Ambassador to the United States complained that 100 tons of parcels containing food, clothing and medicine, supplied by the Polish American Council and the Polish Red Cross were stored in New York awaiting transport promised by the Soviet Ambassador. The story was similar with war material destined for General Anders' Army.[113]

Incredible as it may sound, the Soviet Government imposed import tariffs on food, clothing and medicine for the Polish refugees. It is incomprehensible that while the Soviets were receiving enormous lend-lease deliveries from the United States, the Americans did not insist that relief parcels be allowed to enter the USSR duty free.[114] Relief funds were not unlimited so money used to pay the tariffs effectively reduced the number of parcels entering the USSR. The Soviets prohibited the importation of food and used clothing and imposed a 200% tariff on new clothing.[115] They charged duty on relief packages, both entering and leaving the Soviet Union. For various reasons many parcels were returned unopened, and the Soviets charged duty a second time, plus expenses to return the packages to the senders. Some packages were abandoned and some were confiscated and sold to pay the duty. Others were diverted by Soviet officials for their own use.[116]

Soviet interference with the relief parcels and military supplies occurred in October, 1941, the high point in Soviet-Polish relations. It took Sikorski's direct intervention during his talks with Stalin in December of 1941, to get permission to get the relief program underway. Moreover, after his talks with Stalin the Soviets granted the Polish Government a loan of 100 million rubles for the purpose of helping Polish citizens in the USSR.[117] Even then the relief agencies were barely tolerated and their role was being constantly reduced.

The Soviets issued an order that made it a crime for a Polish citizen to receive food at these distribution centers.[118] Even soldiers and potential soldiers going to join the army were not allowed to receive food at these centers. It is difficult to understand the reason for this order which caused thousands of Poles to die from starvation as many were traveling without food or money when the order was issued. The Polish Embassy asked in vain that the order be revoked and that Polish civilians be allowed the same quantity of food as Soviet citizens. It claimed that according to an earlier order signed by the Soviet General, Pikushezyna, those traveling to join the army were to be permitted to receive food at the centers.[119]

Finally, in 1943, Polish relief agencies were liquidated and over a hundred of their employees were arrested.[120] Stalin terminated the relief action partly because food received from abroad was of a higher quality than could be found in the USSR and partly because it was politically embarrassing to admit that he had to resort to foreign aid to feed those upon whom he forcibly imposed Soviet citizenship. In addition, the Soviets claimed that the Poles were using their relief network for espionage.[121]

It seems that although Stalin was able to appreciate the size of the Polish relief network, he overestimated its capabilities for intelligence operations. Nevertheless, the OSS was convinced that some of the Russian charges of Polish espionage in the USSR were true. The legal counsel to Ambassador Kot admitted that some spying was done by the relief agencies, calling it amateurish and done without direction or instructions. The British Ambassador to the USSR reported that Kot confided to him that the relief network was also being used as a spy network. The ineptitude of the erstwhile "agents" was demonstrated when one delegate left a briefcase in a restaurant with a report about the economic situation in the region.[122] The briefcase naturally fell into NKVD hands and the incident served as a pretext for arresting more than 100 delegates and for closing the relief offices. When the Russians closed the relief agencies, in 1943, a Polish delegation went to Moscow to negotiate an agreement to continue the relief program under the control of the Red Cross or jointly by the Polish Embassy and Soviet officials. However, when the delegation was in Moscow the Katyn Affair erupted and the Soviet Union broke off diplomatic relations with the Polish Government.[123]

The Polish-Soviet alliance was under heavy strain. The difficult conditions created for the Polish Army, the constant manipulation of food ration quotas, delays or failure to deliver the promised armaments, obstacles to the relief effort for civilians and a suspicious insistence on an immediate dispatch of parts of the Polish Army to the front--

could not but raise Polish suspicions about Soviet intentions and make them doubt that an alliance and cooperation with the Soviets was possible or desirable. The mysterious and inexplicable disappearance of thousands of officers from the three POW camps in Kozelsk, Starobielsk and Ostashkov made it particularly difficult for Poles to believe the Soviets had good intentions. The Soviet side had its own reasons for disappointment. They were aware that the predominant mood in the Polish Army was unfriendly to them. The refusal of the Polish command and the government to commit to battle those units that were, according to the Soviets, combat ready raised the question whether the Poles wanted to fight at all. The presence of a Polish relief network on Soviet territory, practically independent of Soviet authorities and disposing of its own food supplies, must have been a thorn in the side of the totalitarian government used to exercising absolute control over the souls and bodies of people under its jurisdiction. Therefore it is not surprising that both sides began to consider the possibility of evacuating the Polish Army from the USSR as the best compromise solution for both sides.

**Koltubanka**

A defacto Jewish unit, (technically the 9th Regiment of the 8th Division), in the Polish Army was created at Koltubanka in the USSR and continued for several months during the winter of 1941-1942. The unit was part of the 8th Division which was one of the first to participate in the evacuation and one of the first to be disbanded when the army was reorganized. Estimates of the number of Jewish soldiers at Koltubanka range from 600 to 900.

Anders was pressured from two sides. The Irgun (Merek Kahan)[124] wanted an identifiable Jewish Unit and the opposition (Rabbi Rosengarten, among others) saw a Jewish unit as a ghetto. The Koltubanka unit was abolished at the time of the first evacuation, according to Meir Lustgarten, who served in the unit. Koltubanka was a compromise. It was not called a Jewish unit and there were non-Jews scattered through the ranks, but defacto it was a Jewish unit. Kahan finally relented and told Anders he would have no objections to disbanding so the unit was abolished.

Ari Weinberg did not serve at Koltubanka but his brother in law, Ignacy Bochenek was an officer and did serve there. Weinberg admitted he was considering desertion, especially after it was suggested by Polish friends, but he did not desert at the behest of his wife's brother and uncle who were officers in Anders' Army. The interview with Weinberg was routine until he mentioned his brother-in-law. He then produced a set of photographs which had belonged to Bochenek (deceased) who said he wanted them used in some historical record, where upon permission was granted to use them in this book.

The photographs were shown to Rabbi Rosengarten who was able to recognize Lt. Bochenek, a Jewish ATS, (later identified as Julia Goldbaum) the unit commander and his family, a number of Jewish soldiers and himself. The photographs show the soldiers wearing boots and heavy overcoats, which according to Rosengarten were issued just prior to the dissolution of the unit.

There were other units at Koltubanka, including a staging area for soldiers who were to be transferred to the Navy and Air force. According to Witold Kociejowski the Jewish unit wasn't the first or the last to get new boots and heavy coats. (Letter dated November 7, 1991.)[125]

## Collaborators and Spies

Parsadanova, said, "Of course there were Soviet spies in the Polish Army, there are spies in all armies." There definitely were British spies in the Second Corps, according to Howarth. The general consensus among officers interviewed was that there were a minimum number of spies in the Second Corps, although an officer said he knew of two Ukrainians and one Byelorussian who were arrested for spying.

A bigger problem, according to Racieski, was women who had close relations with ranking officers. He mentioned the name of one woman who was a KGB plant. Once they left the USSR she admitted to being a spy. On his first trip to London, Anders went by way of Cairo and left her there.

Perhaps the most famous collaborator was General Leon Kozlowski, a former minister in the prewar government. A former officer and deserter from Anders Army, he was court martialled in absentia and sentenced to death by Anders. He was killed in an allied bombing of Berlin.

A British "most secret" report found in an unclassified American intelligence file, lists [126] the names and activities of Polish agents who were working for the Germans. Included on this list were persons who were supposed to convince Anders to tell his army to lay down their arms and join the Germans against the Russians.[127]

## APPENDIX "A"

Jan Romanowski:

Jan Romanowski escaped to France in 1939, only to volunteer to return to Soviet occupied Poland to organize and operate an anti-Soviet underground. At the Romanian-Soviet border there was a shoot out and he was wounded. The local mountain people, known as Rutherians "sold him" to the NKVD. Ten months later he was tried as a spy and terrorist in the Russian courts and was sentenced to be executed on July 7, 1941. The German invasion on June 22, saved his life. He was released from Lubienka prison on August 31, a month after amnesty was granted and the next day reported for duty. He was the 13th officer to join the newly formed army and was assigned to be the aide to Anders' Chief of Staff. Romanowski left the USSR during the second evacuation to Iran where due to the death of an ADC to Anders, he was named to replace him and served as Anders' ADC until after the war ended. Romanowski's position gave him a unique opportunity to observe many events and personalities during this period.

## APPENDIX "B"

Anders had four major aide d' camps:

–Captain Jerzy Klimkowski, who served from the time in the USSR until he was jailed by Anders when they were in the Middle East.

–Captain. Jan Romanowski who served from the time in Iran until after the war and was Anders' longest serving ADC.

–Captain Ludwik Lubienski, former Secretary to Foreign Minister Jozef Beck, served as a special assignment officer for General Anders.

–Captain Eugene Lubomirski, who also served as Anders's interpreter.

Footnotes

1. Documents on Polish-Soviet Relations, 1939-1945 (London: Heinemann, 1961), v. I, p. 141-142. Maisky wrote a book, "Who Helped Hitler?", which could be a treatise on rationalization. He concludes that France and Great Britain helped Hitler by forcing the Soviet Union to enter into an agreement with Germany and argues that the Second World War could have been avoided if the Soviets, British and French had stood up to Hitler in the early years. He claims the unwillingness of Britain and France to enter into an agreement with the Soviets forced the Russians to form an alliance with Hitler for self-protection. He blames the Poles for not agreeing (until it was too late) to allow Soviet troops to pass through Poland, if necessary, to fight the Germans. He argues it was necessary for the Soviets to take a portion of Poland to prevent German troops from being massed on the Soviet border. From the Soviet point of view there may be some merit to Maisky's contention, but the Polish Government knew that once in Poland, it would be difficult, if not impossible, to evict the Red Army. See, Maisky, Ivan.Who helped Hitler? 1964, Hutchinson, London.

2. M. Kukiel, General Sikorski: Zolnierz i maz stanu Polski walczacej (London: Instytut Polski, 1970), p. 174-175.

3. FO 371/26757/C8598.

4 A. Eden, The Memoirs of Anthony Eden, (Boston: Houghton Mifflin, 1965), v. 3, p. 273.

5. FO 371/26757.

6. J. Retinger, Memoirs of an Eminence Grise (Brighton: Susex UP, 1972), p. 123. In 1930, Pilsudski appointed General Sosnkowski, Commander-in-Chief of the Polish Army. He was known as Poland's best military strategist and enjoyed wide popularity.Surprisingly Parsadanova called him "loyal and straight". When he was "fired," in 1944, he went to Canada where he spent the rest of his life. For more about Sosnkowski, see NA 61513X;FR1944 vol iv p.995; FO 371/39481 and FO 371/26579/C9315.

7. Retinger, Memoirs of an Eminence Grise, p. 120-121.

8. A copy was obtained by American military intelligence, National Archive, Poland #6940, #6010.

9. FO 371/267757. General Haller was never found.

10. HI, Mikolajczyk coll., Box 1.

11. W. Anders, An Army in Exile, p. 44-51.

12. Z. Bohusz-Szyszko, "General broni Wladyslaw Anders" in General Wladyslaw Anders: Zycie i chwala (London, 1970), p. 14.

13. HI, Borkowski file, box 1 (1941).
14. Anders wife, daughter and son in law drove to Italy and arrived unannounced at his headquarters.
15. Anders' letter to Sikorski (August, 14 1941) in GSHI, PRM 42/4. The infamous article 54, Paragraph B of the Ukrainian Penal Code and Article 58, Paragraph B, of the All-Soviet Code were used to justify the death penalty or long prison terms. The Ukrainian Penal Code which applies throughout the Soviet Union, provides "Any foreigner who does an act which is contrary to the Soviet conduct of the war, or in any way is a hazard to the Soviets will be sentenced to death or imprisonment." The language of the codes was interpreted in such a way as to apply to non-Soviet citizens. Based on this interpretation a non-Soviet citizen forcibly brought to the USSR was required to be loyal to the Soviet Union. In addition, the code was interpreted in such a way that it allowed for a prosecution of non-citizens for deeds in their home country. This concept of extra-territorial application of Soviet law was used to justify the execution or imprisonment of Polish citizens who, while in Poland, did something that would be punishable if done by a Soviet citizen in the USSR.
16. Documents on Polish-Soviet Relations, 1939-1945, I, p. 147-148.
17. Ibid, p. 147-153.
18. A resolution of the State Defense Committee signed by Stalin (December 25, 1941) in Novaia i Noveishaia Istoriia 2 (1993), p. 73-75; FO 371/26760/C10394/3226/55.
19. Documents on Polish-Soviet Relations, 1939-1945, v. I, p. 156.
20. General Anders asked the survivors to submit written testimony of their experiences in the Soviet Union. There are 10,000 of these reports in the Anders' Collection in the Hoover Institute and they formed the main source basis for this subject.

21. "Polish-Soviet Relations, 1941," HI, Borkowski collection, box 1; also "Polish-Soviet Agreement 1941 The Final Text" HI, Mikolajczyk collection, box 16. At first "collaboration statements" were only for officers enrolled at the Villa, but after amnesty the NKVD tried to get all officers to sign the statements. Although torture was not used to coerce signing, sometimes pressure was applied and some officers were not immediately released to give the NKVD time to work on them. General Rudnicki admitted signing but said it was under duress and in the belief his release was predicated upon signing the statement. The signer of this simplistic statement was agreeing to inform the NKVD of anything he learned that might be of interest to Soviet Intelligence. The appointment of General Rudnicki as a division commander is the best evidence that Anders did not treat these statements as a serious matter.

22. Excerpts from Politburo minutes of August 12, 1941, forwarded to Beria in Novaia i Noveishaia Istoriia 2 (1993), p. 63-64.

23. Izvestia (August 13, 1941).

24. State Defense Committee decision #4956.

25. Dokumenty i materialy po istorii sovetsko-pol'skikh otnoshenii, (eds.) I.A. Khrenov, N. Gasiorowska-Grabowska (Moscow 1973), v. VII, p. 264.

26. The preceding and the following paragraphs are based on testimonies in HI Anders coll., box no. 81.

27. A.-L. Moats, Blind Date with Mars (Garden City, N.Y.: Doubleday, Doran, 1943), p. 433.

28. S.W. Slowes, The Road to Katyn: a Soldier's Story (Oxford, U.K.; Cambridge, Mass.: Blackwell Publishers, 1992), p. 1

29. Beria's report to Stalin and Molotov (November 1, 1941) in Noviai i Noveishaia Istoriia 2 (1993), p. 65-67.

30. HI, Mikolajczyk coll., box 16.

31. Beria to Stalin (October 1, 1941) in Novaia i Noveishaia Istoriia 2 (1993), p. 66-67.

32. V.S. Parsadanova, Sovetsko-pol'skie otnosheniia v Gody Velikoi Otechestvennoi voiny, 1941-1945 (Moscow, 1982), p. 49.

33. A report from Beria to Stalin and Molotov (October 1, 1941) in Novaia i Noveishaia Istoriia 2 (1993), p. 66.

34. Retinger, Memoirs of an Eminence Grise, p. ??

35. HI, Borkowski coll., Box 1.

36. GHSI, A. XII. 1/56.

37. Anders, An Army in Exile, p. 94-95.

38. Panfilov's report (September 19, 1941), Tsentral'nyi Arkhiv Ministerstva Oborony Rossiiskoi Federatsii (Central Archive of the Ministry of Defense of the Russian Federation) [cit. furth. TsAMO], f. 280, op. 768407, d. 45, l. 12 and Beria's report to Stalin (October 1, 1940) in Novaia i Noveishaia Istoriia 2 (1993), p. 66; also see Documents on Polish-Soviet Relations, 1939-1945, v. 1, p. 201-202.
39. FO 371/26760/C10394/3226/55.
40. Beria to Stalin (November 30, 1941), in Armia Polska w ZSRR 1941-1942 (ed.) W. Materski (Warsaw, 1992), p. 18.
41. Anders, An Army in Exile, p. 54.
42. Daily Telgraph (October 6, 1941).
43. Panfilov to Stalin and Molotov (December 18, 1941), TsGAMO, f. 280, op. 768407, d. 45, l. 18.
44. Documents on Polish-Soviet Relations, 1939-1945, v. I, p. 205.
45. Documents on Polish-Soviet Relations, 1939-1945, v. I, p. 207-208, 210.
46. A. Prazmowska, "Polish Refugees as Military potential: objectives of the Polish Government in Exile," in: Refugees in the Age of Total War, (ed.) A. Bramwell (London, Boston: Unwin Hyman, 1988), passim.
47. Documents on Polish-Soviet Relations, 1939-1945, vol. I, p. 231-243. Apparently only Sikorski was scheduled to represent the Poles. Sikorski asked Harriman, the American envoy to the USSR to arrange for Kot and Anders to be invited to the meeting.
48. Anders, An Army in Exile, p. 89.
49. Jews in Eastern Poland and the USSR, 1939-46, N. Davies, A. Polonsky (eds.) (Houndmills, Basingstoke, Hampshire: Macmillan, 1991), p. 58, n. 86. Anders issued an order dated November 14, 1941 stating that there shall not be any religious or ethnic discrimination in the army. A second order, dated November 30, 1941 was contradicitory and is considered anti-Semitic Anders maintains the second order is a forgery. Copies of the orders are in HIPSZ box 8 folder 59. See als, Unequal Victims pp. 336-7 and Kot's Dispatches, pp. 465-6
50. Documents on Polish-Soviet Relations, 1939-1945, v. 1, p. 243.
51. S. Mikolajczyk, The Rape of Poland: Pattern of Soviet Aggression (New York, Whittlesey House, 1948), p. 23.
52. Anders, An Army in Exile, p. 90.
53. Resolution of the State Defense Committee (25 XII 1941) in Armia Polska w ZSRR 1941-1942, p. 40, 42, 44.

54. Documents on Polish-Soviet Relations, 1939-1945, v. I, p. 251-253.
55. Documents on Polish-Soviet Relations, 1939-1945, v. I, p. 344-348.
56. Times (October 3, 1941); Anders, An Army in Exile, p. 51.
57. NA 5935.
58. Interview with Alexander Zvielli.
59. V.S. Parsadanova, Sovetsko-pol'skie otnosheniia v Gody Velikoi Otechestvennoi voiny, 1941-1945, p. 81.
60. A telegram from Zhukov to Molotov (February 6, 1942), in Armia Polska w ZSRR 1941-1942, p. 46.
61. Panfilov to Stalin and Molotov (undated draft, after March 1, 1942), TsGAMO, f. 289, op. 768407, d. 45, l. 27-29.
62. Daily Telegraph (October 6, 1941).
63. W. Anders, An Army in Exile, p. 97.
64. Documents on Polish-Soviet Relations, 1939-1945, v. I, p. 163-164, 279-280.
65. Panfilov to Stalin (March 17, 1942) in Armia Polska w ZSRR 1941-1942, p. 74, 76.
66. Dokumenty i materialy po istorii sovetsko-pol'skikh otnoshenii, VII, p. 287.
68. Beria to Stalin (March 14, 1941) in Armia Polska w ZSRR 1941-1942, p. 48.
67. Documents on Polish-Soviet Relations, 1939-1945, I, p. 301-310.
69. Minutes of the meeting of the joint Soviet-Polish commission (March 28, 1942), TsGAMO, f. 289, op. 768407, d. 45, l. 27-29. l. 76-77, 79-80.
70. Beria's memo to Stalin (March 31, 1942) in Armia Polska w ZSRR 1941-1942, p. 88.
71. TsGAMO, f. 289, op. 768407, d. 50, l. 218-219.
72. Documents on Polish-Soviet Relations, 1939-1945, I, p. 368-369.
73. Dokumenty i materialy po istorii sovetsko-pol'skikh otnoshenii, VII, p. 198-199.
74. P. Zaron, Armia Andersa (Torun, 1996), p. 39-40, 106.
75. Documents on Polish-Soviet Relations, 1939-1945, v. I, p. 173, 175-176.
76. Documents on Polish-Soviet Relations, 1939-1945, v. I, p. 210-211.
77. Documents on Polish-Soviet Relations, 1939-1945, v. I, p. 182.
78. W. Anders, An Army in Exile, p. 76, 121-122.

79. FO 371/24481.
80. FO 371/39468/C2240.
81. FO 371/39485/C6788.
82. HI, Ambasada USSR, Box 16, folder 97.
83. London Times (October 3, 1941); the information that they were released to serve in Anders Army was untrue.
84. NA Palestine 5129.
85. Documents on Polish-Soviet Relations, 1939-1945, v. I, doc. p. 200-201, 227-228.
86. HI, PSZ coll., box 6, folder 39, doc. #911.
87. Federal Register, v. 111 (1943), p. 322. For the adventures of a Polish soldier trying to get out of the Red Army and into Anders' Army see, F. Virski, My Life in the Red Army (New York: Macmillan, 1949).
88. Jews in Eastern Poland and the USSR, 1939-46, p. 43, 379; S. Kot, Conversations with the Kremlin and Dispatches from Russia (New York: Oxford UP, 1963), p. 269.
89. Panfilov to Stalin (September 19, 1941), TsAMO f. 280, op. 768407, d. 45, l. 12
90. HI, Mikolajczyk coll., box 16.
91. Undated report by Panfilov to the State Defense Committee, TsGAMO, f. 280, op. 768407, d. 45, l. 26; Minutes of the joint Soviet-Polish commission (March 28, 1942), ibid., d. 40, l. 81-82.
92. Beria to Stalin (March 14, 1942) in Armia Polska w ZSRR 1941-1942, p. 48-72.
93. Beria to Stalin (July 24, 1942) in Armia Polska w ZSRR 1941-1942, p. 98. There was no evidence that Klimkowski was in contact with the NKVD after leaving the USSR. He was jailed and reduced in rank ostensively for misappropriation of a vehicle, which seems a cover story for more important mischief. Klimkowski was among the first to return to Communist dominated Poland and was actively engaged in the campaign to smear Anders' name. Everyone seemed to know about Klimkowski schemes, plots, involvement with the NKVD, etc.Why did Anders keep Klimkowski as his ADC when his reputation was so bad.? Romanowski's answer is that Anders was very trusting and loyal to a fault, to the people around him.
94. Beria to Stalin (November 30, 1941) in Armia Polska w ZSRR 1941-1942, p. 18-28.

95. It included: Gen. Wolkowicki (deputy commander of the 6th Division), Col. Grobicki (deputy commander of the 5th Division), Maj. Dorman (chief of staff of the 6th Division), Lt-Col. Felshtein (chief of staff of the Reserve Regiment), Lt-Col. Pawlik (commander of the 16th Infantry Regiment), Maj. Lis (deputy commander of the 6th Artillery Regiment), Beria to Stalin (November 30, 1941) in Armia Polska w ZSRR 1941-1942, p. 24.

96. Such views were reportedly held by three generals (Krogulski, Rakowski, Wolkowicki), three colonels (Szmidt, Marszalek, Felsztyn) and Major Domon, a report by Beria to Stalin (March 14, 1942) in Armia Polska w ZSRR 1941-1942, p. 52.

97. Ibid. p. 52, 54.

98. Ibid. p. 24, 54.

99. Ibid., p. 58, 60.

100. Ibid., p. 24, 52, 60, 62, 64.

101. Ibid., p. 18, 20, 48, 50, 66.

102. Ibid., p. 32, 34, 36, 38, 64.

103. HI, PSZ box 8.

104. There was no love between the Bishop and Sikorski. In a secret American intelligence report dated May 19,1943, which as yet has not been fully declassified, it is stated Sikorski considers Gawlina as a camouflaged Pilsudskite while Gawlina is disturbed about Sikorski being "surrounded by free masons, who are said to exercise a strong influence over him." NA Special Rept.IDS No.263 rpt London, HJ 18-B Klimkowski named Gawlina as one of his co-conspirators and Romanowski suggested not ruling out that possibility. See,OSS X10506.

105. Although Polish citizens of Ukrainian nationality constituted a large, if not the largest minority in prewar Poland, the Polish soldiers questioned could not recall more than a handful of Ukrainians in the Second Polish Corps. The news of Ukrainian units in the German Army added to the Pole's mistrust. No examples were found of Ukrainians holding important positions in Anders' Army. The general consensus was that the Ukrainians in the army were pro-German, yet Ukrainian soldiers are buried at Monte Cassino and other Polish military cemeteries in Italy. Sikorski accused the Ukrainians of spreading Nazi propaganda and called them, fifth columnists. The hostility increased when it became known that the Germans had used Ukrainians as police and militia in German occupied Poland.

106. There were relatively few Protestants in Anders' Army and the first Protestant chaplain was not appointed until late 1943, due, in part, to fact the soldiers deported to Russia were from Eastern Poland and the Protestants in Poland were concentrated in Western Poland. No one was able to provide an example of a high ranking Protestant officer. The statements from Protestants who had served with Anders followed a pattern, first denial of any prejudice and then they expressed their grievances. In a few cases the person being interviewed had served a term in the German Army but didn't offer that information until asked. There are very few Protestants participating in the activities of the large Polish exile community in London. An explanation given for the prejudice against having Protestant chaplains in the army was that the only way a Roman Catholic could get a divorce under Polish law was to become a Protestant. The Roman Catholic chaplains were fearful that making Protestant chaplains available would result in conversions as a first step towards getting divorced. This was discussed with two ministers who served as chaplains each one denied converting a single soldier while serving the Second Polish Corps.

107. Daily Telegraph (October 6, 1941).

108. American Joint Distribution Committee Archives (New York) [furth. cit. AJDC], file #425 (dated January 14, 1944).

109. AJDC, file #424.

110. Nowy Swiat (June 20, 1942). Colonel Berling later accused Anders of withholding food, medicine and other supplies. Berling assumed, wrongly, that the storehouses were under Anders' control. He should have been criticizing Kot instead.

111. Nowy Swiat (June 8, 1942).

112. S. Kot, Conversations with the Kremlin and Dispatches from Russia, p. 23.

113. "Memorandum on the subjects submitted by the Polish Ambassador to the Secretary of State in conversation on October 14, 1941," HI, Buzkowski coll., Polish Ambassador to the USA files.

114. The American Red Cross had an agreement with the Soviet Government that relief should be distributed only through the Soviet Red Cross. The American Red Cross relief went to the Red Army or stayed in storage in Teheran because the Poles wouldn't agree to its distribution through the Soviet Red Cross, NA, Palestine, #5129.

115. Nowy Swiat (June 3, 1942).

116. AJDC, file #424.

117. Dokumenty i materialy po istorii sovetsko-pol'skikh otnoshenii, VII, p. 271-273.

118. Dokumenty i materialy po istorii sovetsko-pol'skikh otnoshenii, VII, p. 245-278.

119. HI, Ambasada in the USSR, box 17.

120. AJDC, file #425 (January 14, 1944).

121. The allegations were contained in a Joint Distribution Committee memo dated December 29, 1943, from Simon Segal to Mr. Gottschalk.

122. Dobkin's report (November 19, 1942). The Polish Embassy's representatives were known as "delegates." The Soviet decision to treat all persons living on lands occupied by the USSR in November 1939 as Soviet citizens had its ramifications for the selection of the delegates. According to the representative of the Jewish Agency, when the Polish Embassy named Jewish delegates, they were rejected by the Soviets on the basis that the Jews were Soviet citizens, Jewish Agency records (Jerusalem).

123. Daily Worker (June 11, 1943).

124. Merek Kahan was a private in Anders' Army and something of a mystery man. He was interviewed many times and was very helpful, but would give evasive answers when asked about himself. Engel calls Merek Kahan an unofficial advisor to Polish intelligence. He was at least that. Kahan spent a year in Iraq with Ander's Army but his only answer to "why?" is that it was "for my health." It's not difficult to guess that it would not have been healthy for him if the British found him. He was close to Z. Racieski who probably was an Polish Army intelligence officer. There is much yet to be learned about these two and the Irgun-Polish Intelligence relation.
See Engel, Facing a Holocaust, p. 248. Engel refers to two other Irgun leaders as "unofficial advisors", Miron Sheskin, a civilian and M. Buchweitz, a Jewish officer attached to the Documents Bureau.

125. For more about Koltubanka, See, HI Anders Box 70, Doc. 139-140 and HI PSZ box 6, folder 41, Doc.966. A list of the names of soldiers who served at Koltubanka can be found in HI Ambasada, USSR, box 17.

126. NA 51396.

127. For more on this subject, see NA XL 12049; FR 1944,vol.III, p. 1341; FO 371/24481/C6384.

# CHAPTER THREE

# THE EVACUATIONS FROM THE USSR

The evacuation of the Polish Army from the USSR was and still is a hotly debated topic. Much of the controversy which subsequently surrounded General Anders had to do with his decision to take his army and accompanying civilians out of the USSR. During his career Anders made many important decisions, the consequences of, which affected many people, but the decision to evacuate from the Soviet Union was undoubtedly the most significant of his life. Many people question whether this was the right decision under the circumstances.

Evacuation of the Polish Army from the USSR was not only a dramatic movement of over a hundred thousand people, it was also a delicate political decision of the greatest caliber, both for contemporaries and posterity. Two days after Germany invaded the USSR, General Sikorski wrote a memo in which he called for "unorganized evacuation from the territory of the Soviet Union." He outlined four evacuation routes, the first being "through the Caucasus-

Iran, or Turkey, into Palestine or India."[1] He later changed his mind and opposed a total evacuation, favoring instead formation of the largest possible Polish Army in the USSR. Predicting that the liberation of Poland would come from the east, he wanted a Polish Army that would come to Poland along with the Soviets.

The idea to use the army in the Middle East appeared quite early as there was apprehension that the British would use the Polish Army against Japan, which was threatening to conquer India and invade Iran and the Middle East. There was also a possibility of using Polish troops to garrison Iran and the Middle East in order to release British soldiers for the Japanese front.

In the fall of 1941, Sikorski and Anders considered the possibility of transferring the Polish Army to the Caucasus, both thinking that it should be concentrated in one place. Anders' plan was to transfer the Polish Army to the Caucasus which would make evacuation from the USSR possible if the Germans defeated the Soviet forces in Southern Russia. Sikorski didn't want to make this suggestion directly to Stalin for fear that Stalin would question his motives. Instead he tried to persuade the British to broach the idea to the Soviets.[2] The British preferred to avoid getting involved and refused, saying any suggestion to the Soviets about moving the Polish Army should come from the Poles. However, they authorized Sikorski to tell the Soviets that they would have no objection to such a move. They were also willing to support the Polish initiative in this matter indirectly, by informing the Soviets that they would speed up the transfer of equipment to the Poles if the "Polish troops were placed on the left of the Soviet line, for example in the Caucasus..."[3]

In October of 1941, Churchill offered to take over the burden of maintaining and arming the Polish Army if it were to be evacuated to Iran, where it could replace the five Red Army Divisions stationed there. In this way the British would take over the entire responsibility for protecting the

Iranian oil fields. Stalin rejected Churchill's suggestion thinking perhaps that this was a ploy to deprive the Soviet Union of its influence in Iran.[4]

In a telegram to Kot, dated October 28, 1941, General Sikorski explained that if the Soviets could not feed and supply Anders' Army it should be concentrated in a single area accessible to British supplies, either in Iran or in the Caucasus.[5]

This idea was then broached by Sikorski to Stalin during their talks, in December, 1941. Sikorski made it clear that he wanted the army to return to the USSR after it was equipped and had rested in the Middle East, and offered Stalin his personal assurances on that score. Stalin evidently did not like the idea. Mentioning that Churchill and Harriman had also proposed evacuating the Polish Army from the USSR, he fumed that the whole idea was inspired by the British who needed Polish troops in the Middle East. To prevent this he agreed to increase the size of the Polish Army in the USSR to seven divisions and to ensure that it would be supplied with sufficient amounts of food and arms. He also consented to Sikorski's request for the transfer of 25,000 soldiers from the USSR to Polish units in England and the Middle East. After extracting these concessions from Stalin, Sikorski gave up the idea of evacuating the army to the Middle East.[6]

When, at the beginning of March, 1942, the Soviets warned Anders that they would soon cut the number of food rations to 26,000 or 30,000, Anders, citing a telegram from Sikorski, told Panfilov that the surplus personnel whom the Soviets could not provide for would have to be evacuated to Iran.[7] On March 18, 1942, Anders met with Stalin and, after the latter's repeated refusals to provide the Polish Army with more than 44,000 rations, they agreed that all personnel over and above that number should be evacuated to Iran.[8]

On March 24, 1942, Kot told Vyshinski that he was distressed when he learned of the evacuation plan. He claimed that neither he nor Sikorski were in favor of the evacuation, and that it was not initiated by the Polish Government and was against its wishes. He still hoped the Polish Army would participate in the struggle against the Germans on Soviet territory and that this would strengthen ties between the two nations, hopefully having a positive affect on their future relations. Vyshinski assured Kot that the evacuation was caused by circumstances beyond the control of the Soviets.[9]

The evacuations were not the first withdrawal of Polish soldiers from the Soviet Union. At the beginning of his liaison mission in Moscow, General Szyszko-Bohusz asked for the evacuation of nine hundred airmen and seamen sorely needed for the Polish Navy and Air Force in Great Britain. Arrangements for their transfer were made as early as August, 1941. Sikorski periodically instructed Anders to transfer large numbers of soldiers to Great Britain. At one point Sikorski directed Anders to evacuate twenty thousand soldiers from the Soviet Union as soon as possible: five thousand to bring the Independent Carpathian Brigade to division strength, five thousand for the Air Force and Navy in England and ten thousand to stay in the Middle East.[10] Anders complied with these orders but didn't like them, especially after some of his soldiers were lost when their transport ship was torpedoed.

According to Romanowski, the transfer of personnel to England was a major source of disagreement between the two generals. The motive for the request was clearly to reduce Anders' strength. Sikorski's defenders argue that the request was not politically motivated, and that he needed these men for the invasion of the continent. But D-Day was still more than a year away.[11] At one point, when Sikorski asked for fifteen hundred Polish cadets to be transferred to Britain Anders refused and Sikorski did not press the issue. The sequence of events suggest that Sikorski was not prepared to take the risk of a confrontation with Anders on an issue which he was likely to lose.

The British agreed with Anders in the Anders-Sikorski debate on how many soldiers were to be sent to England. From their point of view it made little sense to bring Polish soldiers from Russia and the Middle East to England where they would be inactive at a time when there was a shortage of soldiers in the Middle East. The British Ambassador in the USSR supported Anders and suggested that only trained airmen be transferred to Britain. Sikorski's reaction was to ask Eden to instruct His Majesty's Ambassador to support his request for large numbers of Polish soldiers to be sent from the USSR to England.[12]

In December, 1941, Sikorski received Stalin's permission to transfer 25,000 men to Great Britain for Navy, Air Force and tank units, more than twice the number he had earlier told Kot he needed for these purposes. The rationalization for transferring the soldiers from Anders' force was to enlarge the units in England which were short of soldiers while they had more than enough officers. The best estimate is that ultimately twenty thousand soldiers were sent from Russia even before the issue of evacuation of the whole army arose.[13]

The first wave of the evacuation from the USSR started in March of 1942. On April 1, Sikorski advised Churchill by telegram that 35,000 soldiers were en route from the USSR to Iran, and an additional ten to fifteen thousand were expected shortly. He estimated that ultimately 77,000 soldiers and an unspecified number of civilians would be evacuated. Sikorski informed Churchill that he agreed with the Soviet decision that the main concentration of the Polish Army, two or three divisions, should be in the Middle East,[14] which contradicts Kot's statement that Sikorski opposed the evacuations.

However, Sikorski's telegram to Churchill of April 1st, is also evidence that he wanted only part of the Polish Army to leave the USSR for the Middle East.[15] He was still interested in maintaining a significant Polish Army presence fighting at the side of the Soviets when they reached Polish territory. On April 30th, the Polish Cabinet approved the evacuation which had just been completed, but at the same time resolved "to leave on Soviet territory part of the Polish armed forces to fight side by side with the Red Army."[16] Instructions to that effect were sent to Anders by Sikorski on June 12, 1942.[17]

When the British were planning the evacuation of Anders' Army, they contemplated two alternative routes, through Turkey or Iran. The Turks had allowed British and Greek troops to escape though Turkey when the Germans occupied Greece, but by the spring of 1942, with Germany menacing her borders, it was unlikely that Turkey would be willing to incur the German wrath by allowing the passage of Polish troops. This left Iran as the only practical route. The first leg of the evacuation was by railroad from camps in Tashkent and Iangi-Iul' to the port of Krasnovodsk on the Caspian Sea. The next leg was by ship across the Caspian Sea to the Iranian port of Pahlevi. Looking at the map, it might appear that an overland journey by trucks from Tashkent and Iangi Iul to Iran would be best, but a lack of fuel made this route impracticable for large groups. General MacFarlane advised the Soviets that British authorities in Iran had claimed they could not accept more than 2,500 Polish soldiers per week. They explained that they had limited facilities and needed fourteen days notice of the arrival of the Poles to get the necessary equipment and supplies from Teheran to Pahlevi. General MacFarlane's advice was ignored and almost all of the evacuees arrived at Pahlevi at nearly the same time.[18]

Conditions in Krasnovodsk were horrible and overcrowded and the evacuees waiting to board ships suffered from lack of food. Anders begged the British, to no avail, to send two weeks' rations for 27,000 people to Krasnovodsk as the evacuees boarding the ships were literally starving to death. The trip from Krasnovodsk to Pahlevi (Iran) varied from 24 hours to three days, depending on the ship, most often taking 30 hours. After having suffered in Soviet prisons and labor camps the evacuees were so afraid of Soviet duplicity that even while boarding the ships they had a lingering suspicion that either they were not really leaving the USSR or that the Soviets would change their decision and turn them back at the last minute. The first ship, overcrowded with seasick passengers, arrived at Pahlevi on March 28, 1942. Even after they had arrived the refugees feared they might be forced back to the Soviet Union. When they saw Soviet soldiers on shore in Iran they panicked. It took time to dispel their apprehensions of a horrible trick being played on them and that they were still in the USSR.[19]

In the first eight days of April over 29,000 evacuees arrived in Pahlevi with Colonel Boleslawicz in charge at the Iranian port.[20] According to information sent on April 13, 1942, to the Polish Embassy in Washington by Sikorski the first wave of evacuees included 30,000 soldiers, 12,610 civilians, 100 cadets and 1,150 women from the ATS.[21] According to Soviet figures the transports brought 29,099 soldiers and 12,155 civilians to Pahlevi.[22] Thus, the number of evacuees quoted by Polish sources exceeds by 1500 the number given by Soviet sources. The conclusion is that some civilians managed to avoid Soviet controls and got onto the ships bound for Iran.

The NKVD reported that the Polish Army received news of the evacuation with mixed feelings. Many officers were so anxious to fight the Germans that they were prepared to go into battle immediately. They supported the Soviet policy of immediate departure of Polish units for the front and saw the evacuations as an unnecessary delay. These officers were not necessarily pro-Soviet. In July of 1942, Beria reported to Stalin that part of the Polish High Command reacted negatively to the decision to evacuate to the Middle East. In a discussion with Major Zhukov, Colonel Okulicki, Anders' Chief of Staff, expressed concern about Polish troops becoming a colonial army for the British. Okulicki asked Anders in public, "Why aren't we at the Front?" but he got no reply. General Szyszko-Bohusz told Zhukov that "to Egypt want to go people, who believe in the defeat of the Red Army and the break in communications between the Soviet Union and its Allies, and since I believe in the strength of the Red Army, more than many other Polish citizens, I would not like to leave the USSR."[23]

After the first evacuation the Soviets blocked further recruitment into the Polish Army. On May 4, Ambassador Kot, in a note to Molotov, protested this as well as the recruitment of Polish citizens into the Red Army. He reminded Molotov that during their March 18th meeting Anders and Stalin agreed the Polish Army could continue to recruit from among Polish citizens and evacuate those in excess of the 44,000 who were to remain in the USSR.[24] Sikorski and Kot were told that it was now Stalin's policy not to permit further recruitment for the Polish Army because there wasn't enough food available to feed an army not in combat.[25]

After April 1942, the Soviets told the Poles there would be no more evacuations and to dismantle the evacuation organization. However, on June 30, 1942, Molotov informed the British Ambassador that the Poles had three divisions trained and ready to fight and that the Soviets were willing to permit those divisions to be transferred to British command.[26] A week later Molotov gave the British Ambassador in Moscow a copy of Stalin's statement to the Poles that he "had no objection to the transfer of Polish troops in the USSR to the Near East and suggested that three divisions be transferred."[27] The British welcomed and accepted this offer although they knew there would be opposition in the Polish Government. Obviously the British played an important role in getting Stalin to agree to the evacuation. Harold MacMillan wrote that "after Germany attacked Russia, we pleaded with the Russians to let them [i.e. the Poles] free."[28] The Foreign Office liked the idea of Anders' Army in its entirety leaving the Soviet Union. Romanowski believes Anders made up his mind about evacuating the entire Polish Army after discussing it with Churchill. In his first meeting with Churchill in London,

April 22, 1942, Anders tried to impress upon him the need to evacuate the entire Polish Army from Russia. Churchill agreed, but it's not clear whether Churchill convinced Anders or Anders convinced Churchill.[29]

In 1952, Robin Hankey told Keith Sword that it was Churchill who persuaded Stalin to let Anders leave the USSR with his entire army and accompanying Polish civilians. According to Hankey, the British wanted the Polish Army in the Middle East and the Russians didn't want the Poles in the USSR unless they could be made to be pro-Communist, something that was not likely.[30] In a message to Stalin on July 18, 1942, Churchill pointed out that if the Polish troops did not get to Iran and the Middle East it would be necessary to send additional British troops there.[31] Soldiers who would otherwise be available for the opening of the Second Front would have to be diverted to the Middle East. Churchill knew the "Second Front " was at the top of Stalin's agenda.

In 1942, the Soviets were carrying the greatest part of the burden of fighting the Nazis and Stalin was continually complaining about the failure of the Western Allies to open the "Second Front." Above all else, Stalin wanted a Second Front to relieve pressure on the Red Army by forcing the Germans to shift some divisions away from the Russian Front. Churchill's motives in encouraging the Soviets to let the entire Polish Army leave for Iran were military as well as political and humanitarian. He resisted pressure to prematurely start the Second Front and denied Stalin's request that British troops be sent to the Russian-German Front.

According to Anthony Eden, Churchill wanted to bring home eight battalions of British soldiers from Palestine, replacing them with Polish troops whose loyalty to Great Britain was unquestioned. Churchill saw British troops in Palestine as being wasted and wanted them greatly reduced in number.[32]

Romanowski's recollection that Churchill wanted soldiers in the Middle East whom he could trust, is consistent with Anthony Eden's statement. Churchill's reasoning appears to make sense but there is an inconsistency. If the British troops in Palestine would be wasted, doesn't it mean that the Polish soldiers replacing them would also be wasted? Many soldiers of the Second Polish Corps felt they had already been "wasted" for two years and were anxious to get into battle. Another inconsistency is that Churchill had a propensity, which he himself admitted, to use non-British soldiers in battles where high losses were anticipated. The exchange of Polish for British soldiers was not consistent with such thinking because by the time Anders arrived in Palestine the threat of German Armies linking up in the Middle East had passed.

On July 8, Anders was notified by the Soviets of their agreement to a second evacuation. In thanking Stalin, Anders declared that "the Polish Army will fight wherever she will be for the common victory" and stressed how important it was to fight the Germans in the Middle East. He also repeated his request for the resumption of recruitment of Poles in the Soviet Union into the Polish Army, saying this would elevate the mood of the whole Polish nation. He tried to persuade Stalin by resorting to flattery and declared: "I turn to you, since I'm convinced you will review and decide the question with the same good will you showed me until now."[33] This of course had no effect and no additional recruitment was allowed.

By the time of the second evacuation, the Polish Army supposedly had 44,000 soldiers. The Soviets said 70,000 Poles could leave in the second evacuation, which meant that 26,000 civilians could be evacuated. According to the British, the total number of Poles permitted to participate in the two evacuations was 75,000 soldiers and 38,000 civilians, for a grand total of 113,000.[34]

The British and the Poles had prepared for a second evacuation even before it was approved by the Russians.

The British Foreign Office representatives in Iran complained they could not handle the large volume of soldiers and civilians that might be coming from the USSR. The British bureaucracy seemed to treat the evacuations as a nuisance rather than as an opportunity to save human lives.

The Soviets knew that, contrary to orders, Anders was arranging for Polish civilians to be included in the second evacuation, especially families of soldiers and civilians deemed important. From the middle of May, 1942, 1,149 civilians were added to the evacuation list. Of these only 28 were fit for military service, the rest were old people, women and children. Zhukov demanded that Anders stop putting civilians on the evacuation lists and threatened to arrest civilians found in places where the army was waiting for relocation.[35] Nonetheless over 25 000 civilians were able to join the second evacuation.

By the last day of August, 1942, the main part of the second evacuation had been completed. The official total for the two evacuations was 115,000, including 75,000 soldiers. These figures are on the low side as soldiers and civilians sent directly to England were not included. The following statistics include those who went by ship and those few who went by the overland route between August 12 and November 2, 1942: the army 39,558, the ATS 1,794, the Cadets 2738, and 26,000 civilians.[36] According to a report submitted to Churchill, the second evacuation included 43,569 military and 25,970 civilians. 1,400 evacuees came by the overland route.[37] The Soviets give a slightly lower figure of 69,917 evacuees (41,103 military and 28,814 civilians).[38]

The truck route via Ashkabad was used by the last group of soldiers, who had stayed behind under the command of General Rudnicki to take care of final details and attempt to get more people evacuated. A few hundred additional Polish citizens were able to get out of Russia going by train to the Iranian border and then by truck to military camps in Iran and Iraq.

The Polish officer who coordinated the second evacuation at the Soviet end was Lt. Colonel Berling, who told General Rudnicki that he would catch up with him in Iran. Instead, Berling took a car and documents and joined the Red Army. Berling alleged that Anders had told him that Jews, Ukrainians and Byelorussians could not join the evacuation and that fifty Jews waiting in Kransnovodsk would be expelled from the army. There is nothing to confirm the truth of this allegation.[39]

After the second evacuation a considerable number of Polish soldiers and civilians were waiting and hoping to leave the USSR, but all hope ended when the Soviets terminated diplomatic relations with Poland in the spring of 1943. Although there were reports to the contrary, Stalin did not permit any significant numbers of Poles to be evacuated after 1942.

A small number of children was allowed to leave the USSR after the second evacuation. They left in two groups of 77 and 88 in December, 1942, and January, 1943. Very little is known about these evacuations but it appears they may have been part of the group of Jewish children known today as the "Teheran Children." The confusion may have been caused by the fact that the Jewish children had been given Polish names and school uniforms for their journey to Palestine. In the Anders Collection at the Hoover Institution, there are several notebooks containing lists of names of children evacuated from the USSR. Included in these files are depositions from Jewish children who were evacuated at this late date.[40]

The evacuation of the entire Polish Army from the USSR raises the question of did Anders disobey the orders issued to him by his Commander-in-Chief, General Sikorski? The issue here is whether Anders had the authority to make a major military policy decision, and to resolve questions concerning Polish civilians. In both areas Sikorski had the final authority and Anders was clearly his subordinate.

Anders' critics often accused him of disobeying Sikorski's orders, so it has to be established exactly which orders he disobeyed. Clearly Sikorski not only agreed with the first evacuation, but was involved in its technical planning. The accusation of disobedience can therefore be raised only in relation to the second evacuation. In a set of instructions dated May 1, 1942, Sikorski explained to Anders in no uncertain terms that it was vital to maintain an army in the Soviet Union in spite of all the hardships that its personnel had to bear. The entire army could be evacuated only in case of a total Soviet collapse,[41] according to Sikorski, so evacuating the whole army clearly contradicted both the letter and spirit of these instructions.

Anders never denied that Sikorski sent him a telegram saying a portion of the Polish Army was to stay in the USSR.[42] He wrote,

> "I had to make such a decision against orders from London. I was convinced that the order resulted from a lack of understanding of our situation. The head of the government (Sikorski) was badly informed by the Polish Ambassador (Kot) in Moscow. Remaining in Russia was contrary to the Polish national interest. The decision to get out of there I took on my own responsibility and God granted that it was a right one."[43]

What would have happened if Sikorski had convened a court-martial to try Anders for disobeying orders? This is pure conjecture as there is no evidence that a court-martial was ever considered. If Sikorski ever considered court-martialing or removing Anders from command he kept it to himself. Charging Anders with disobeying orders would have further divided the Poles and would not have served their common objective of restoring Polish independence. Sikorski wisely avoided a confrontation that could only have been divisive. A court-martial of Anders or his dismissal from command might have gained backing from a majority of the National Council (the representation of major political parties) but it is hard to believe that the soldiers and civilians evacuated by Anders would not have supported him. Any attempt to punish Anders might have ended in a mutiny and the Polish people should be thankful to Sikorski for never prompting such a confrontation.

Anders' decision was and still remains a subject of a bitter controversy. Not unexpectedly, Poles evacuated by Anders say he made the correct decision, and tend in general to approve of Anders' other military and political decisions. Conversely, those who criticize his evacuation decision tend to be critical of other aspects of his military and political career. Those who were evacuated with Anders speak of him as if he were a candidate for sainthood. His detractors consider him partially responsible for Poland's loss of postwar independence and indirectly for the loss of thousands of Polish lives. As far as Anders himself was concerned he never seemed to have had any doubts about his decision. This was confirmed by his widow and his two aides-de-camp. According to Mrs. Anders, her husband ranked the evacuation from Russia as one of the major achievements of his life.[44]

How can we judge his decision a half century later? At first glance a decision which probably saved 125, 000 Polish citizens from hunger and oppression seems incontestable. Those evacuated would otherwise have faced starvation, disease and death. Anders gave them a chance for survival. Many survivors believe fervently that they would have died if they had not been taken out of the USSR.

There are two main criticisms of the evacuation decision. The first is that Poland might have been independent after the war had there been a strong Polish Army present when the Soviets pushed back the Germans and occupied Poland. The second criticism is that evacuation saved some Polish lives, but worsened the situation for the overwhelming majority of Poles remaining in the USSR. The withdrawal of General Anders' Army and the subsequent termination of diplomatic relations between Poland and the Soviet Union that followed a year later, left hundreds of thousands of Poles without any assistance from the Polish Government or the army. Those left behind became completely vulnerable to Soviet whim.

Who were the critics? The first and most understandable group were those who were left behind. The second consisted of those opposed to General Anders on political grounds. The third group were those who were not anti-Anders, but still concluded that Anders made the wrong decision. They believed he acted in good faith and in accordance with what he considered to be the best interests of the Polish people, but his decision was wrong.

The last group of critics argued that evacuation helped Stalin achieve many of his objectives, e.g. it strengthened the claims of the "Union of Polish Patriots" and other Soviet puppets that they represented the responsible Polish leadership. It is doubtful that the presence of Polish forces during the liberation of Poland could have made any difference as the size of the Red Army guaranteed that the Soviets could do as they pleased. According to some critics, if there had been a strong, independent Polish Army when the Germans were chased out of the Polish territories, the non-Communist Poles would have been able to remain in control or at least to have a greater role in the postwar Polish Government. This is what Ambassador Kot thought and this apparently was General Sikorski's first inclination. Kot never seemed to waiver from this opinion.

The sad truth is that it was the Teheran and Yalta conferences which determined the future of Poland. Stalin wanted to control a buffer area between the Soviet Union and the West, and as long as the Red Army was engaged against the Germans the Western Allies, clearly, were prepared to give Stalin what he wanted. Even an independent Polish Army of ten to fifteen divisions entering Poland with the Soviets would not be viable against two hundred Red Army Divisions. Perhaps with American and

British participation, the Poles could have defeated the Soviets but any discussion of a military confrontation between the Soviets and the Western Allies was nonsense because the Western Allies were not about to go to war against the Soviet Union on behalf of the Poles. There was no reason why Stalin would give away his absolute control of Poland, given his political and military power. If a Polish-Soviet confrontation had ever occurred the Polish Divisions would have been annihilated. What we know of Stalin tells us that he would not have shirked before a large scale massacre. To claim that the presence of an independent Polish Army would have stopped Stalin from imposing Soviet rule over postwar Poland is unrealistic. It is difficult to see how postwar history could have been changed if Anders had kept his army in the Soviet Union.

The second argument against evacuation was that the Poles left behind were at the mercy of Stalin, and their status would have been better if General Anders and his forces had remained in the Soviet Union.

But this begs a question whether Anders would have been in a position to improve the plight of the refugees even if his army had remained in the USSR. The fact is that diplomatic relations between the Soviet Union and Poland were not terminated by the 1942 evacuations, but by dramatic developments in Polish-Soviet relations caused by the Katyn affair which will be discussed in the next chapter. One can therefore conclude that the presence of Anders' Army in the Soviet Union could not have helped the Poles. It could only have resulted in an armed conflict between Poles and Soviets, the results of which would have been disastrous for the Poles and would have weakened the alliance against Germany. With the benefit of more than 50 years of hindsight, Anders had little choice but to try to evacuate as many Poles as he could. Thus it can be said he acted wisely on behalf of the people for whom he felt responsible.

## The Jewish Issue in the Evacuation[45]

One of the most controversial questions connected with the evacuation is the extent of discrimination against Jews in the selection of candidates, both military and civilian for evacuation. This is a very sensitive and important issue as perceived discrimination in the evacuation was a main Jewish grievance against Anders. Even competent historians tend to paint a rather one-sided picture of what actually happened. For example, Neal Ascherson stated that at the last moment Anders beat off a Soviet attempt to keep Polish Jews from evacuating.[46] On the other hand, in Lenni Brenner's account, the Soviets are portrayed as faultless in every respect, while the Polish Army was depicted as doing nothing right[47] The truth is much more complex.

Perhaps the most telling piece of evidence pertinent to the issue is a protocol of the Polish-Soviet military commission about the evacuation of the army and military families signed by Anders and Zhukov on July 31, 1942. It stipulated that "family members of soldiers of the Polish Army from among the inhabitants of Western Ukraine and Byelorussia of non-Polish nationality are subject to evacuation only in the case where it is documentarily established that they really are the closest relatives of the military in the Polish Army in the USSR (parents, spouses, children, minor or sick siblings supported by a military person)." Family members of soldiers of non-Polish nationality had to be put on special lists, to which certificates signed by the army, Chief of Staff, divisional commanders or their chiefs of staff or commanders of training centers had to be attached.[48]

To this has to be added the fact that Soviet authorities had set an absolute ceiling of 70,000 people who could be included in the second evacuation.[49] In this situation, each time a Jew was accepted to fill the quota, it meant that one more Pole would be left behind.

Notwithstanding Sikorski's order that there be no discrimination in the Polish Army and Anders' declaration of

May 4, 1942, that "Jews have been treated on the basis of full equality and they will continue to be treated in the same way" a document exists which proves that the Polish Army did in fact distinguish between Jews and Poles when selecting civilians for evacuation.[50] This document, signed by Anders and Szyszko-Bohusz, bearing the title, "A Memo about the Jewish question during the evacuation of the Polish Army from the Soviets to Iran" states:

> "It is a fact that in the area of stationing of the Polish [military] units the largest concentration of Polish Jews was to be found... While the majority of families of Polish soldiers were scattered among the collective farms of distant areas of Northern Kazakhstan, Aktiubinsk, Semipalatinsk and Altai regions or even further north (Northern Russia, Siberia). With the number of Polish soldiers and their families subject to evacuation restricted by the Soviet authorities to 70,000 as the inviolable number, the Command of the Polish Army in the USSR had to set down a just rule for sending of civilians to Iran taking into consideration first of all the good of the Polish cause."[51]

According to this memo the pool of Polish citizens living close to the army consisted of 27,000 Poles and 17,000 Jews. Moreover, there were 2,000 closest family members of soldiers who could be brought from their places of residence in time for evacuation. For these 44,000 civilians there were only 26,000 evacuation "slots" (70,000 minus 44,000 soldiers).

Among those evacuated in the second wave were 1,570 Jews not including the uncertain number of Jews who evacuated overland. A simple calculation shows that the Polish authorities evacuated almost all Poles (ca. 24,000 out of 27,000) and a very small percentage of Jews (at most 2,000 out of 17,000). This, to the Polish military authorities was apparently the "just rule" to which the document quoted above referred. As the document conceded "A comparison of the number of citizens of Polish and Jewish nationality demonstrates, that even if there had been no restrictions from the Soviet authorities, a just departure rule had to be set, because the very [geographical] distribution of the population created unjustified and unacceptable advantages to the Jews, to the detriment of the Poles."[52]

Anders claimed that he refused a Soviet demand to expel the Jews from the army and asserted that no one was purged from the army on religious grounds. To support his claim he cited statistics of soldiers expelled between July 1, 1942, and the end of the evacuation on September 1, 1942: 188 Roman Catholics, 125 Jews, 13 Greek Catholics and 24 others[53]

There are documents confirming his claim. When the Soviets asked him to hand over ten Jews who had left with the first evacuation (they wanted to put them on trial on the charge that they were Soviet citizens who had illegally left the USSR) Anders did not comply.[54] According to a marginal note on a report of the United States Army Counter Intelligence Service "the USSR permitted evacuation of Jews only after the repeated intervention of General Anders."[55]

General Rudnicki was adamant that it was the Russians who limited Jewish participation in the evacuation. Both during my interview with him and in his book he went into great detail about Soviet efforts to limit the number of Jews leaving the USSR.[56] According to the Poles, Soviet officers reviewed every list and demanded that people ineligible for evacuation be taken off the train but the task of evicting them fell on Polish officers. Some Polish officers admitted that they took Jews off the trains, but argue it was done only when it became apparent that if it was not done the entire train would be detained.

General Szyszko-Bohusz blamed the Russians for limiting the numbers of Jews to be evacuated, and claimed that it was only because of intervention by him and other Poles that a total of 2,870 Jews were able to leave during the second evacuation. For his efforts to help Jews to evacuate he was presented with a written expression of gratitude "signed by Orthodox Rabbis and Jewish intelligentsia."[57]

On March 3, 1942, the Jewish Telegraphic Agency accused the Poles of preventing Jews from leaving the USSR. It cited the NKVD source which stated that the NKVD didn't care if Jews left, claiming that the Poles were the problem. It is interesting that in this rare instance the JTA quoted the NKVD as a reliable source of information.[58]

In September, 1942, an official of the Jewish Agency, Shertok complained to a Jewish representative on the Polish National Council, Dr. Schwarzbart, that relatively few Jews were included in the evacuation. According to Shertok there were only 6,000 Jews among 130,000 evacuees, while Jews constituted from one third to one half of all Polish citizens in the USSR and that 140,000 were registered at the Kuibyshev Embassy. He thought the Soviets were responsible for preventing Jews from leaving because they refused to recognize Polish citizenship of those inhabitants of Eastern Poland who were not ethnically Polish. Schwarzbart agreed that it was the Soviets who were not permitting the Jews to leave.[59]

A distinction should be made between an official policy of discrimination and actions of individuals. When I asked a group of former Polish officers about discrimination in the Polish Army, one of them denied it, and the others laughed at his statement and told me that,of course, there was prejudice at work when evacuees were selected. Their laughter was startling, but they were not laughing at the predicament of the Jews, but at the denial that discrimination had existed.

Jews questioned on this point gave conflicting statements. A Jewish soldier said he had successfully passed as a non-Jew until an anti-Semitic Polish officer ordered him off the train. In contrast, an elderly Jewish woman blessed a Polish officer who had given her military clothing and smuggled her onto the train. A sympathetic Polish officer took overcoats and hats from embarking Polish soldiers to put on Jewish civilians so they could pass as soldiers. The Soviets checked civilians much more closely than soldiers. Mrs. Alexander Zvielli said she experienced no discrimination when she was evacuated. She felt General Michal Tokarzewski-Karaszewicz was especially helpful in giving Jews a chance to be evacuated. She saw him put on the train two "soldiers" with heads bandaged and only later did she realize that these were rabbis who in this way hid the beards which they refused to shave.[60] Buchweitz said he did not see any discrimination during the evacuation and that he helped a Jewish woman get out of Russia by saying she was his aunt.[61] When one, Captain Raczkowski, refused to take a Jewish woman because he did not want to risk his military career, she was helped by Chaplain Cienski, even though she refused to accept a certificate of baptism which he was handing out to Jews to help them evacuate.[62] A Jewish soldier, who later served with the Polish Army until the end of the war, was removed from a train but a Polish friend helped him get on another one.[63]

On the other hand, some Polish officers were reported to be zealous in excluding Jews from evacuation trains. justifying their conduct by claiming that some Jews had welcomed the Soviets, in 1939. Racieski told of an incident where a sergeant removed a group of Hasidic Jews from a train even though they had authorization from the Roman Catholic Bishop to board. They appealed to the Bishop who forced the sergeant to put the Jews back on the train.[64]

On August 3, 1942, a delegation of rabbis met with Anders to request that more Jews be permitted to participate in the evacuation. Anders pointed out that he had been able to get the Soviets to make some exceptions to their rules against evacuating Jews, but blamed the hardened Soviet position on the conduct of the evacuated Jews who had made anti-Soviet statements to the American press as soon as they were safely outside the USSR. Such statements drew attention to the fact that the Jews had been evacuated in violation of Soviet law. He also complained that the evacuated Jews were also making anti-Polish statements, which discouraged Polish officers from helping the remaining Jews. He wondered why they should take risks to smuggle out Jews who would criticize Poland and the Polish Army at the first opportunity? In spite of his criticism of Jewish behavior Anders agreed to help.[65]

In return Anders asked the rabbis to help prevent anti-Polish statements and asked them to sign statements saying there was no anti-Semitism in the Polish Army. Once they were away from the Polish Army, the rabbis who had signed these statements recanted, saying they had signed untrue statements because this was the only way to be evacuated. They didn't seem to care that their recanting worked against the Jews still in the Soviet Union.

A list of "special" people to be evacuated was made up by a civilian rabbi, who took money and valuables from Jews wanting to be on the list. The son of Rabbi Hagar went to Iangi-Iul' to talk with this rabbi about his list and he then went to meet Bishop Gawlina, who said the list was bogus. The Bishop promised Rabbi Hagar's son he would intervene on behalf of the rabbis to make possible their departure from Russia. Bishop Gawlina was so committed to this that on one day alone he had three conferences with General Anders on this subject and in return he asked Rabbi Hagar to organize world Jewry to intervene for the Catholic priests left in Russia.[66]

The immediate families of most Jewish soldiers being evacuated were allowed to go with them. According to the Jewish Telegraphic Agency, if 500 Jews were dismissed from the army and denied evacuation, it meant that 500 Jewish families were left behind. Did every Jewish soldier have his family with him? Perhaps the answer was "yes" because Jewish soldiers who were allowed to leave temporarily adopted a Jewish family if they didn't have one.

According to one interviewed Jewish soldier, many of them forged documents to get Jewish civilians out of the USSR. He took six Jewish civilians as his "relatives" and was asked to take more.[67]

According to Romanowski, Anders ordered Czapski to see that no discrimination was practiced and to undo it wherever it occurred in the evacuation process. There is a general consensus that many Jewish lives were saved by this order. One assignment was to review all lists of people to be evacuated. When Czapski saw Jewish names scratched from the list, he would reinstate their names, or if the group had already departed, put those names at the top of the next list. All lists had to be approved by the NKVD and signed by Anders.[68]

On August 19, at a meeting with Zhukov and General Szyszko-Bohusz, Jechiel Szlechter, representing Jewish interests, was told that no more minorities were to be evacuated. Zhukov said however, that he would accept for evacuation Jews who until November 29, 1939, had lived in areas west of the Ribbentrop-Molotov line, but that two witnesses had to be provided as proof.[69]

Szlechter and Rabbi Kanner appealed to Anders who told them that 1,500 Jews were in the first evacuation and asked Szlechter to prepare a list of 500 Jews he wanted evacuated. Anders told them that on three occasions he had appealed to the Soviets for permission to evacuate specified groups of Jews, but his appeals were denied. The Soviets were not permitting any more Jews to leave and he suggested that the Jewish representatives contact the Soviets. He promised that if Szlechter got the Soviets to permit evacuation of additional Jews he would also approve it. Szlechter noted that 36 Jews were arrested for entering Iran illegally, but were released after his talk with Kot.[70]

On the policy level, the issue was not really about anti-Semitism but about a territorial dispute between the Soviet Union and Poland. For a person denied evacuation it did not make any difference if it was done as anti-Semitism or because of a border dispute between the Soviet Union and Poland. All he knew was that he was forcibly removed from the train by an officer wearing a Polish uniform.

According to a historian who specialized in Polish-Jewish relations during the war, David Engel, anti-Jewish restrictions during the evacuation were forced on Anders by the British and the Soviets. Engel, who does not hesitate to criticize Anders and the Polish Government in Exile for their treatment of Jews, argues that in this case the British and Soviets skillfully created the impression that the restrictions were imposed by the Polish Army for purely anti-Semitic reasons. In Engel's opinion;

> "the Soviets, aware of the strained nature of Polish-Jewish relations in the West and hoping to cultivate that strain to their own propaganda advantage, laid a trap for the Poles: they told them that they would not permit Jews to leave (and that they would curtail Polish evacuations if Jews were included among them) but later denied that they had done so when confronted with Jewish protests. In this fashion they were able to embarrass the Poles, make them appear liars and present them as the sole obstacle to Jews wanting to leave the USSR. The Soviets really didn't care whether several thousand Jews left the country with the Polish troops; such small numbers would not undermine their claim that the Jews of the annexed territories were Soviet citizens. This, of course, cannot be proved or disproved without reference to material presumably located in Soviet archives, but it seems to be the most plausible explanation for the behavior that Polish and Jewish sources report."[71]

At first the British didn't seem concerned with the issue of recruiting Jewish soldiers into the Polish Army in the USSR. If the Polish Army was to stay in the Soviet Union there was no reason for them to be concerned.

However, after the evacuation got underway, the British became worried about the large numbers of trained and armed Jews coming to the Middle East as part of the Polish Army. At the same time the British Prime Minister was lobbying Stalin in favor of the evacuation, the British Foreign Office was becoming uneasy about a possible influx of Jewish soldiers into the Middle East. The British were highly suspicious of the relations between the Polish military, the Polish Government, and the Jews. The British suspicions were heightened by reports that the Polish Government in Exile was cooperating with the Zionists and making statements favorable to the idea of a Jewish homeland in Palestine. The British were particularly afraid that the Polish Army might create Jewish units that would attract Palestinian Jews with Polish roots. This could lead to creation of a Jewish Army that the British would have to deal with at a later date.

There is incontrovertible evidence that from March 30, 1942, onward, the War Office and the Foreign Office pressured the Poles not to take many Jews out of the USSR. They did it because, to quote a memo by Frank Roberts "we should not want a large number of Polish Jews in the Middle East."[72] Interviewed after the war, Roberts denied that the British had any influence over the number of Jews who came to the Middle East with General Anders' Army. Indirectly, however he conceded that the British did try to restrict the number of Jews coming out of Russia by saying it was necessary to "keep the right balance of Arabs and Jews."[73] In view of the documentary evidence his denial is hardly credible. The negative position of the British is also confirmed by their rejection of a request by the Palestine-based General Committee of Polish Jewry to assist its efforts in getting Zionists out of the USSR.[74]

British opposition to the influx of Jews into the Middle East also explains the curious, and totally uncharacteristic wording of a letter which Anders wrote to the British Ambassador in Moscow, Cripps, on October 13, 1942. Anders, while asking Cripps to persuade Stalin to allow further evacuations, assured him that, "amongst them are at least 60,000 men of "pure Polish blood." Nothing else attributed to Anders contains that kind of language.[75] It can be explained by Anders' desire to reassure Cripps that he would not be bringing more Polish Jews to the Middle East.

Another indirect evidence that the British, in fact, did try to persuade the Poles to restrict the number of Jews evacuated to the Middle East is a letter by the Secretary of State for Colonies to the British High Commissioner in Palestine telling him that General Sikorski told Churchill that "the bulk of the Jews in Polish Army in Russia are concentrated in divisions which are remaining there."[76] Unless one believes in coincidence the statement attributed to Sikorski would seem to confirm that the British did pressure Sikorski to leave the Jews in Russia. One might even venture a hypothesis that it could have been Churchill himself who exerted the pressure. In the end about from 3,600 to 4,200 Jewish soldiers and from 2,500 to 3,600 Jewish civilians left the USSR with Anders' Army.[77]

**The Evacuation of Soldiers' Families**

Churchill kept his promise to Anders and petitioned Stalin to allow families of the Polish soldiers to be evacuated to the Middle East. Churchill's letter of July 18, 1942, addressed to Stalin, acknowledges the burden of feeding the dependents, and states, "We think this burden is worth accepting...."[78]

Churchill was not really very eager for the families to be evacuated and may have just gone through the motion to appease Anders. The first group of family members arrived in Iran on March 31,1942. Churchill's reaction at that time was revealed when he wrote two days later, "Are we going to get nothing but women and children?" Oliver Harvey from the Foreign Office did not want any more civilians coming out of Russia, calling them a nuisance and suggesting a "no civilians" policy.[79] Fortunately, there were others in the Foreign Office who knew the morale and effectiveness of the Polish soldiers was directly related to the circumstances of their families. Anders was told by the British, the Polish Government in London, and the Russians to stop bringing civilians out of Russia, but they kept on coming.

Kot and General Tadeusz Klimecki, Sikorski's Chief of Staff, demanded that Anders stop evacuating civilians but he continued to ignore these instructions. Kot was told about the evacuations after the fact and complained it resulted in a flood of Poles moving south.[80] Anders got a telegram from Klimecki indicating British unhappiness about bringing civilians to Iran.

There was a continuing battle with the Soviets concerning the evacuation of soldiers' families. Anders made the point that the soldiers would not be at their best if concerned about families left behind. Considerable efforts were made by Anders to get families of soldiers evacuated, but this met with limited success.

Footnotes

1. NA 6940, 6010, Poland.
2. A telegram to General Hastings Ismay (September 26, 1941), (copy), GSHI, A. XII, 1/56.
3. GSHI, A. 11.49/Sow/6; NA Poland 5935.
4. GSHI, PRM coll., box. #39-b, doc. #132.
5. Documents on Polish-Soviet Relations, 1939-1945 (London: Heinemann, 1961), v. I, p. 185.
6. Documents on Polish-Soviet Relations, 1939-1945, v. I, p. 237-242, 244.
7. Panfilov to Stalin (17 III 1942) in Armia Polska w ZSRR 1941-1942 (ed.) W. Materski (Warsaw, 1992), p. 76; W. Anders, An Army in Exile (London: Macmillan, 1949), p. 98.
8. Documents on Polish-Soviet Relations, 1939-1945 (London: Heinemann, 1961), v. I, p. 301-305.
9. Vyshinsky to Stalin and Molotov (March 24 1942) in Armia Polska w ZSRR 1941-1942, p. 82, 84.
10. FO 371/16762/13356.
11. Interview with Romanowski.
12. GHSI, A.11.49/Sow./6.
13. FO 371/16762/13008.
14. GSHI, A. X11, 1/57 and PREM, 204/354/1.
15. Documents on Polish-Soviet Relations, 1939-1945, p. 319-320; FO 371/16762/13356.
16. Documents on Polish-Soviet Relations, 1939-1945, p. 342.
17. Ibid., p. 369-370.
18. A letter from the British Military Mission in Moscow to the Foreign Relations Division of the Soviet Ministry of Defense (March 10, 1942), TsAMO, f. 380, op. 768407, d. 53, l. 206.
19. An interview with Romanowski. In the autumn of 1941, at the height of the battle for Moscow, when Stalin needed all the help he could get he kept five fully equipped divisions in Iran. GSHI PRM 39-B, no.132
20. GSHI, A. 11 49/Sow./2, No. 216.
21. HI, coll. MSZ, box #234.
22. Beria to Stalin (April 4, 1942) in Armia Polska w ZSRR 1941-1942 (ed.) W. Materski (Warsaw, 1992), p. 90.
23. Beria to Stalin (July 24, 1942) in Novaia i Noveishaia Istoriia 2 (1993), p. 88-89.

24. Documents on Polish-Soviet Relations, 1939-1945 (London: Heinemann, 1961), v. I, p. 348-349.
25. GSHI, PRM, 70, No. 223.
26. Sovetsko-angliiskie otnosheniia vo vremia Velikoi Otechestvennoi voiny 1941-1945 (Moscow, 1983), v. I, p. 520.
27. Documents on Polish-Soviet Relations, 1939-1945, v. I, p. 399.
28. H. MacMillan, The Blast of War (New York, Harper&Row, 1968), p. 429.
29. David Engel seems to be saying the British maneuvered Anders into a no-win situation, In the Shadow of Auschwitz: the Polish Government-in-exile and the Jews, 1939-1942 (Chapel Hill: Univ. of North Carolina Press), p. 146.
30. Interview with Keith Sword.
31. Perepiska Predsedatelia Soveta Ministrov SSSR s Prezidentami SShA i Premer Ministrami Velikobritanii vo Vremia Velikoi Otechestvennoi Voiny 1941-1945 gg. (Moscow, 1957), v. I, p. 53.
32. A. Eden, The Memoirs (Boston: Houghton Mifflin, 1965), v. 3, p. 118.
33. Anders, An Army in Exile, p. 112; a telegram to Stalin (July 31, 1942) in Novaia i Noveishaia Istoriia 2 (1993), p. 89-90.
34. E.L. Woodward, British Foreign Policy in the Second World War II (London, 1970), v. II, p. 616-617.
35. Beria to Stalin and Molotov (July 24, 1942) in Novaia i Noveishaia Istoriia 2 (1993), p. 88.
36. HI, PSZ coll., box #2.
37. PRO, PREM, 3/354/7.
38. Koptelov to Stalin and other leaders (September 7, 1942) in Armia Polska w ZSRR 1941-1942, p. 106.
39. J. Ciechanowski, "Armia Polska w Rosji w Swietle dziennika Szefa Sztabu z 1942 r." Zeszyty Historyczne (Paris), v. LVII (1991), p. 97-99. It was only after the second evacuation that General Rudnicki realized how much food, clothing and equipment was left behind. See, Last of the War Horses, K.S. Rudnicki, p. 249. Food had been taken to the embarkation points but it was confiscated by the Russians.
40. HI, Anders Coll., Box 42.
41. Documents on Polish-Soviet Relations, 1939-1945, v. I, p. 346-348.
42. Anders, An Army in Exile, p. 109.
43. W. Anders, Bez ostatniego rozdzialu (Newton, 1950), p. 191.

44. Interviews with Mrs. Renata Anders, Jan Romanowski and Lubienski.
45. About 10% of Polish Jews who were in Poland in 1941 survived the Holocaust. The largest group to survive were those deported to the USSR in 1940-1941. As bad as conditions were in Siberia, more than 10% survived.
46. N. Ascherson, The Struggles for Poland (New York: Random House, 1987), p. 122.
47. L. Brenner, The Iron Wall: Zionist Revisionism from Jabotinsky to Shamir (London: Zed Books, 1984), p. 127.
48. GSHI, KGA 24.
49. "Memorjal w sprawie zydowskiej podczas ewakuacji W.P. z Sowietow na teren Iranu," p. 4, (September 18, 1942) signed by Szyszko-Bohusz and Anders, in GSHI, KGA 24.
50. For Anders' declaration see Jewish Telegraph Agency Bulletin (May 5, 1942).
51. "Memorjal w sprawie zydowskiej podczas ewakuacji W.P. z Sowietow na teren Iranu," p. 4.
52. "Memorjal w sprawie zydowskiej podczas ewakuacji W.P. z Sowietow na teren Iranu," p. 4.
53. Letter of October 20, 1942 in HI, Ambasada USSR, Box 17.
54. GSHI, A. XII, 22/30, doc. 164, p. 252.
55. Jerusalem Postal and Telegraphic Censorship, Special Report No. 216, NA, Palestine, 5129.
56. An interview with General K. Rudnicki; also his Na polskim szlaku (Wspomnienia z lat 1939-1947) (London, 1983), p. 200-201.
57. GSHI, KGA, 24.
58. Jewish Telegraphic Agency (March 3, 1942).
59. Jewish Telegraphic Agency (May 24, 1942).
60. An interview with Mr. And Mrs. Alexander Zvielli.
61. An interview with Menahem Buchweitz.
62. Testimony of Chawa Kestenbojm, publ. in Jews in Eastern Poland and the USSR, 1939-46, N. Davies, A. Polonsky (eds.) (Houndmills, Basingstoke, Hampshire: Macmillan, 1991), p. 335.
63. An interview with Zelig Goldberg.
64. An interview with Racieski (London, November 6, 1989).
65. Engel, In the Shadow of Auschwitz: the Polish Government-in-exile and the Jews, 1939-1942, p. 279.
66. HI, Anders coll., box. 63.
67. An interview with Zelig Goldberg.

68 An interview with Jan Romanowski.

69. GSHI, KGA, 24.

70. GSHI, KGA, 24.

71. A letter from David Engel to the author.

72. Jews in Eastern Poland and the USSR, 1939-46, p. 46.

73. An interview with Frank Roberts (London, July 7, 1992).

74. HI, Anders Coll., Box #60.

75. GHSI, PREM, 3/354/7.

76. FO 371/31099, p.36.

77. For various assessments see, GSHI, KGA, 24 and Kol. 138/213; NA Palestine, 5129; Anders, An Army in Exile, p. 113.

78. The Correspondence between the Chairman of the Council of Ministers of the USSR with the Presidents of the United States and the Foreign Ministers of Great Britain during the Great Patriotic War of 1941-1945. 1976, Moscow, vol. 2, pp. 64-68.

79. FO 371/31082

80. Anders, An Army in Exile, p. 101.

# CHAPTER FOUR

# GENERAL ANDERS' ARMY IN THE MIDDLE EAST

## Arrival and Conditions in Iran

The country into which Anders' Army arrived after its escape from the USSR was far from friendly to the Allied cause. Iran had been occupied by British and Soviet forces since August 29, 1941. On January 29, 1942, the Iranian Government was suborned to sign a treaty with the USSR and Great Britain, legalizing what was a de facto British-Soviet occupation.[1] Not surprisingly the Iranians felt a certain sympathy for the Germans. German agents had operated in Iran from the beginning of the war but their presence had no significance before Germany invaded the USSR. In the fall of 1941, the British arrested 70 Nazi agents and sympathizers in Teheran with expectations of arresting hundreds more. They predicted that if German planes reached Teheran the Iranian people would spontaneously attack the soldiers of the occupying powers.[2] This opinion about Iranian hostility to the Allied cause was shared by the OSS.[3]

The Poles arriving in Iran were in a deplorable physical condition. They were extremely emaciated by starvation. Half of the civilians were infected with diseases, typhus being the most common. In addition they suffered from dysentery, malaria, and other diseases related to food and vitamin deficiencies. Overcrowded conditions on the boats crossing the Caspian Sea further deteriorated their health. Although British facilities in Iran were waiting for them with food and medical care many people were beyond saving. Of the 12,000 civilians who arrived in the first evacuation 6,200 had to be hospitalized and 453 died soon after arrival. Altogether 1,344 soldiers and civilians (about 3%).of the first evacuation wave died soon after reaching Iran. By November of 1942, between 22 to 28 percent of those who had come with Anders from Russia had died.[4] The roads through Palestine, Iraq and Iran were lined with the graves of Poles.

As 40% of the evacuees were lice infested, everyone had to go through a delousing camp which meant that their clothes had to be relinquished to be burnt. Some evacuees resisted this as they had been issued new uniforms and clothing just before leaving the USSR. Eventually medical officers were able to convince everyone of the necessity of destroying all clothing brought from the Soviet Union in order to curtail the infections and diseases to which they had been exposed. The evacuees were then issued new, clean uniforms or civilian clothing.

Although the Poles were overwhelmed by the availability of food, and Iran seemed to them a land of plenty in comparison with the Soviet Union, in fact when they arrived there was a food shortage. According to Hankey, the shortage was caused by Iranian corruption which made it impossible to organize a rationing system. This immediately resulted in open hostility between Poles and the local people who were convinced that the Poles were given the most and the best food and this had caused the shortages. It appeared to the Iranians that Polish children were getting better rations than their own children. Riots ensued caused by the

Iranians' belief that food shortages and high prices were created by Allied soldiers especially the Poles. Relations improved somewhat when food supplies improved and towards seeing "moneyed Polish refugees leaving food shops heavily laden."[5]

Even though the Polish press attempted to give the impression of an unbridled Iranian affection for the Poles, there were many instances of hostile acts against them. Not surprisingly, Iran being a Moslem country, public imbibing of alcohol by Poles, perhaps making up for three years in Soviet captivity, was a major source of friction. Religious Iranians were offended by the "idleness and gay life" of Poles living outside the camps. To avoid incidents, the Iranian Government pressed for a reduction in the number of Poles allowed to live outside the camps, especially those who were unemployed. The British wanted to get the Poles out of Iran as soon as possible--not only because their presence contributed to tensions with the Iranians but also because it clogged the main supply route to the Soviet Union and was a source of political embarrassment.[6]

American intelligence reports gave a mixed, and often contradictory assessment of the evacuated soldiers. All the reports stressed their high morale and discipline, their desire to fight Germans and their dislike of the Soviets, but differed concerning their state of health and military training. One report asserted that they were well trained and in good health. There was also a difference of opinion as to whether the Polish forces would be combat ready by January, 1942.[7]

A less flattering picture of the Anders' Army was painted by James Aldridge, a New York Times reporter known to be anti-Polish. He wrote that Polish Forces in Teheran were controlled by an "elite of Polish officers and wealthy Polish women" and went on to accuse the Poles of selling British uniforms and blankets to the Iranians. The Polish elite, he reported, was selling relief packages on the open market. According to him Polish Jews were put into a ghetto and camps were segregated by social class. He stated also that the army was conducting an anti-Russian campaign and had pressured Iraq not to let Jewish children pass through to Palestine. Aldridge's column looked as if it had been prepared in NKVD offices in Moscow. Hankey called the Aldridge story "a pack of lies or quite gross distortion of the facts."[8]

There were, however, continued reports of anti-Semitism in the army. One claimed that Jewish civilians were given the worst living quarters and another that they were refused food and shelter. The Jewish Telegraph Agency reported that in one town 250 Jewish soldiers were sleeping in the streets and were denied food and shelter by the Polish Army. After British intervention the Jewish soldiers were sent to Teheran. The Jewish representative on the Polish National Council, Schwartzbart, charged that Jews were being discriminated against in the selection process for the army. Responding to Schwartzbart 's criticism, Anders ordered an investigation which concluded that no discrimination occurred and claimed that among men of military age the percentages of Jews and non-Jews who were accepted was similar, but that one third of Jews given a clean bill of health by the medical commission did not report for duty and were smuggled into Palestine by Jewish organizations. Furthermore, the report explained that those who were found ineligible for service were not deprived of uniforms, since no other clothing was available, and the basis for the accusation that the army was not feeding Jewish soldiers, was that they were wearing uniforms but they were not soldiers. Both Anders and his Chief of Staff, Colonel Okulicki found the conclusions of the investigation satisfactory.[9]

Jewish groups charged the Polish Relief Committee in Iran with withholding adequate supplies from Jews because of anti-Semitic tendencies among the administrators.[10] However in September, 1942, a delegate of the Jewish Agency in Teheran, in a lengthy report to the World Jewish Congress, commented favorably on the aid being provided by Polish relief agencies operating out of

Teheran to Polish Jews still in the USSR.[11] Similarly representatives of the American Jewish Joint Distribution Committee testified to good cooperation in matters of relief efforts between Poles and Jews in Iran. In fact, out of the total cost of the Joint's Teheran operation of $2,780,000, over $1,000,000 was covered by the Polish Red Cross and the Polish Government, while $1,200,000 was provided by relatives (of which $750,000 came from Palestine, $240,000 from the U.S. and the balance from England, Australia and South Africa).[12] The only way to account for the inconsistencies in these various reports are the differences in time and place.

If cooperation between Jewish and Polish relief agencies was relatively smooth it can be contrasted to the strong conflict that developed between the Polish agencies and the American Red Cross. American Red Cross workers protested against not being able to give aid directly to individuals, accusing Polish relief agencies of "dishonesty, unfairness, inefficiency, waste and extreme selfishness." They accused the Poles of trying to force out American Red Cross representative, MacDonald, because he allegedly discovered their gross misuse of Red Cross supplies.[13]

Neither the army, nor the majority of civilians accompanying it, stayed in Iran for long. Between August 10 and September 8, 1942, the army was transported to Iraq where it was joined by Polish units coming from Palestine.[14] Most civilians were evacuated to India and Africa but a few stayed in Iran after the bulk of the Polish population left and found jobs in the civilian economy or in American army camps. In 1944, the British Legation in Teheran reported that several hundred Poles were living in the city "by their own wits and who have for many months been disowned by the British Legation." An additional 200-300 Poles who supported the Communist administration which the Soviets had installed in Poland, chose not to depart from Iran with Anders' Army.[15]

**Reorganization in Iraq**

The main body of Anders' Army reached Iraq without any serious obstacles. At first Iraq was merely a stop on the road to Palestine but the Poles found it an excellent training area, and using it as such took some of the pressure away from Palestine where so many foreign forces were stationed. It was therefore decided to bring Polish soldiers commanded by General Zajac, the Carpathian Brigade (formed in 1940 from Poles who fled to the Middle East via the Balkans) and Anders' soldiers from the first evacuation, from Palestine to Iraq. In Iraq they joined soldiers under the command of Anders who had come from the USSR in the second evacuation. By November, 1942, the Polish forces in Iraq numbered 70,000 soldiers.

A major problem however was to find a way to get Jewish civilians through Iraq to Palestine. According to agreements between the two governments Iraq had no control over the transit of military personnel through Iraqi territory. As part of their appeasement policy the British accepted a transit visa requirement for civilians passing through Iraq, which applied to all civilians but with restrictions against Jews. Iraq opposed any movement of Jews westward towards Palestine and agreed to the stationing of the Polish Army on its territory only after the Poles assured them they would not be taking any Jewish civilians to Palestine.

Jewish civilians therefore had to be ferried by ship around the Arabian peninsula and through the Suez Canal to Palestine. The trip by ship lasted weeks compared to traveling by truck which was measured in hours. Evacuation by sea was also hampered by a lack of shipping. To facilitate the transportation, General Sikorski worked out a confidential arrangement with the Iraqi Legation which allowed the transit of a number of Polish civilians (mostly Jews) without a visa, which probably involved bribery. As a result some Jewish children were smuggled through Iraq wearing Catholic school uniforms. Whatever the special arrangement was, it ended in the summer of 1943, when

General Sikorski died tragically in an airplane crash. Two months later the Polish Government gave the British assurances that in the future only bona-fide military personnel and civilians with Iraqi visas would be transported across Iraq in military convoys[16]

The British ambassador in Baghdad was very upset about this deception. He complained to the Foreign Office that such illegal convoys were tarnishing the British Embassy's reputation for "dealing fairly with the Iraqi Government" and warned that he was not prepared to accept such a risk indefinitely. The British Embassy in Teheran advised Baghdad that these were exceptional circumstances and only bona fide military and eligible civilians would be in future convoys.[17]

It is inconceivable that Anders was not aware of the illegal smuggling of Jewish civilians in Polish military convoys across Iraq. In fact Anders was explicitly instructed by the British that no illegal travelers were to be included in future Polish military convoys going through Iraq to Palestine. It is to Anders' credit that the British Ambassador accused him of violating those instructions and getting Jewish civilians into Palestine illegally.

The Polish soldiers arriving from Iran were first stationed in the region of Qizil Ribat, near the Iranian border, where Anders established his headquarters in September of 1942. The army stayed there for several months before moving to training sites in the oil region around Kirkuk and Mosul. In October-November, 1942, the troops were concentrated at Khanaqin, in Northern Iraq.[18]

In Iraq the Polish Army was placed under the British 10th Army commanded by General Wilson. An immediate benefit to the British was that the Poles took over the protection of the oil installation in Northern Iraq, relieving the 8th Indian Division which could then be transferred to the Mediterranean Theater.[19]

During their stay in Iraq the Polish Army was completely reorganized, to conform to the British organizational model. A British liaison unit, headed first by Brigadier Way and later by Brigadier Firth, was established at General Anders' headquarters. There was also a U.S. liaison officer, Lt.-Colonel Henry Szymanski.

The original plan for the reorganization of Anders' Army was submitted by Sikorski's Chief of Staff, General Klimecki in August of 1942.[20] The plan called for the three infantry divisions which Anders had led out from the USSR plus the Carpathian Brigade from Palestine to be transformed into an "Army" consisting of two "Corps" (each of 2 infantry divisions) and two tank brigades. The army was to number 56,000 soldiers and those remaining were to be transferred to the United Kingdom.

Under British pressure the plan was significantly modified. Instead of an army the Poles had to do with a Corps of two infantry divisions, one tank and one infantry Brigade plus a full complement of Corps units. The Corps was to number about 71,000 soldiers. Since 3000 soldiers were to be sent to the United Kingdom there was a deficiency of 4,000 personnel. On September 8, 1942, Sikorski approved the plan proposed by the British.[21] Thus was born the Second Polish Corps.

Following reorganization, important changes were made among the commanding officers. General Joseph Zajac, who had been sent by Sikorski from London to command the Polish Forces in the East was to be Second-in-Command under General Anders. Anders got rid of General Zajac as soon as possible, replacing him with General Tokarzewski-Karaszewicz who had come with him from the USSR. Zajac wasn't Anders' or anyone else's enemy but the consensus was that he wasn't strong enough for the job. There was some sympathy for Zajac especially among the older officers who felt that Anders was pushing him aside. Other important nominations included the appointment of former commander of the Carpathian Brigade, General

Kopanski, to head the Third Carpathian Infantry Division and of General Rakowski as the Corps' Chief of Staff.[22]

Relations between the Polish Corps and the Iraqi population were no better than they had been in Iran. Iraq, like Iran, had also been pro-German and in April-May, 1941, was occupied by the British which did not dispose the Iraqis favorably towards the Allied soldiers. Soon after arrival in Iraq a series of unpleasant events started to haunt the Polish forces. The most important reason why Polish soldiers were resented in Iraq was a food shortage and an increase in food prices, which the local population attributed to food purchasing by the army and by individual soldiers. In addition, the undisciplined behavior of Polish soldiers stirred hostility towards them. Also burglaries and break-ins occurred which did not improve the situation. The British let Anders handle these matters on his own, lest his enemies exploit them to undermine his position.[23]

By the summer of 1943, with the reorganization and training of the Corps largely completed, it was moved to Palestine and was stationed in the area between Gaza and Tel Aviv. The schedule called for embarkation to Egypt by December 15, 1943, the last stop before Anders' Army was to engage the enemy in Italy.[24]

## Palestine: Relations with the Jewish Population

It is ironic that the Polish Army found itself stationed in Palestine. For 900 years Jews had been a minority in Poland and now Poles where living in an area which Jews regarded as their national territory. There were Polish soldiers and civilians in Palestine from 1940 until the spring of 1948. Elements of Anders Army arrived in Palestine in 1942 and the army left for Egypt in December, 1943. Until the arrival of the evacuees from the USSR, the Polish armed forces in the Middle East consisted only of the Independent Carpathian Brigade and a few stragglers. In late March, 1942, the British began preparations to receive Anders' Army in Palestine but they had no clear idea at that time how many Poles would be arriving. Their estimates varied between 10,000 and 100,000, but the actual number was close to 110,000 (70,000 soldiers and 40,000 civilians). The British had not anticipated that the Poles would be arriving in organized military formations; they had expected they would arrive as disorganized individuals.[25]

The Poles traveled from Iran to Gedera in Palestine through Habbaniya in Iraq on trucks organized by the British 10th Army beginning in April, 1942. They traveled in truck convoys, with each truck transporting about 600 soldiers, with the women (nurses and ATS) traveling in smaller groups of no more than 100. There were four separate camps in the Gedera area: Gedera, Yibna, Al Mughar and Bash Shet, with a total capacity of 14,000. There were two other groups of camps, one with a capacity for 15,000 people and the other for 16,000. These were designated as Castina group and Julis group. Women were sent to a camp in Rehovath and cadet schools were set up in Gaza and Barbara (non-existent today), near Ashkelon. The headquarters of the army was divided between "km 89" (near Gaza) and Rehovath with only a small liaison office in Jerusalem. Obviously at different times there were different numbers of Poles stationed in Palestine.

Anders' Corps was moved to Iraq for training and then brought back to Palestine in August and September of 1943, where Polish forces comprised over 64,000 soldiers, 3000 women of the ATS and 3000 cadets.[26]

Palestinian Jews were a diverse group, but in 1942 the Polish language was widely spoken among them, and their leaders were almost all Polish born. It was said you could cross Palestine and never be in an area where Polish was not spoken. For Polish soldiers in a foreign country it was a novelty to find a Polish speaking population.[27]

The friendly reception of an allied army decreases as numbers increase and its stay lengthens. For example, the first American soldiers arriving in England received a warm reception, but with time, and as their numbers increased, the public attitude towards them became less favorable. The same was true for the Polish Army in Palestine. A Polish officer from the Carpathian Brigade said that when the Brigade was the sole Polish unit in Palestine the soldiers had excellent relations with the Jews. Relations deteriorated when the Polish Army arrived from Russia in 1942.[28]

The first Polish soldiers to reach Palestine were received very well. They had come to fight the Germans and had brought news from home and Polish-born Palestinian Jews were anxious to hear what was happening in their native towns. Many had been in Palestine for five or ten years but still had thoughts of friends and family in Poland with whom all communications had stopped when the the war started There were several reunions with soldiers from their native towns, during which, at least for the moment, the negative side of Polish-Jewish relations was forgotten. The first soldiers into Palestine were invited by Polish Jews into their homes. The Poles were sympathetic to the Jews and in those early days attended many cultural events with the Jewish population and played sports against local Jewish clubs. Polish soldiers who had been farmers in their civilian life, would, when off duty, go to a kibbutz to work where they were badly needed because so many kibbutzniks were away in the British Army. Jewish attitudes and willingness to work hard for their new country impressed the Polish soldiers and gave them a new respect for Jews. Some soldiers even remember that Polish-Jewish relations in Palestine were excellent.[29] The History of the Polish Armed Forces in the Second World War, published by the Sikorski Institute in London, also describes the army's relations with the Jewish community in Palestine as good, in spite of Jewish desertions and Jewish political activities.[30]

However a few serious incidents arose between Jews and Poles. A newspaper in Tel Aviv claimed that some anti-Jewish riots in which at least one Jew was killed had been provoked by Poles. According to the Polish consul in Jerusalem, during the summer of 1942 a Polish soldier killed a Jew. It turned out that the reason was neither political nor racial but personal--they were fighting over a girl. The soldier was sentenced by the Polish Army court to serve five years of hard labor in prison.[31]

The good relations between Polish soldiers and Palestinian Jews were initially damaged by events outside Palestine when Jewish civilians, newly arrived from Poland, told about wide-spread anti-Semitism in Poland. They reported that under German occupation, the Poles had become more anti-Semitic, and the Polish underground was doing nothing to halt this. They had heard that some Poles were turning Jews over to the Germans in order to receive a reward, which was often the home and the property of the Jews they had betrayed.

Although the Polish underground, in 1942, formed an organization called Zegota to assist Jews and to punish Poles who denounced Jews, this organization didn't come into full strength until 1944. For most Jews the activities of Zegota were less visible than the anti-Semitism of a considerable number of Poles. Additional anti-Polish sentiment was generated by the arrival in Palestine of 14 Jewish children from a Polish shelter in Kenya, who complained that they had been abused by the Polish children, who were very anti-Semitic.

These accusations and incidents created an unfriendly attitude towards the Poles in Palestine. Jewish soldiers were asked by Palestinian Jews why they were staying in the Polish Army. In an attempt to repair their image the head of General Anders' Documentation Bureau, suggested that whenever Poles make an anti-Semitic remark they should be told they are hurting Poland, and that Zegota would execute those Poles in occupied Poland who betray Jews to the Germans.[32] Some Jews who left the army in Palestine may have exaggerated anti-Semitism, in order to justify their desertion, which also helped turn public sentiment against the Poles. Mutual resentments were also provoked by commercial dealings. Jews thought that the Polish soldiers, who had cash, were buying watches and jewelry at very low prices exploiting the Palestinian Jews who needed the cash. Polish civilians who arrived in Palestine with a few valuables to sell felt exploited by Palestinian Jews who paid them very low prices.[33] It has also been argued that because supporters of the anti-Semitic National Democratic party gained control of the Polish institutions in Palestine, Polish Jews in Palestine who, in 1940, were well disposed toward Polish refugees, later began to regard them as enemies.[34] It is therefore impossible to accept as true a U.S. intelligence report attributing anti-Polish attitudes in Palestine to Communist inspiration. Attributing the anti-Polish sentiment to Soviet propaganda was not realistic as it relieved the Poles of responsibly for any anti-Polish attitudes.[35]

Some Poles and some Jews harboring a preconceived animosity for each other looked for incidents to justify their prejudices. One Jew said he hated all Poles based on a name calling incident in a cafe. A Pole told me he hated all Palestinian Jews because a shop keeper had overcharged him. The Jewish Chronicle reported that a group of ten Polish criminals, expelled from the army in Palestine, had a cellar club house in Tel Aviv which denied entry to Jews. Mysteriously the club house was destroyed and the Tel Aviv police could not find the vandals.[36] A few "incidents" happened because some Poles had difficulty understanding that the Jews in Palestine would not take the verbal abuse they had taken in Poland. Most incidents occurred when Polish soldiers were drunk and except for these rare incidents the relations were good.[37] In March, 1944, after a majority of the Second Polish Corps had left Palestine, there were anti-Jewish disturbances in Palestine for which several Polish soldiers were sentenced to prison by the British. Rabbi Meir Berlin, upon arriving in New York, said that the stories of Poles in Palestine causing anti-Jewish riots were grossly exaggerated and added that anti-Semitic remarks by Polish soldiers were not representative of the Polish leaders.[38]

In general, the total number of "incidents" was very small, considering the large number of soldiers and the length of their stay in Palestine. Anders issued an order informing his soldiers "they must refrain from confrontations and incidents involving the local population." When drunk the Polish soldiers usually brawled with British and Australian soldiers while fights with Jews were very rare. According to one interviewee Polish soldiers had better relations with Jews in Palestine than later on with the civilian population in Italy.[39]

In fact, contacts between Polish soldiers and Palestinian Jews were limited. The soldiers spent most of their time in military training and time off was spent sightseeing. Things were dull and the soldiers were bored. Even when they got weekend passes, life in Tel-Aviv came to a standstill from Friday evening until sundown on Saturday as the Jews were observing the Sabbath.[40]

The Polish Government in exile was quite supportive of the idea of a Jewish homeland in Palestine. Representing the Ministry of Information, Professor Olgierd Gorka explained to a group of Zionist leaders that his government was hoping the Jewish Homeland would serve as a place of settlement for Polish Jews and prevent those who had fled the Germans from returning to Poland after the war. He was also hoping that its support of Zionism would gain it Jewish support against the USSR and would help persuade Palestinian Jews to join the Polish Army.[41]

The Prime Minister and the Commander-in-Chief, General Sikorski, declared his support for the concept of a Jewish Brigade in the British Army.[42] The British learned about it when his speech was reported in the Jewish Telegraphic Agency Bulletin on August 17, 1942. Sikorski's statement upset the British who called it part of "Sikorski's tendency to appease Zionists at Great Britain's expense" and inconsistent with the assurances Sikorski had given the British. The official response to the British complaint came from Stronski, Polish Minister of Information, who explained that Sikorski's statement was intended to make the point that Jews will not be forced to leave Poland.[43]

It is undeniable that the Sikorski Government's pro-Zionist position was largely motivated by a desire to gain Zionist support for Poland in the inevitable confrontation with the Soviet Union, an unrealistic calculation. Zionists were not going to antagonize the Soviets, whose support they needed for creation of the State of Israel, moreover the Soviets were carrying the brunt of the fighting against Nazi Germany. As far as Polish efforts to recruit Palestinian Jews to Anders' Corps, the results were not very impressive as only a very few enlisted. For Jews who wanted to fight Nazis there were better alternatives, i.e. enlisting in the British Army or in Jewish units created by the British. For the Jews who were in Palestine illegally, service in the British Army seemed to promise legalization of their status after the war.[44] It's possible that Sikorski and other Poles knew they could make gratuitous statements inviting Palestinian Jews to join the Polish Army knowing that few, if any, Jews would accept.

## Polish Military Training for the Jews of Palestine

The history of the Polish Army providing military training to Palestinian Jews goes back to prewar days and continued through the first years of the war. Most of the activity took place with Irgun Zvai Lemmi, (known as the "Irgun") but at least one group of Haganah members is known to have gone to Poland for secret training by the Polish Army.

Yaa'cov Meridor was the acting head of the Irgun, when, in 1939, he went to Poland for a training program conducted by Polish officers for 26 high ranking Irgun members. It was part of a prewar plan to encourage Polish Jews to immigrate to Palestine.

The prewar training program is traceable to meetings between Ambassador Edward Raczynski and V.Jabotinsky, in 1936 and 1937. The 1937 meeting was attended by Jabotinsky and Kahan and Polish Secret Service people plus Ludwik Lubienski, later an aide to General Anders.[45]

When it looked like the German Army might reach Palestine, the Polish Army in Palestine trained the Jews there in sabotage. Ely Tavin, for example, received espionage and explosives training. and participated in a course on guerrilla warfare. The training was continued in Palestine until the start of 1944 when the Irgun commenced their actions against the British.

According to Merek Kahan, the Polish Army destroyed all documents showing cooperation with Jews after the Irgun killed some British soldiers. The Polish Army had every incentive to deny cooperation with the Jews.[46] An OSS report[47] on the Irgun, which has many discrepancies, refers to two Polish generals who had come to Palestine with Anders, conducting a training program for Irgun recruits. Tavin's recollection was that the program was conducted by Polish sergeants and a captain.

The OSS and other American intelligence agencies were perplexed by the cooperation between the Polish Army and the Irgun. The following are some samples from Intelligence reports:

> "...the Irgun is procuring arms from the Polish Forces stationed in Palestine. The amount is said to be appreciable..."[48] (Tavin says the amount was insignificant)
>
> "...incontrovertible evidence of collaboration between Polish elements and the terrorist gangs..."[49] (This comment originated with the Jewish Agency)
>
> "One of the Colonels of the old Deuxieme Bureau is now a leader of the Irgun..." (Kahan?? Very unlikely)[50]

"The Irgun was greatly strengthened by the arrival of Polish Troops in Palestine."

The source of much of the intelligence "information" undoubtedly was the Jewish Agency which was strongly anti-Irgun. An OSS report, in 1945,[51] reads like anti-Irgun, anti-Polish propaganda:

> "Palestinian Jewish terrorists are receiving aid and comfort from Polish sources. The Poles are furious with the British for selling them down the river to the Soviets and are interested in embarrassing Britain by every means. Although Poland is not popular among Jews because of her past anti-Jewish record, the extremists among the Jews are inclined to accept this aid against the common British enemy."

Nothing was found which links Anders to the prewar military training of Jews. The training of Jews for the possible German assault on Palestine was mostly done prior to Anders arrival in Palestine. However the OSS reports indicate there was cooperation between the Irgun and the Polish Army during the time when the Second Polish Corps was in Palestine.[52]

## Politics in the Army

The Polish Army in Palestine was heavily politicized as a number of political factions existed within the army. Apart from supporters of Sikorski and his administration in London the most important factions were the Pilsudskites and "Endeks." The Pilsudskites supported the Polish prewar military regime, while the "Endeks" were right-wing, nationalist and heavily anti-Semitic. There was also a small group of pro-Soviet communists. Each group tried to court Anders because of the personal loyalty the soldiers of the Second Polish Corps had towards him. Anders was constantly accused of belonging to this or that orientation, yet nothing was found which tied him to any particular political group. The only political force benefiting from this political division was the Communists.

Polish soldiers in Palestine had a great interest in keeping informed about military and political affairs so an inordinate number of Polish language newspapers and bulletins were published in Palestine.53 The most important among them was the daily Gazeta Polska (The Polish Gazette), published in Jerusalem and devoted to political matters and supporting London Government. A cartoon magazine Parada, a counterpart to the British Parade, was published jointly with the British Ministry of Information. A daily mimeographed Camp Bulletin was issued for all Polish armed forces in the Middle East. The Union of Polish Patriots in Palestine, a branch of the Soviet puppet organization which existed under a similar name in the USSR, circulated clandestinely (it lacked a license for public distribution) Biuletyn Wolnej Polski (Bulletin of Free Poland), a weekly printed in Jerusalem. The "news" in the Biuletyn came from Soviet sources and for all practical purposes functioned as the mouthpiece of Soviet propaganda. Its editor, Jozef Broda was a professional criminal who had served time in a Polish prison before the war and was released from the Polish Army on a medical discharge.[54]

From the time of signing the Sikorski-Maisky Agreement the Polish Government in London and the Soviets were conducting a propaganda war. This war followed Anders' Army (to which the Soviets had access in a variety of ways) to Palestine. In addition to the Communist party of Palestine, which was always small, there were left wing Socialists and some who temporarily supported cooperation with the Soviets. According to U.S. intelligence, the year 1943 saw a growth in pro-Soviet tendencies among Arabs and Bethlehem was the center of Communist activities in Palestine. The report attributed the substantial pro-Soviet support among Arabs to the 100 or so (Russian) Orthodox schools managed by the Palestinian Orthodox Society and concluded that most of the pro-Soviet and pro-Communist Arabs knew Russian and of the Orthodox religion.

There had been rumors in Palestine that in February, 1944, the Second Polish Corps had court-martialed, for political reasons, a substantial number of Polish officers. In late February the "rumor" was repeated in the American press, claiming that from 15 to 500 officers and soldiers were sentenced. At the beginning of March, newspapers in London carried a story that the Polish Army in Jerusalem had sentenced one Polish officer to life imprisonment and 22 other officers and soldiers to 20 years imprisonment. The articles alleged that they were punished for expressing sympathy for the Soviet Union and for desiring to join a Communist-dominated Polish Army organized in the USSR by Colonel Berling. The articles were repeated by the Soviet press agency.[55]

Two and one half months later the Polish Telegraphic Agency carried a denial of those stories and announced that only six Poles were court-martialed at the time indicated by the press.[56] The six included: Captain K. Rozen-Zawadzki, Lieutenant R.L. Imach, 2nd Lieutenant S. Szczypiorski, 2nd Lieutenant F. Kukulinski, Sergeant L.T. Strzalkowski and Corporal R. Gadomski. Three of the four officers were found guilty of "deliberately acting to the detriment of the Armed Forces of Poland in time of war." 2nd Lieutenant Kukulinski was found guilty of the same charge but his actions were not deemed deliberate. All four officers were also found guilty of "creating an illegal revolutionary organization, supported by the Palestinian Communist Party." The court found that they had encouraged soldiers to disobey their superiors and had spread rumors that the Polish Army was kept in the Middle East because the London Government didn't want to fight for the liberation of Poland. They were also accused of spreading rumors that the British had killed Sikorski and that the British would force the Polish Army to fight in Burma. The purpose of the rumors was to weaken the discipline and fighting ability of the army. Imach and Szczypiorski were also found guilty of espionage, both having confessed that they passed bad intelligence and tactical information, as well as code books, to Soviet officers. Rozen-Zawadzki was sentenced to life imprisonment, Imach and Szczypiorski to fifteen years and Kukulinski to two years in prison.

Strzalkowski was found not guilty and all charges against him were dismissed. Gadomski's case was separated from the others but, after further investigation, he was also sentenced to a prison term.[57]

In December, 1945, after the war ended, the Warsaw Government demanded the release of six officers and soldiers who, it claimed, had been sentenced for political opinion and were being held in the military prison at Quassassin in Egypt. They were Rozen-Zawadzki, Imach, Cadet Stanislaw Willowicz (sentenced to 10 years), Corporal Wladyslaw Spychala (4 years), Private Wladyslaw Czernic (8 years) and Sergeant Jan Zebrowski (sentenced to "several years"). Postwar Communist authorities in Warsaw demanded that they be immediately released and given the chance to return to Poland, where their convictions would be annulled. Warsaw asserted that there were other political prisoners in Quassassin prison but did not know their names. It appears that the British complied with this request.[58]

Soldiers were not arrested just for having pro-Soviet sentiments. Those who were arrested were found guilty of the more specific crimes of forming an illegal organization in the army and conducting agitation detrimental to army morale. Officers who were merely sympathetic to the Soviets and had been prominent pro-Soviet activists in the "Villa of Happiness" (Lt.-Colonel Dudzinski, Lt. Tyszynski, Lt. Tomala and Lt. Szczemigalski) were not prosecuted but had to submit to a "Court of Honor" composed of their peers.[59]

## Crime and Punishment in the Army

Every army has problems with discipline and must have the means for enforcing it. The Polish Army in Palestine was not an exception. However, being an army in exile, existing and operating in unusual circumstances, its methods of dealing with disciplinary problems had certain unusual features.

Normally an army has several options available for dealing with its criminal elements: execution (obviously for extreme cases), dishonorable discharge, and long and short term imprisonment. For Anders' Army each of these options presented difficulties. For one, the British did not permit the army to execute soldiers in areas under their jurisdiction. Even so there were rumors that as many as seven Polish soldiers and officers were executed while the army was in Palestine, but no evidence of executions exists. It is difficult to believe that such executions could have been kept secret from the British authorities. When officers who had been in a position to know were interviewed, they categorically denied any executions took place.

Long term imprisonment was also problematic due to the circumstances in which the Second Polish Corps found itself. Even if necessary facilities had existed this form of punishment would create difficulties: it would mean a loss of manpower for administrators and guards, costs, etc. The major difficulty from the point of view of the Polish Army was that it was only passing through the Middle East and it was not clear whether it would ever return. It was possible to incarcerate Polish soldiers in British facilities but no army and no government wants it soldiers and citizens to fall under foreign jurisdiction and to serve sentences in foreign prisons.

Short term jail sentences were a viable punishment from the logistical and legal point of view but were clearly inappropriate for the more serious crimes as they could deprive the punishment of its deterrent effect, and hence lead to an increase in crime. Transporting prisoners along with the army would also be awkward. Obviously, the manpower issue was paramount and no one wanted to create an option allowing a soldier to shirk combat duty by committing a minor crime.

To deal with the problem the British suggested that the Polish Army set up a disciplinary camp at Latrun, half way between Tel-Aviv and Jerusalem. The British also helped with its organization and turned over sections of the British camp to the Poles. The camp started operating on January 1, 1944, and was used to detain Polish military personnel accused of criminal as well as "anti-Polish " offenses. In January, 1944, the camp had 156 inmates (14 officers and 142 soldiers). On March 1, 1944, 23 additional officers and soldiers were sentenced to the Latrun camp. The Soviets claimed the camp was set up to punish soldiers and officers who had criticized General Anders and who favored working hand in hand with the USSR.[60]

The British soon started questioning who was sent to the camp and for what reasons as they were concerned that soldiers were being imprisoned for Communist views or pro-Soviet sympathies. General Tokarzewski-Karaszewicz instructed the camp's commandant on how to respond to these questions, which, according to Tokarzewski-Karaszewicz, were coming mainly from British officers of Jewish origin. Tokarzewski-Karaszewicz told him to explain that only those soldiers who were accused of violating the penal code are to be sent to the camp, that accusations should be brief and vague and that gaps are to be filled in later. He directed the commander of the camp to seek the assistance of the army commander in handling difficult questions.[61] Tokarzewski-Karaszewicz's instructions confirm that Latrun was used not only for criminal but also for political prisoners. The Poles obviously suffered from Russophobia, but who could blame then after their experience in the USSR? They knew about the Villa of Happiness and that Soviet agents were operating in the Second Polish Corps.[62]

Polish authorities also considered the possibility of opening another camp for civilian criminals or of sending them to the military camp in Latrun. The Polish Consul General in Palestine was ordered to cooperate with the authorities "towards checking the evil if done by Polish citizens." He gave the British a list of Poles with a record of criminal convictions and a list of suspected criminals. The second list included persons "whose past and present conduct give cause to serious fears that they might become harmful to the community." He suggested immediate "isolation" of people from the first list (which included two people who had been sentenced to life imprisonment by Polish civilian courts before the war) in the Latrun camp and police surveillance for people on the second list. The Consul estimated that among the Polish refugees in Palestine there were more than 100 criminals. Anders had agreed to accept these civilian criminals at Latrun camp, provided they were brought there by British police and if the Polish Ministry of Work and Social Welfare covered the costs of internment. However, the London Government decided that only the President had the authority to intern Polish civilians and that internment could be done only through a Presidential decree. The whole thing came to naught because the British authorities refused to imprison civilians in a military disciplinary camp. Preventive confinement is after all, an anathema for the Anglo-Saxon concept of criminal justice.[63]

This brings us to dishonorable discharge and expulsion from the army as the last option for punishing insubordinate or criminal soldiers. This was an option exercised extensively by Anders, because it was the least undesirable. Expulsion meant turning criminals loose in Palestine which, from the point of view of Anders' objectives, was a viable alternative.

According to Antoni Patak, a representative of the Ministry of Work and Social Welfare, at least 25 soldiers who had been expelled from the army in Iran were later sent to Jerusalem. He reported that 300 more soldiers were awaiting discharge on the grounds of psychological disorders or criminality. Some of the discharged soldiers were not turned over to civilian authorities but were detained in the Latrun camp.[64]

## Between the British and the Jewish National Movement in Palestine

From the beginning of their arrival in Palestine the Poles found themselves in an unenviable situation between British colonial authorities and the Jewish population. The British authorities in Palestine were opposed to bringing the Polish Army into the country because they expected it would have a significant number of Jews in its ranks. In January, 1942, more than two months before the first evacuation, the High Commissioner of Palestine, Harold MacMichael voiced his concern that the Polish Army might bring a large number of Jewish soldiers to Palestine. He was particularly opposed to formation of a Jewish Unit in the Polish Army, because it "could unite with other scattered Jewish units in the Allied Armies to form the nucleus of a Jewish Army," and such an army would present a threat to the security of Palestine. He was, however, overruled by the British War Office which regarded Palestine as the best area, from the military point of view, for stationing the Polish Corps. The Foreign Office could not but defer to the War Office on this question but it emphasized that "It is in particular desirable that such units should contain as low a proportion as possible of Polish nationals of Jewish race, and that in no circumstances should Polish Jews be formed into separate military units within the Polish forces in the Middle East."[65]

The apprehension of the British authorities in Palestine was caused by a report that Polish forces in Russia included at least one purely Jewish battalion and other units where the proportion of Jews was as high as 30%."[66] The Colonial Office tried to remove these apprehensions by stating that, in fact, the percentage of Jews in the Polish units brought to Palestine would be small."[67]

Of course Polish leadership was appraised of British concerns. Sir Cecil Dormer, British Ambassador to the Polish Government, was directed to tell them that "so far as is possible to avoid posting many Polish troops of the Jewish race to Palestine" and that Polish Government support was needed "in avoiding any undesirable repercussions from the choice of Palestine as a concentration point for Polish military units."[68] The British knew that General Sikorski had Zionist contacts and had spoken about finding more room in Palestine for Polish Jews after the war. MacMichael feared the Polish Government would directly or indirectly encourage "Zionist aspirations in Palestine." MacMichael's fears were confirmed when he learnt that after a meeting held on January 25, 1942, Polish and Jewish representatives announced during a press conference that the Polish Government favored a Jewish Army and a Jewish State in Palestine.[69] Dormer was instructed to warn Sikorski against embarking on any policy regarding Zionism which might be embarrassing to the British Government.[70]

Needless to say, the Poles were dependent on the British, and therefore British opinion had to color their judgment on Jewish issues. The Polish Government agreed to take all precautions necessary to prevent any political action by Polish Jews which would be against British policy and instructed the Polish civil and military personnel in Palestine to act accordingly.[71] On March 31, 1942, Frank Savery reported that Frankowski, temporarily in charge of the Polish Ministry of Foreign Affairs, had assured him that the Poles would not be bringing a large number of Polish-Jewish soldiers to Palestine and would not create Jewish units in the Polish Army.[72] Dormer reported that he had received written assurances from the Polish Acting Minister of Foreign Affairs that "the Polish Government (will) prevent any political action on the part of Polish Jews which might appear to be inconsistent with the interests and views of His Majesties Government."[73] The British officials seemed satisfied with these Polish assurances. Frank Roberts minuted, "Satisfactory, Sir C. Dormer might be instructed to thank the Polish Government for this assurance and the action they are taking."[74]

The Poles were to refrain, first of all, from forming Jewish units within the army. The British felt very strongly on this issue as is demonstrated by the Minister of State for

Colonies' statement that "unless the Poles agree not to form a Jewish Legion in Palestine, the Polish troops will have to be accommodated elsewhere." On March 16, 1942, a communication from 10 Downing Street directed the Foreign Office to advise the Polish Government in London that if there were Jewish Units in the Polish Army, the army would not be "accommodated" in Palestine.[75]

The British authorities did not see the incongruity between its efforts to discourage Polish anti-Semitism and its pressure to reduce cooperation between Jews and Poles. The tone of the Colonial Office and other British official documents clearly reflect the attitude that they expected the Polish Government to do as it was told. This begs the question of whether the Polish Government in London was ever a sovereign government. In the end the British got what they wanted--only a limited number of Jews came to Palestine and no Jewish units were formed in the Second Polish Corps.

When, in January of 1944, the Irgun started attacking the British, the main force of the Second Corps had already moved to Egypt, although its headquarters, schools, hospitals, etc, remained in Palestine. Some Polish cadets in Palestine believe the Irgun went out of its way to avoid injuring Poles during its raids on the British. For example, they claim that at one Polish school an anonymous telephone call advised that planned excursion to a beach on a day when the Irgun would attack British installations there be canceled.[76] Apparently, the Polish Army listed certain areas "out of bounds" at the advice of the Irgun, which gave advance warning to the Poles of its planned anti-British activities. Poles were constantly advised to make sure that on their vehicles and clothes there was something identifying them as Poles since their shoulder patches saying "Poland" were the sole distinguishing feature of their British uniforms.[77]

Army officers, however, dispute the testimony regarding it as unlikely that the Irgun would give advance warning of their future actions, but these officers were already on their way to Italy when the Irgun started its underground activities against the British.[78]

The Poles were neutral in the British-Jewish conflict but showed mild pro-Jewish sympathies in the Arab-Jewish conflict. A majority of non-Jewish soldiers were supportive of the idea of a Jewish Homeland in Palestine, seeing it as analogous to their own aspirations for a national Polish state. Generally, they had no sympathy for Arabs in Palestine tending to favor the Jewish side. However, the Poles were sympathetic to the food shortages suffered by the Arabs as they could identify with that because of their experiences in the Soviet Union. The Poles found it very upsetting to see the British destroy food rather than give it to needy Arabs.[79]

## Desertions

One of the most important consequences of coming to Palestine was the wave of desertions which affected the Second Polish Corps. Much of what has been written about the soldiers who deserted from the Corps is incorrect. Some accounts are intentionally misleading for political reasons while others are inaccurate because the people involved do not want to open old wounds. "Deserter" is an ugly word and even after fifty years some "deserters" from the Polish Army refused to allow their names to be used. In describing what they had done they prefer to employ euphemisms like "escape" or "departure" instead of "desertion." It is difficult to call soldiers who changed armies deserters, although there is no denying that excepting the very few who were officially discharged from the Corps, the majority of Jews who "escaped" were technically deserters. In discussing motives for desertion a distinction should be made between those who left military service altogether and those who joined another army and merely changed uniforms.

Most deserters in Palestine were Jews and almost all found refuge in a kibbutz or a settlement town. At first, Palestinian Jews were hesitant to hide deserters as they were afraid of possible consequences, but soon the kibbutzim became the main sanctuary for deserters from the Polish Army. The number of Polish Jews who "deserted" from the Second Polish Corps in Palestine between the end of 1942 and the end of 1943 was substantial.

The number of Jews in the Second Polish Corps cannot be known precisely because some Jews hid their identity. Also, an unknown number of soldiers did not consider themselves Jews but were considered Jews by others. Various sources give different figures for both the number of Jews there were in the Anders' Army at the time of its arrival in Palestine and for how many deserted. According to Alexander Zvielli, 4,200 Jews came to Palestine in the ranks of Anders' Army and 3,000 deserted. Out of that number 2,000 enlisted in the British Army, including the Jewish Brigade, while the remainder joined the Hagannah, the Irgun, or the settlement police.[80] The same figures are accepted by Polonsky and Davies.[81] Terlecki estimates that only 2,450 out of 4,226 (i.e. 58%) who came to Palestine with Anders abandoned its ranks.[82] Of all the estimates his is the lowest. A semi-official history of the Polish Armed Forces in the Second World War states that about 600 Jews deserted between August of 1942, when the desertions began, and the end of 1942. It puts the number of Jewish deserters, in 1943, at "several thousand" including "a significant number of trained instructors" and estimates that about 1,300 Jews remained in the army and a few deserters returned.[83] In January of 1944, the British High Commissioner in Palestine, MacMichael reported that 2,580 Jews deserted from the Polish Army and complained that the Polish command had not provided any statistics on desertions. When approached about this, Anders told him that 2,580 was about right and to expect several hundred more desertions as they were not greatly deplored from the military point of view by the Polish command.[84] According to a recently declassified U.S. intelligence report, in September of 1942, the Polish Army had 4,300 Jewish soldiers, of whom only 1,328 remained by March 1, 1944.[85] In April of 1944, Frank Savery of the British Foreign Office reported that in early 1943 Anders' Army included 146 Jewish officers and 3,255 Jewish soldiers and that by April 24, 1944, only 1,000 remained. According to these figures the Jewish desertion rate was 71%.[86] The few Jewish deserters who returned to the Polish Army[87] were given light punishment, reduced in rank, and returned to duty.

The kibbutzim presented an ideal place for Jewish deserters to hide and work. The kibbutzim needed work and manpower for protection against marauding Arabs, so they were especially pleased to attract Jews with military training.[88] There were a few clashes between kibbutzniks and British Police, but very few resulted in arrests. The police had little success in determining which kibbutzniks had been there for years and which were recent Polish Army deserters, so without the cooperation of the Polish Army, ferreting out deserters was virtually impossible.

The idea of a commanding general permitting large scale desertions is alien to all military tradition yet General Anders did little to discourage Jewish soldiers serving in his Corps from deserting. When the desertions began, a few deserters were arrested by Polish military police as there are records of a few courts-martial for Jewish deserters when the Second Polish Corps first arrived in the Middle East. There is, however, no indication that these courts-martial ever took place and it seems likely that some of the court-martial documents were a sham, placed in the files to appease the British. For example, there is a record of Hiam Novik, a Jewish soldier sentenced by court-martial, for desertion, to six years imprisonment, yet there is no sign that he ever served his sentence.[89]

Romanowski recalls that a handful of Jewish deserters were arrested in Iraq but when they were brought before Anders he told the Military Police to release them and not to arrest deserting Jews. In Iraq an oral order was issued that Jewish deserters were not to be arrested, the order had to be oral so as not to provoke the British. Anders told some officers confidentially that "Jews are fighting for their freedom and I won't stand in their way, as they have a fight before them."[90] Anders of course could not make such statements publicly because of Polish dependence upon the British.

Some of Anders' critics cannot accept that he might have been motivated by humanitarian reasons for turning a blind eye to Jewish desertions, so they offer several alternative explanations. First, they argue, that, as a practical matter Anders had no alternative but to let the Jews escape. Yaccov Meridor, a former commander of Irgun Zvei Leumi, expressed respect for Anders, but said the general was wise not to chase after deserters because he wouldn't have caught very many.[91] Rabbi Rosengarten claimed that Anders simply could not pursue deserters because most left the ranks just as the Polish Army was departing Palestine for Italy. Furthermore, the Polish Government wanted to gain American support against the Soviets so he was therefore loathe to arrest and possibly kill Jewish soldiers who would resist, which would further increase the perception that Poles are inherently anti-Semitic.[92] Finally, to conduct an extensive search for deserters would have required a commitment of many soldiers. Once caught, the deserters would have to be fed, tried and guarded. In other words, because of the magnitude of the problem, the whole army would have to be engaged in chasing deserters instead of training for combat, so arresting deserters would reduce, rather than increase, the number of soldiers available for battle.

Rabbi Rosengarten expressed the opinion that General Kopanski was responsible for persuading Anders to allow Jews to desert, and that at first Anders did not agree, but went along with Kopanski's recommendation.[93] His opinion however, is contradicted by others, especially by Raczynski. who said he remembered that it was Anders' decision to let Jewish soldiers desert in Palestine and Sikorski concurred.[94]

The British were constantly challenging Anders about not arresting Jewish deserters and not cooperating with British policy. For example, the Polish Army could never find any photographs of the Jewish deserters, which infuriated the British, who repeatedly asked for them.[95] MacMichael made it clear that General Anders did not cooperate in searching for deserters. When pressed, Anders insisted that it must be done by Poles alone and he told MacMichael that "if present conditions (remain) unchanged I would feel obliged to give up all further search for deserters in general." The British offered the assistance of their Military Police for conducting searches in the kibbutzim which Anders turned down, saying he had his own military police. He commented that if the British intention was to arrest all Jews who had been trained as soldiers in the Polish Army they would need at least two Divisions.[96]

There is one report which represents Anders' position differently. The British High Commissioner MacMichael told a representative of the Jewish Agency that Anders complained about the high number of Jewish deserters and asked for British assistance in finding them in the kibbutzim.[97] It seems that MacMichael purposefully misrepresented Anders' position in order to persuade the Jewish Agency not to encourage Jews to desert. If Anders had really asked for British assistance the British would have complied and there would have been scores of "incidents."

The Polish refusal to persecute Jewish deserters made it impossible for the British to catch them since the deserters were under the jurisdiction of the Polish Army and were not violating British law except to the extent that they could have been in Palestine illegally. So when Palestine Police caught Polish deserters they had to turn them over to the Polish military authorities.[98] The British were also aware that some deserters were now in the British Army while others had joined the Palestine Police.[99]

To appreciate properly the attitude and policy towards deserters that Anders and the Polish Second Corps adopted, one has to bear in mind that they were totally dependent upon British goodwill. General Anders knew he was taking a risk every time he did something that placed him in conflict with the British. We know the British were very upset about the number of deserters and about Anders' refusal to prosecute them. Anders refused to budge on this issue in spite of British pressure. Was this due to his identification of his own aspirations for restoring his Polish homeland with Jewish aspirations to create their homeland in Palestine? None of the numerous books about the formation of the Israeli Army mentions that Israel received almost half a brigade of trained soldiers, thanks to General Anders.

Trying to reconstruct the motives of the Jews who deserted is a complicated matter. When interviewing individuals who had deserted they were reluctant to talk about it nor were they candid when they agreed to talk. There was a natural propensity for the deserters to rationalize their acts even though a few, unexpectedly, were more open about their answers. First of all it has to be stated that it is very unlikely that Jewish deserters were motivated by fear of combat. Those who entered the kibbutzim came under the general authority of the Jewish Agency and the Hagannah and if their motive was avoidance of combat they had certainly come to the wrong place, since the kibbutzniks were constantly involved in heavy fighting against both Arabs and the British and suffered severe casualties.

Since the largest numbers of desertions took place when the Polish Army first arrived in Palestine, and when it was getting ready to depart for the Italian front, an argument could be made that the motivation was indeed cowardice. Although cowardice may have been the main reason behind desertion for some soldiers, the timing cannot be taken as sufficient proof that it really was so, especially since everyone knew that a fight with the Arabs and the British was inevitable. In fact, the semi-official history of the Polish Armed Forces notes that the first large wave of desertions occurred in August of 1942, that is, at the time the British allowed Jews to form their own national defense squads. This caused many Jewish soldiers to desert from the Polish Army to help the Palestinian Jews. Prior to that time, according to the Official History, there had been few Jewish desertions.[100]

One can certainly discount cowardice as a motive for those who deserted to join the British Army. It has been estimated that about 20% of deserters joined the British Army.[101] There were several reasons why the Jews would want to switch to the British Army. Many felt that general conditions were more favorable there: pay (although later equalized) was better and more benefits were available. This was important for those who had families in the Middle East. It was also a perceived that the British Army afforded more opportunities for advancement. Finally, there was a hope that service in the British Army would guarantee British citizenship after the war or the legal right to settle in Palestine. The British made efforts to quell false rumors that were circulating about this.[102]

Deserters who joined the British Army. found that the British did not particularly want more Jewish soldiers with advanced training and front line experience. Instead they preferred to use the Jews as "pioneers" in construction or labor battalions. Ostensibly the reason for putting Jews in "pioneer" units was to avoid offending the Arabs who saw armed Jews as a potential nucleus of a Jewish Army. Some of the deserters joined the Jewish Brigade formed by the British and later fought in Italy on the left flank of the Second Polish Corps.[103] Rabbi Casper in his book about the Jewish Brigade makes no mention of Polish Jews or of the fact that some of them had deserted from the Polish Army. It seems that Casper intentionally gave the impression that the soldiers of the Brigade were all from English speaking countries. Passing over of the inconvenient fact that some of the soldiers of the Brigade had been deserters might be attributable to a universal disdain for "deserters" of any kind.[104]

Another possible explanation for Jewish desertions would be Polish anti-Semitism. The difficulty lies in the fact that it is impossible to measure the level of anti-Semitism in the Second Polish Corps. Those who claimed they deserted because of anti-Semitism have every incentive to exaggerate its intensity. A U.S. Army intelligence report from November of 1943 attributed the desertions of Jews from the Second Corps to their brutal treatment, but according to another, undated report, "the allegations of anti-Semitism in the Polish Army, which are being spread, are grossly exaggerated, to say the least, and are most unfair to the Polish soldier."[105] According to one Polish soldier there was very little friction between Polish and Jewish soldiers. He said that conflicts in the tents tended to be chronic poker losers against the winners (poker was a popular pastime) rather than Poles against Jews.[106] One source of resentment towards Jews was that they frequently received short-term passes enabling them to attend the synagogues on Jewish holidays, which precluded other soldiers from getting their fair share of passes.[107]

Jews who didn't desert gave sharply differing opinions about anti-Semitism in the Corps. Some felt that it existed but was no worse than what they had experienced in prewar Poland and was mostly limited to name calling. Other Jews, for whom the army was the first prolonged experience of close interaction with non-Jews, were less able to cope with anti-Semitic slurs. Although Jews who spoke only Yiddish were not "represented" in the Polish Army there were secular as well as religious Jews who had very little experience in dealing with Poles before the war.

The official policy of the Polish Government condemned and forbade demonstrations of anti-Semitism in the armed forces. On August 5, 1940, Sikorski issued an order in which he stated that "my principle is that a Polish soldier now fighting for the common cause has thus given sufficient evidence that he is a Pole irrespective of his origin and religion. I strictly forbid the showing to soldiers of Jewish faith any unfriendliness, through contemptuous remarks humiliating to human dignity" and promised, "all such offenses will be severely punished."[108] This didn't end anti-Semitism or prevent some officers and NCOs from engaging in anti-Semitic behavior, but the general consensus of those interviewees who didn't desert was that anti-Semitism might have been a contributing factor for some but it was not the major reason for desertion. This is confirmed by the equal rate of desertions among Jews who served in the Carpathian Brigade, where anti-Semitism was minimal.

The best answer to why the desertions occurred in Palestine is that the majority of deserters felt their future was in Palestine. They felt they had nothing to go back to in Poland, since their families had perished and nobody was waiting for their return. In other words, they did not desert because they hated Poland or the Poles. Like many other Polish citizens, Jewish and gentile, they left because they felt their future to be elsewhere. A certain group pressure undoubtedly also played a role. As one soldier said: "everyone expected me to desert, the soldiers in my tent, the officer in charge, my friends at the kibbutz, so I deserted."[109]

At least 800 and probably as many as 1,000 Jewish soldiers continued to serve in the Second Polish Corps until the end of the Second World War.[110] Most former soldiers when asked why they did not desert, simply said that they were not deserters. For them the desire to avoid the stigma of deserting was the overriding consideration. They were embarrassed by the large number of Jews who had deserted and were their most severe critics. For some of these it was a matter of soldierly pride, wanting to prove (to the Poles or to themselves) that Jews could be good soldiers. Not surprisingly this group won more than their fair share of medals in Italy. Some said that they never considered deserting because they were Polish citizens as well as Jews or that they felt more Polish than Jewish. This explanation was given mostly from secular Jews who had integrated into the Polish way of life while retaining their Jewish identity. One said that his father and grandfather had been officers in the Polish Army and he was not going to disgrace their names by deserting. Another did not want to embarrass his uncle and brother-in-law who were officers in the Second Polish Corps and had implored him not to desert. At the same time he was friendly with a Polish Major who suggested he should desert because Jews would have no future in postwar Poland.[111] Most of those who remained in Polish ranks were not Zionists, had never participated in prewar Jewish youth groups, and spoke little or no Yiddish or Hebrew. Some of them wanted to return to Poland after the war and had hopes of finding some of their relatives. A handful of non-deserters indicated that their overriding consideration was to fight Germans and expected that the Polish Army would eventually be in the thickest part of the battle.

What was the most surprising about those who did not desert was that in retrospect they felt they had made a mistake by not deserting. What they meant was that they should have stayed in Palestine where Jewish soldiers were needed. They were apologetic not for serving in the Polish Army but for failing to serve in the Jewish Army.

Interestingly, the largest identifiable group of non-deserters were Jewish doctors. There was only one Jewish medical officer who "escaped" from the Second Polish Corps. Approximately 60% of medical doctors serving with the Polish Army in Italy were Jews which should not be unexpected as a similar percentage of Jews were in the medical profession in prewar Poland. The low percentage of deserters among doctors may be attributed to their officer rank which shielded them from the whims of malicious officers or NCOs with anti-Semitic prejudices. In addition, soldiers going into combat would not want to offend a doctor whom they might meet later in an operating room. The overriding consideration which kept doctors from deserting was their professionalism: they felt the Polish Army needed them and even if they were not sure whether they would want to return to Poland after the war they still felt an obligation to it as doctors, if not as Polish citizens.

The attitude of the Polish Corps' officers towards Jewish desertions reflected that of their commander, General Anders. A number of them felt that if Jews regarded Palestine instead of Poland as their homeland then it was reasonable to expect them to stay there. Even those like Lieutenant Dowgiallo, who criticized the Jews for trying to force their way into the Polish Army in the USSR, said that the Jews had abandoned the ranks for ideological reasons and not cowardice.[112] Some Polish officers were even proud that "their Jews" (i.e. the Polish Jews) played such an important part in creating a Jewish homeland in Palestine and in the Six Day War. An officer, reminiscing about his Jewish friend, the Irgun leader, Marek Kahan, recognized that Kahan's Jewish patriotism was fully compatible with his loyalty to the Polish Republic.[113] According to other testimony, however, reaction to Jewish desertions among Polish soldiers was mixed--some felt that Jews found their homeland, others that the Jews didn't want to fight.[114]

From descriptions of circumstances surrounding the Jewish desertions it is clear there was little or no hostility among the Polish soldiers, who usually knew in advance about a Jewish colleagues intention to desert. In camp conditions, with people living together in tents with no privacy, it was impossible to keep any secrets form ones tent mates. The first and obvious indication of intent to desert was by the items a soldier packed for his one-day leave. Nobody going on a one day leave would take a toothbrush. Deserting soldiers would quite openly say good-bye to their tent mates. In some cases farewell parties were thrown for departing Jews.[115]

Although there was some criticism of the desertions by Poles the majority of critical comments came from Jews who hadn't deserted. The latter were upset that the departing Jews had added to the perception that Jews were not good soldiers. A few Poles were also critical. One women felt that the deserters disgraced themselves, the Polish nation and their fellow Jews.[116] In the main, however, Poles were very understanding and undoubtedly some bigots were glad to see the Jews go.

The few Poles who were unsympathetic to deserters demonstrated a highly emotional and extreme patriotism and were highly sensitive to any comments that could be even remotely construed as critical towards Poland. Curiously, they could not excuse Jewish desertions, even though their idolized Commander General Anders, had done so. This almost fanatical group was in the minority. Their reaction was not so much attributable to anti-Semitism as to extreme patriotism. It is interesting that in contrast to the majority of interviewees, those who were unsympathetic to Jewish desertions tended also to adopt a pro-Arab position in the Israeli-Arab conflict.

Jewish desertions gave raise to another issue which made the British unhappy with the Polish Army and its command, namely the flow of weapons from the Polish Army to Jewish paramilitary groups. In 1942, the British were adamant about stopping the influx of weapons to the kibbutzim, even though the latter were constantly under the threat of Arab attacks. The British were unconcerned about the safety of the kibbutzniks, their concern was that at some future date the weapons would be turned against them. At first the Polish Army cooperated with the British Army in searching for weapons in the kibbutzim. In November, 1943, the British Police, accompanied by hundreds of Indian soldiers, conducted a major search of the Jewish settlement of Ramat Hakowesz. Ostensibly they were looking for Polish Army deserters and to make that claim credible a Polish officer and two Polish soldiers accompanied them. A Jewish newspaper reported that these Polish soldiers "expressed their regret for being dragged into this search, which disgusted them."[117] The Poles understood that "arms (were) needed by Jews for their very existence." The reports of this incident in the Jewish press were very complimentary towards the Poles. Clearly the Polish Army wanted no part in these searches.[118] Anders refused to cooperate with the British search for weapons as he had earlier refused to cooperate in the search for deserters. His position was that he did not want to get Poles involved in what he called "local politics."[119]

Former soldiers gave differing answers to the question of whether or not soldiers sold or gave away weapons to Palestinian Jews or Arabs. Some said that this never happened, other said it was a common occurrence. However, it is unlikely that weapons were taken by deserters since most of them deserted when they were on leave and those going to town on leave were not allowed to take weapons. It became clear during the interviews that Polish soldiers must have sold weapons, or, in a few instances donated them, to Jews or Arabs. Even after fifty years this was a sensitive topic and the officers interviewed were reluctant to admit that it had taken place. The disappearance of weapons became a problem for the Polish Army but it was not acknowledged or discussed openly because Anders feared that if the British got wind of this they might impose stricter controls on weapons supplied to the Polish Army. The Poles had a strong incentive to avoid reporting the theft of weapons. A few soldiers reported that their weapons had been stolen by Arabs when in fact they had sold them to Jews. According to Elly Tavin, a former Irgun intelligence officer, there were so many small arms available at a low price, that it wasn't necessary to resort to stealing, and that no effort by the Irgun or any other Jewish group to buy or steal weapons had been organized and the incidents of Polish soldiers selling or giving away their weapons was negligible. It seems that most stolen weapons had come from supply depots rather than from individual soldiers, who faced being court-martialed for losing their weapons.[120]

The Jews who had chosen to remain in Anders' Corps felt it necessary to prove themselves. At least 800 of them fought in Italy where they had a particularly good military record due to the self-selection process which took place among Jewish soldiers. Those who stayed were committed to fighting the Germans and to proving that Jews could be good soldiers, and knowing of the Holocaust, knew why they had to defeat Nazi Germany. By the end of January, 1945, 118 Jewish soldiers were decorated for honorable action, courage, and bravery: 5 were awarded the highest Polish military order of "Virtuti Militari;" 55 received the "Cross for Valor," 33 were given the Silver Cross of Merit and 25 received a Bronze Cross of Merit. In addition, numerous Jewish NCOs and officers were promoted in recognition of their action on the field of battle.[121]

Finally, to round-off the discussion of the desertions, it should be kept in mind that not all deserters were Jews. According to a report prepared by Colonel Mokrzycki, among the soldiers who deserted between 1940 and November 1, 1943, from the Polish Armed Forces in the Middle East, there were 628 non-Jews (523 Roman-Catholics, 54 Greek Catholics, 50 Orthodox and 1 Protestant) as well as 2091 Jews. However, from January until November,1943, i.e. during the time the bulk of the army was in Palestine there were 124 non-Jewish and 1448 Jewish deserters.[122] Moreover, 40% of the non-Jewish deserters came back. The number of committed non-Jewish deserters was closer to 400.[123]

Among them three groups could be distinguished. First, there were the common criminals a group significantly larger than one might expect. Second, were "normal" deserters who can be found in any army, especially when it is about to enter combat. The third group were soldiers who didn't want to leave their families or friends. Apparently a number of Polish soldiers married Jewish women and either became Jews or at least became identified as Jews.

## Katyn and the Soviet Break of Diplomatic Relations with the Polish Government in Exile

While Anders' soldiers were training intensively to take part in the expected assault by the Western Allies on the European Continent, a gruesome discovery was announced by the Germans on April 13, 1943. They claimed to have found mass graves containing thousands of corpses of Polish officers in the Katyn forest near Smolensk.[124] Twelve days later the Soviet Union broke off diplomatic relations with Poland. This event had grave implications for the soldiers of Anders' Army. It raised a possibility that the

Soviet Union had its own plans for Poland, namely that it was preparing to install a Communist dominated government. If this happened Anders' soldiers would not be able to return to their homes even after Germany had been defeated.

By 1943 the world had become inured to mass murder. A few thousand victims in one mass grave was less than an average daily quota in each of several Nazi death camps. The irony was that it was the Germans who called the world's attention to the mass murder in Katyn Forest, and who knew more about mass murders than the Germans? With a "holier than thou" posture, the Germans pointed an accusatory finger at the Soviets. There is grim irony in the righteous indignation expressed by the Germans in appealing to world opinion and calling for the International Red Cross to investigate the massacre.

The Katyn discovery provided a solution to the riddle of the missing officers. Their inexplicable absence and the strange, evasive or absurd Soviet explanations appeared in a new light. It was only now that those strange words, uttered in the spring of 1941, before a group of Polish officers (Berling, Gorczynski, Tyszynski) in the "Villa of Happiness" by the deputy head of the NKVD, Merkulov made sense. Merkulov was talking about a possibility of organizing a Polish Red Army unit and when Berling said that officers from the camps of Kozelsk, Starobelsk and Ostashkov could be used, Merkulov reportedly said: "No, not them. With them we committed a great error."[125]

Today we know that on March 5, 1940, the Soviet Politbureau (Stalin, Beria, Voroshilov, Molotov, Mikoian, Kalinin, Kaganovich) passed a formal resolution to liquidate 14,736 Polish POWs and 10,685 Polish civilians. The actual number of those executed was slightly smaller: 14,552 military and police personnel (from the camps in Kozelsk, Starobelsk and Ostashkovo) and 7,305 civilians from prisons in Western Byelorussia and Ukraine.[126] Among the officers of the Polish Army murdered in the spring of 1940, there were as many as a thousand Jews, which means that virtually all Jewish officers interned in the USSR were killed.[127] A detailed study by Simon Schochet identified at least 262 Jews among the officers who were killed. Katyn was thus an atrocity perpetrated on both Poles and Jews, who died in a common cause.[128]

The discovery of the Katyn graves caused the most serious crisis in Soviet-Polish relations. The Soviets no longer had any need for the Polish Government in London. With the Soviet Army victorious at every front Stalin did not need the Poles as allies. He was much more interested in retaining the portion of Poland that the Soviet Union had acquired in the Ribbentropp - Molotov Pact and in subjugating the rest, than in trying to achieve a good neighborly relation with a Poland that was headed by an independent government. It is very likely the Soviets were only waiting for a pretext to break off relations, in a way that the Polish side could be blamed for it, and Polish reaction to the Katyn affair provided them with such an opportunity.

It didn't take the Polish Government in London long to conclude that the German accusation that the Soviets were to blame for the massacre was correct. All circumstances indicated that the massacre occurred in 1940, and therefore it was the Soviet authorities who were responsible. When Anders found that the names of corpses identified by the Germans coincided with the names on his missing officers list, he immediately sent a telegram to Sikorski demanding that the government take a public stand on the issue.[129] On April 17, the Polish Government announced that it had asked the International Red Cross to investigate the German claim.[130]

The Soviets treated the Polish reaction as an affront to their dignity and honor. On April 21, 1943, Stalin warned Roosevelt and Churchill that he was breaking relations with Poland because, "the Sikorski Government is striking a tremendous blow at the Soviet Union to help Hitler tyranny."[131] On April 25, the Soviets terminated diplomatic relations with Poland. In their note they accused the Polish Government of allying itself with Nazi Germany in order to extract from the Soviet Union concessions on the border issue.[132]

The British were not prepared to risk their alliance with the Soviet Union for the sake of the Poles. As long as the war with Germany lasted cooperation with the Soviets was the paramount consideration for Churchill. Now he was asking the Poles to do what he had done, namely to place the needs of an alliance with the Soviets over his own aversion to Communism in general and Stalin in particular. He felt deep sympathy for the Poles over their loss but severely chastised them for bringing the International Red Cross into the matter, regardless of whoever was responsible for the crime. As he said to Sikorski "if they are dead nothing you can do will bring them back."[133] He asked the impossible of the Poles. Added to the injury of being victimized by the Soviets they were supposed to bear the insult by pretending that nothing had happened. Eden, at Churchill's instruction, told the Polish Government in London that if they would publicly blame the Germans for Katyn, Stalin would not break off diplomatic relations. Sikorski, known to be the Polish leader most likely to make concessions to the Soviets in order to help the Grand Alliance against the Nazis, refused to comply with Churchill's demands. He agreed to withdraw the request to the International Red Cross for an independent inquiry but refused to announce publicly that it was the Germans and not the Soviets who had committed the murders.[134]

Churchill knew the truth but was willing to sacrifice almost anything and anyone to defeat the Nazis. To him the events of 1940 were old business and he wasn't going to destroy the Grand Alliance over this incident.[135] The British Government's position was that both the Poles and the Soviets had made mistakes. The Poles' mistake was to call in the International Red Cross and it was the Soviets' mistake to terminate diplomatic relations.[136] With the benefit of 50 years of hindsight, Churchill was right. There was no sense for the Poles to complain about the Soviets when they didn't have the military strength to do anything more than complain. One might wonder however what Churchill's stance would have been had the Soviets murdered British officers.

Wladyslaw T. Bartoszewski, in the forward to Road to Katyn sees a connection between Katyn and the creation of Auschwitz, both occurring before the Germans invaded Russia. He writes that, "it appears that the murders of Oswiecim (Polish name for Auschwitz) and Katyn were conceived at the same time and in collusion."[137] This interesting comment would probably not be treated seriously if not for the excellent reputation of its author.

Both Churchill and Roosevelt tried to persuade Stalin to change his mind and restore diplomatic relations with Sikorski, but their efforts had no effect. Stalin suggested only that the three Great Powers take steps towards "the improvement of the composition of the present Polish Government from the point of view of strengthening the unified allied front against Hitler."[138]

## Sikorski's Trip to the Middle East and His Death

In April, 1942, General Boruta-Spiechowicz warned Sikorski that a group of officers in the Polish Army in the Soviet Union were agitating in favor of replacing him as the Commander-in-Chief with Anders. These officers were headed by Anders' aides-de-camp, Captain Klimkowski, the same person who told Beria that he was willing to arrest Anders.[139]

The depressing news about Katyn, followed by the breaking of diplomatic relations by the Soviets prompted rumors and fears in the Polish Army in the Middle East. The soldiers whose families had been left in the Soviet Union were increasingly worried about their fate, creating a fertile ground for a mood of opposition and hostility towards Sikorski and his government. A few officers saw the whole situation as a failure of the London Government and became hostile to Kot and Sikorski, and to a lesser extent to Anders. Bitterness also mounted against the British. A few officers even concluded that Poland should ally itself with Germany against the Soviet Union.[140]

Indeed it seems there really was a circle of officers who favored replacing Sikorski with Anders. This conclusion is based on interviews with persons who did not want to be named and who claimed to have been members of this group who said that if they were named they would deny everything. There were even rumors about plans to assassinate Sikorski. These rumors seem to have originated either with the Pilsudskites who wanted to force Sikorski to resign or with Captain Klimkowski. Anders must have been aware of the scheming officers but nothing was found to indicate he encouraged or discouraged them.[141]

The real culprit in this matter was boredom, according to Racieski.[142] The army had been stationed in the Middle East for over a year, and, apart from training the soldiers had nothing to do. Boredom was rampant and political intrigues were the result. When the British got wind of the agitation and plotting they warned Anders to restrain any "hot-headed talk."[143] Worried by a possibility of unrest in the Polish Army in the Middle East, the British urged Sikorski to visit the army to put an end to this unhealthy and dangerous situation and to assure himself that Anders was not involved in a conspiracy. The "plot" to get rid of Sikorski was idle talk according to Patrick Howarth and Zhukov, and almost everyone else, except British Intelligence.

To Sikorski these rumors must have been worrisome, especially since it was known that on some crucial political issues he did not see eye to eye with General Anders. Anders believed that Sikorski never understood the Soviets,[144] was badly informed about conditions in the Soviet Union and had made a major mistake by not going public about the extent of Polish-Soviet differences and conflicts.

In February of 1943, after the Soviets notified the Polish Government that they would no longer recognize the Polish citizenship of inhabitants of Western Byelorussia and Ukraine, Anders wrote both to Sikorski and to President Raczkiewicz suggesting that Sikorski and the the whole government should resign in protest against the Soviet action. Such a gesture, in Anders view, should have opened the eyes of the Western Allies to the Soviet danger.[145]

There was nothing to suggest that Anders himself wanted to replace Sikorski. The best proof that Anders didn't covet Sikorski's position is that after Sikorski's death he made no effort to assume control over the Polish Armed Forces. According to one of his aides-de-camp Anders never wavered in his loyalty to Sikorski.[146]

At the end of May of 1943, General Sikorski set out on an inspection tour of Polish Forces in the Middle East in order to reassert his control, to calm down the agitation and to put to rest all rumors about plots against him. The tour lasted for over a month and during this time, according to most sources, Sikorski and Anders settled their differences. According to Anders, everything was smoothed out between them, and Sikorski came round to his view of the Soviets and the differences between them were settled during a meeting which took place after the Katyn revelation. By then Sikorski knew he couldn't trust the Soviets.[147] This is confirmed by the British Foreign Office representative in Cairo who reported that "Sikorski is said to have expressed himself subsequently after the meeting in satisfactory terms about Anders." In his view Anders was "completely dominated by Sikorski's personality." He quoted Sikorski as saying "Anders was like a small boy who had done wrong and was now contrite and forgiven, but who had to watch his step in the future." Sikorski referred to the need to remove some of the officers in Anders' command but not Anders himself."[148]

The testimony of the Foreign Office representative was confirmed by General Beaumont-Nesbitt who had been told by Sikorski that he felt thoroughly satisfied with Anders and that he had been able to clear up many misunderstandings.[149] According to Anders' aide-de-camp. Lubienski, the night before his death Sikorski told him that "he and General Anders had reached an understanding" and the next morning he said, referring to his previous differences with Anders, "I am very happy, everything is well again."[150]

In spite of the evidence quoted above, the opinion which is still held by some is that the "real" purpose of Sikorski's visit to the Middle East was to relieve Anders of his command. This hypothesis is based on very flimsy evidence, namely, the absence of Anders at the departure ceremony for Sikorski, held at the Cairo airport. This supposedly proved that Sikorski had dismissed Anders. There is however another and simpler explanation for Anders failing to be at the airport. According to at least two credible witnesses, Anders had an attack of malaria, with high fever, and was confined to bed by order of General Szarecki, the Chief Medical Officer.[151] Moreover, Sikorski left Anders a farewell note in which he wrote: "I wish you a speedy recovery, general, and good work in Poland's cause."[152] On June 15 he gave Anders a copy of his book about the Polish-Soviet war of 1920 with the following dedication: "For the Army Commander, General Anders to whom I entrusted with full confidence the priceless treasure of the Polish nation, i.e. the soldiers serving under him in the Middle East."[153] This is the best proof that the two generals had settled their differences amicably. Anders discharged those officers who had been particularly active in political agitation, including Captain Klimkowski.[154]

There is, however, one report which can be construed to mean that upon departure from the Middle East, General Sikorski was planning to dismiss Anders when he returned to London. An unsigned OSS report dated July 4, 1943, claimed that"Sikorski had said there would be some changes in the high command and also in the government in London."[155] The report didn't say to whom or when the

General had made this statement. There is a remote possibility that by "high command" Sikorski meant Anders. As far as changes in government was concerned he probably meant the dismissal of Professor Kot and General Kukiel in order to appease Stalin in order to facilitate the restoration of diplomatic relations with the Soviet-Union.

We will never know what his plan were. On July 5, 1943, General Sikorski was killed in a plane crash. The cause of the crash is still one of the unsolved mysteries of the Second World War and has been the subject of at least three books. The big question has always been whether the crash was an accident or an act of sabotage.

The bare facts of the crash are the following. A Liberator bomber was to fly Sikorski and his entourage from Cairo to London with a stopover at Gibraltar. The plane crashed on take off from Gibraltar and the sole survivor was a Czech pilot, who had been selected by Sikorski. When Sikorski's aircraft crashed in 1943, attention was drawn to previous attempts on his life. In March, 1942, a bomb was found on board an airplane in which Sikorski was scheduled to fly from Canada to the United States.[156] Later that year a plane that was scheduled to take Sikorski from Scotland to London was sabotaged.[157] The fact that there were two known attempts on Sikorski's life, both involving sabotage of an airplane and that Sikorski died in an airplane crash, makes it difficult for some people to accept the coincidence.

Ambassador Raczynski argues strongly that Sikorski was murdered, although for a long time he had believed the crash was an accident. When it turned out that the British Secret Service chief at Gibraltar, Kim Philby, was a Soviet agent, he changed his mind, and decided the Soviets were responsible for Sikorski's death. Of all the Polish wartime leaders, Sikorski was the one most apt to cooperate and compromise with the Soviets on the key issue of Poland's eastern border. Therefore, argues Raczynski, "the Soviets wanted Sikorski dead because he was willing to negotiate and compromise, but the Soviets didn't want to negotiate and compromise. They wanted to deal with a Polish leader who would not compromise which would give the Soviets justification for taking over Poland and imposing their own regime."[158] Raczynski's opinion is shared by a majority of the soldiers and officers interviewed.

Conceivably, the British might have wanted to remove Sikorski because he was disturbing cooperation between the Soviets and the Western Powers, which was necessary for the expeditious defeat of Nazi Germany. Raczynski, who had numerous private meetings with Churchill during the war, rejected outright any suggestion that the British had any part in the assassination of Sikorski. In his view Churchill liked Sikorski personally and more importantly, "assassination was not Churchill's style."

Also killed in the crash was Victor Cazalet, the British liaison officer who had become Sikorski's advisor and confidant. Cazalet, a member of Parliament and a Christian Zionist, was an advocate for Poles, Jews and refugees and was very critical of Churchill.[159]

At the trial of General Anders' libel lawsuit, in 1960, ex-Polish Prime Minister Mikolajczyk announced that he held Anders responsible for Sikorski's death. Although he did not believe Anders or his supporters had caused the crash, he felt Anders was "morally liable" because the death occurred while Sikorski was returning from meeting with Anders and reviewing of the Polish troops in the Middle East. If Sikorski had not gone to see Anders, he would not have been in the crash, therefore Anders was responsible for Sikorski's death. This is flawed reasoning.

In 1947, General Gustav Paszkiewicz accused Anders of being involved in a plot which resulted in the death of Sikorski, claiming that one hour before the crash he was called into Anders' office, and Anders had asked him to join the plot. General Paszkiewicz said he told Anders that if Sikorski was murdered, the next bullet would be for him. Paszkiewicz had been a General in the First Polish Corps in

Scotland, and was the first General to elect repatriation to communist Poland after the war. His charges, which were absurd, have never been substantiated and was most likely a part of the Warsaw Government's campaign to discredit Anders.

It cannot be denied that Sikorski had enemies within the London Government and the army, and it was well known that the Polish leaders had disagreements. No evidence, however, has surfaced so far to give credibility to the charge that Polish opponents of Sikorski were responsible for the crash.

The simple answer is that the plane crashed by accident. In addition to mechanical failure, which is always a possibility, there is evidence that the plane was overloaded which may not have been known to the pilot. Although the plane was supposedly guarded the night before the morning flight, it was apparently visited by a number of visitors. No one going to the plane was challenged by a guard. The "visitors" were loading the plane with cases of whiskey and other purchases. Until proven otherwise one should assume that it was a simple accident caused by overloading the aircraft.

Irrespective of the cause of the Gibraltar tragedy, the death of Sikorski was a heavy blow to the Polish cause. Poland lost a leader who enjoyed a high standing among the Allies and who had earned their respect.

### Successors To Sikorski

At Sikorski's death three generals were under consideration as his successor, Anders, Sosnkowski and Kopanski. Although he had some strong support, mostly from the Socialists, Kopanski was considered "too junior" so the choice was narrowed down.

The British had to choose between two candidates, neither of whom were being acceptable to the Russians. The

British Ambassador to Moscow commented that he knew nothing about Sosnkowski, but he knew that Anders was persona non grata to the Russians. Cadogan wrote "the choice is between a known and avowed anti-Soviet, Sosnkowski, and Anders, who I doubt is much better." Cadogan said of Anders, "He does not impress me."

Anthony Eden recommended against Anders because he lacked "authority or stability of character" and called him "a child in politics." The Russians' wanted anyone but these two, and in the end the British viewed Sosnkowski as the lesser of two evils.

Nothing has been found which indicates that Anders was bitter about losing the competition. It was only when the war neared its end that he showed any interest in being a desk general. It was fortuitous that Anders made no effort to campaign for the job as that could have led to suspicions about Sikorski's death.

After Sosnkowski's selection, consideration was given to naming Anders as Deputy Commander-in-Chief. The British were consulted which put them in an awkward position. If they approved the appointment it would strengthen Anders for the future, but they could not disapprove because of his splendid war record, so the British did not reply.

General Sosnkowski was Commander-in-Chief for one year and was dismissed after he issued an order which was critical of the Western Allies and the Russians. The Polish Government found themselves again selecting a Commander-in-Chief. Macmillan predicted "I have a feeling that Anders will take his place." Who else was there? He under-estimated the determination of those who opposed Anders' appointment.

It had been rumored that the President of the exile government was going to name Kopanski, but General Wilson advised the President that Kopanski was unacceptable to the officers and men of the Second Polish Corps. Soon thereafter the President appointed General Bor-Komorowski Commander-in-Chief. But there was a problem, the general was a prisoner of war and was not expected to be released until the end of the war.

Churchill told General Wilson that he didn't want the Poles to appoint anyone as Commander-in-Chief and that the appointment of Anders would end any chance of a Polish-Russian Agreement. The Poles found themselves in the position where the Russians indirectly were choosing the Commander-in-Chief of Polish Forces. The Polish President followed Churchills advice (or was it an order?) and assigned the functions of the position to a committee consisting of the President, the Chief of Staff and generals Kopansk and Kukiel. This Committee functioned until Anders was named Acting Commander-in-Chief in February, 1945. When General Bor was liberated, Anders, in due course and without any visible resentment, resigned in favor of General Bor.

Footnotes

1. A. Hamzavi, Persia and the Powers, an account of diplomatic relations, 1941-1946 (London, New York: Hutchinson & Co., 1946), p. 14. Also see A. Dallin, Soviet Russia's Foreign Policy 1939-42 (New Haven, 1942), p. 407; R. Stewart, Sunrise at Abadan: The British and Soviet Invasion of Iran, 1941 (New York: Praeger, 1988). Hitler associated "Iran" with "Aryan" and this incredibly was the basis of the good relation between Germany and Iran, according to a secret OSS report. NA 20655.It was September 9, 1943, before Iran declared war on Germany.
2. NA, 20655.
3. NA, 19696 and XL 2425.
4. OSS Report (September 10, 1942), NA, Poland, 745022.
5. An interview of Robin Hankey by Keith Sword (1952); NA 19696; FO 371/36691 and W8960.
6. FO 371/36691/180351.
7. NA, Poland, 5935; 6305.
8. New York Times (March 17, 1944); FO 371/39397/C4316.
9. HI, Anders Coll., box 75a, doc #1223; GSHI, KGA 24/13.
10. JTA (June 5, 1942) and (June 17, 1942).
11. AJDC, file 712.
12. AJDC, files 712 and 713.
13. NA, 20655T.
14. P. Zaron, Armia Andersa (Torun, 1996), p. 175; NA, Poland 6905.
15. FO 371/47758/N12610; FO 371/36691; NA 75152.
16. NA Poland, 6905(M.E.) and IG 8100.
17. FO 371/36691, doc. W12805.
18. FO 371/36691, doc. W12844
19. NA 6905, M.E. Poland.
20. GSHI, PRM 345/5; NA 6906 Poland.
21. W. Anders, An Army in Exile. 145-146.The term "Polish Forces in the West" included the Second Polish Corps, but it also included other forces, e.g. the Polish airmen, Navy and the First Armoured Division.
22. HI, PSZ box 3, folders 15, 16; FO 371/39468; Zaron, Armia Andersa, p. 174, 176-177. An "Army" consists of at least two Corps and a "Corps" consists of two divisions. Anders' Army was a Corps and did not qualify as an "Army."
23. Zaron, Armia Andersa, p. 177, 184.

24. FO 371/31089/C11430 and 371/36692/W13336.
25. NA, IG 6905.
26. FO 371/31099/180351 and 371/31099/135871.
27. Zaron, Armia Andersa, p. 227.
28. Polskie Sily Zbrojne w II wojnie swiatowej (London, 1975), v. II, pt. 2, p. 309.
29. An interview with Sas-Skowronski.
30. An interview with Sas-Skowronski.
31. HI, MSZ, box 0613, folder 4.
32. K. Zamorski, Telling the truth in Secret (London: Poets and Painters Press, 1994).
33. An interview with Buchta.
34. A. Bryk, "The Holocaust--Jews and Gentiles in memory of the Jews of Pacanow," Polin, v. II (1987), p. 379.
35. NA 121329.
36. Jewish Chronicle (London) (April 15, 1944).
37. An interview with Goldberg.
38. JTA Bulletin (February 14, 1944).
39. An interview with Sas-Skowronski.
40. An interview with Cynberg.
41. HI, MSZ, box 0611, folder 17.
42. FO 371/31099/C8384.
43. FO 371/31099.
44. An interview with Julian Bussgang.
45. See, Terror out of Zion, Walter Laqueur, p.28.
46. Interview with Merek Kahan.
47. NA 10055.
48. NA87216.
49. NA 92110.
50. Ibid.
51. NA11065.
52. For additional material on this subject see the following: NA JICAME #8873-44; NA 102623; NA rgg.L53363; NA XL15944; NA RGL48292; HI 113/0/11; HI 113/0/20.
53. NA XL 20468.
54. NA 47626.
55. NA 6300 Poland.
56. Nowy Swiat (May 15, 1944).
57. HI, MSZ, box 0568, folder 23.
58. FO 371/4169.

59. GSHI, Kol. 138/213.
60. HI, MSZ Box 153 folder 1 and PSZ, Box 2.
61. GSHI, Kol. 138/213 and 138/245.
62. GSHI, Kol. 138/246.
63. HI, PSZ Coll., Box 2, folder 11 and MSZ Coll., box 153.
64. HI, MSZ Coll., box 153, folder "Elementy przestepcze: Palestyna i Afryka."
65. FO 371/31099, p. 29 and 371/31099/C1274 and 371/31099/135871.
66. FO 371/31099/C2798.
67. FO 371/31099/C2079.
68. FO 371/31099, p. 29; Jews in Eastern Poland and the USSR, 1939-46, N. Davies, A. Polonsky (eds.) (Houndmills, Basingstoke, Hampshire: Macmillan, 1991), p. 46.
69. FO 371/1274/55.
70. HI, MSZ box 0611, Folder 17.
71. FO 371/31099/C4176.
72. FO 371/31099/C3538.
73. FO 371/31099/C4176.
74. FO 371/31099/180351.
75. GSHI, A.XII, 3/40A, 39/74.
76. Interview with Z.K. Jagodzinski. Ely Tavin and Y. Meridor.were questioned on this point and both deny that the Irgun gave warnings of this nature. It's possible that an individual Irgun member made these calls or that there was a misunderstanding.
77. An interview with Szkoda.
78. Interview with Sas-Skowronski and Romanowski.
79. An interview with Hampel.
80. Jerusalem Post (January 6, 1991).
81. Jews in Eastern Poland and the USSR, 1939-46, p. 47.
82. R. Terlecki, "The Jewish Issue in the Polish Army in the USSR and the Near East, 1941-1944" in Jews in Eastern Poland and the USSR, 1939-46, p. 166-167.
83. Polskie Sily Zbrojne w II wojnie swiatowej (London, 1975), v. II, pt. 2, p. 320, 332.
84. C0 733/466/8 and 761/4743.
85. "Facts Concerning the Desertion of Jewish Soldiers from the Polish Army in the Middle East," NA 6320 Poland.
86. FO 371/39484.
87. Polskie Sily Zbrojne w II wojnie swiatowej, p. 332.

88. NA, OSS 53256.
89. HI, Anders Coll., Box 70.
90. An interview with Romanowski.
91. An interview with Yaccov Merridor.
92. An interview with Rabbi Rosengarten.
93. An interview with Rabbi Rosengarten.
94. An interview with Raczynski.
95. MacMichael to the Secretary of State for Colonies (November 27, 1943), CO 733/445/11.
96. HI, MSZ Coll., box no. 0613 and Anders Coll., box 71.
97. CO 733/445/11.
98. CO 733/466/8.
99. According to A. Zvielli estimated that 20% of the deserters joined the British Army (an interview with A. Zvielli).
100. Polskie Sily Zbrojne w II wojnie swiatowej, II, pt. 2, p. 309.
101. An interview with Alexander Zvielli. He has been a reporter for the Jerusalem Post for decades and is considered an authority on the subject. He himself joined the British Army after abandoning the ranks of Anders' Corps.
102. FO 371/39487A/C10504.
103. An interview with Rabbi Rosengarten.
104. B. Casper, With the Jewish Brigade (London, 1947).
105. NA OSS 50051.
106. An interview with Szachnowski.
107. An interview with Zbigniew Racienski.
108. Cit. Poland in the British Parliament 1939-1945, I (ed.) W. Jedrzejewicz (New York, 1946), p. 442.
109. Interviewee asked that his name not be used.
110. Terlecki, "The Jewish Issue in the Polish Army in the USSR and the Near East, 1941-1944," p. 168.
111. An interview with Arie Weinberg.
112. Interview with Frank Rozycki, also HI, Anders Coll., box 75A, doc. #1223.
113. Zbigniew Racieski in Dziennik Polski, (London) (May 7, 1985).
114. Interviews with Scigala and Julian Piech.
115. An interview with Szachnowski.
116. An interview with Helena Gladkowska.
117. CO 733/445/11.
118. HI, Anders coll., box 71, docs. No 165 "W sprawie rewizji w Ramat Hakowesz" and no. 166 "W sprawie rewizji Po Kibucach."

119. HI, Anders Coll., box 71, doc. 163; HI, MSZ, box 613.
120. Interviews with Walter Drzewieniecki, Tavin and Rand, Lubienski and Racieski.
121 Zaron, Armia Andersa, p. 191; a copy of a letter by a Jewish Chaplain Rabbi Steinberg (January 4, 1945) to a Polish-Jewish organization
122. GSHI, Kol. 138/219, p. 1, 10.
123. Ibid., p. 9.
124. Documents on Polish-Soviet Relations, 1939-1945, I (London, 1961), p. 523-524.
125. J. Czapski, Wspomnienia Starobielskie (n.p., 1945), p. 61.
126. Katy : Dokumenty ludobójstwa. Dokumenty i materia y archiwalne przekazane Polsce 14 pa dziernika 1992 r. (Warsaw, 1992), p. 42, also p. 34, 36, 38, 40.
127. S.W. Slowes, The Road to Katyn: a Soldier's Story (Oxford, U.K.; Cambridge, Mass.: Blackwell Publishers, 1992), p. XIV, 3. Its probable that 1,000 is excessive. The report that there were Jews among the victims had a good effect on Polish-Jewish relations. Polish veterans groups in London hold an annual memorial service for the fallen at Katyn. When it was documented that Jewish officers were among the murdered the association of Jewish veterans of the Polish Army was invited, for the first time, to participate in the annual memorial service.
128. An Attempt to Identify the Polish-Jewish Officers Who Were Prisoners in Katyn (New York, 1989).
129. Anders, An Army in Exile, p. 140; HI, Anders Coll. 54/7 and 54/8.
130. Documents on Polish-Soviet Relations, 1939-1945, I, p. 527-528.
131. Perepiska Predsedatelia Soveta Ministrov SSSR s Prezidentami SShA i Premer Ministrami Velikobritanii vo Vremia Velikoi Otechestvennoi Voiny 1941-1945 gg. (Moscow, 1957), I, p. 120, II, p. 60. Thr Polish Ambassador, Romer was telephoned at 2:00AM and asked to come to the Kremlin. Upon arrival he was handed a note indicating that the Soviet Union broke diplomatic relations. He refused the note saying it was too violent. A second note was delivered at 5:00AM and was rejected. Romer then advised his government. NA X41876

132. Dokumenty i materialy po istorii sovetsko-pol'skikh otnoshenii, (eds.) I.A. Khrenov, N. Gasiorowska-Grabowska (Moscow, 1973), v. VII, p. 400-401.
133. W. Churchill, The Hinge of Fate (Cambridge, MA, 1950), p. 759.
134. Documents on Polish-Soviet Relations, 1939-1945, II (London, 1967) p. 698, 701-702
135. An interview with F. Roberts in M. Charlton, The Eagle and the Small Birds. Crisis in the Soviet Empire: From Yalta to Solidarity (Chicago, 1984), p. 25-27; M. Kitchen, British Policy towards the Soviet Union during the Second World War (Houndmills, Basingstoke, 1986), p. 153-155
136. FO 371/34571.
137. S.W. Slowes, The Road to Katyn: a Soldier's Story (Oxford, U.K.; Cambridge, Mass.: Blackwell Publishers, 1992), p. XIII. For more on Katyn See, HI Anders Archives,54/7 54/8; An Army in Exile pp,15-16, 20-21;FO 371/31083/C;FO 371/71610/N2599;FO 371/34571;GSHI P 172-3;GSHI PRM 41/4,p.205 No.149; and The Katyn Forest Nassacre, The Final Report, House ReportNo.2505, 82nd Congress,2nd Session.
138. J. Slusarczyk, Stosunki polsko-radzieckie 1939-1945 (Warsaw, 1991), 176; O. Terlecki, General Sikorski (Cracow, 1983), p. 157-166, 203-204, 210.
139. FO 371/31082/C3950.
140. O. Terlecki, General Sikorski (Cracow, 1983), p. 157-166.
141. GSHI, PREM 3 and an interview with Romanowski.
142. Although he denies it, Racienski was undoubtedly an intelligence officer. He was a private in the army and was associated with Merek Kahan, who was also a private soldier, when they were in Russia together. Racieski boasted that he often had a private breakfast with General Anders. This was not taken seriously until confirmed by Mrs. Anders.
143. NA X41876.
144. FO371/34563/C258 and C/1465/258/55.
145. Anders, An Army in Exile p.93, 136-137.
146. Interview with Lubienski.
147. Anders, An Army in Exile p.148.
148. FO/371/34614/; 371/34614/C6115/; 371/34594/C6892.
149. FO371/34594.

150. C. Thompson. The Assassination of Winston S. Churchill p.53; also J. Czapski The Inhuman Land; p.48.Tompson's title is misleading as it refers to the character assassination of WSC'. He defends WSC against tthe charge he was responsible for Skorski's death.

151. Interview with Romanowski.

152. W. Anders, Bez ostatniego rozdzialu (London 1979) p.172,173.

153. J.L. Englert K. Barbarski (London 1989) p.195.

154. NA CID61243; Terlecki, General Sikorski p.221.

155. NA 6905 (Poland) (ME).

156. GSHI PREM 204/354/1.

157. FO 371/31082/C4034 In March, 1943 Walter Biddle Smith reported to Roosevelt that Sikorski was under fire from the opposition, including some from Polish Forces in the Middle East. He told the President the Russians are unlikely to attack Sikorski personally as his successor would probably be more unrealistic and more anti-Moscow., See, FR 43 VOL.3,P.343, 349. Amb, Racynski comes to the opposite conclusion.

158. Interview with Lidia Ciolkosz, who expressed an opinion opposite Racynski's opinion.

159. Also killed in the crash were Sikorski's daughter and Gen. Klimacki. The only survivor was the pilot.

Author with Count Edward Raczynski, former Polish Ambassador (1935-1945) to Great Britain.

King George VI of England talking with General Anders, Italy, 1944

(From left to right)

Generals Clark (USA), Anders and McCreery (USA)

President K. Sabbat
President of the Polish Government in Exile.
Taken in London, 1988

General Anders and his son, George, in Italy.
June, 1945

(From left to right)
General Anders, General Henry Wilson (British) and the Polish Minister to Iraq.

18 graves of Polish-Jewish soldiers killed in action, at a Polish Military cemetery at Monte Cassino.

The Polish Cave, a reminder of the Polish Army's visit to Israel (then Palestine).

The author lunching with Mrs. Renata Anders,
in London.

A defacto Jewish Unit at Koltubanka
Rabbi Rosengarten is 4th from left.

From left: Capt. Kiedack "ATS", Col. Bakiewick,
Capt. Klimkowski.
1942, Tashkent. USSR

Set of four photos of Winston Churchill visiting Anders in Italy, in 1944. Photos by Jan Romanowski, who quotes Churchill as saying "Stalin will have a fit if he sees these photos - but take them anyway."

L
81170
CAUTION
RIGHT HAND
DRIVE
30

KOMENDA UZUPEŁNIEŃ Nr. 3 A.P. NA WSCH.

M. p. dnia 11. 1. 1944 r.

L. dz. 217/44

ZAŚWIADCZENIE Nr. 6/44

Stwierdzam, że Begin Menachem r. 1913/3?/III w myśl art. 121 ustawy o pow. obow. wojskowym został zwolniony z czynnej służby wojskowej na przeciąg.

12 miesięcy od dnia 4. 1. 1944 do dnia 4. 1. 1945

(Pieczęć okręgu)

KOMENDANT UZUPEŁNIEŃ

KOMENDANT UZUPEŁNIEŃ

DMOWSKI PPLK.

1503/PP&TJ/K/3 6/43.

No. 3 POLISH RALLY RECRUITING STATION

H. A. POLISH ARMY IN THE EAST.

11. 1. 1944 A.D.

Reg. No. 217/44.

CERTIFICATE

I certify hereby that Begin Menachem y. 1913/3?/III conformingly with art. 121 of the Polish law of Military service, is discharged from the active military service for the time of

12 months from 4. 1. 1944 to 4. 1. 1945

No. 3 POLISH RALLY RECRUITING STATION

*The Officer in charge*

KOMENDANT UZUPEŁNIEŃ

DMOWSKI PPLK.

ASSISTANT FOOD CONTROLLER

Reg. 28/?/44

המקור ברשות מכון ז'בוטינסקי

סימול 20פ

M. Begin's honorable discharge papers are on exhibit at the Jabotinsky Institute in Tel Aviv. The false document shown here gives Begin a one year leave and another forged document states that Begin, plus four others (including Merek Kahan), are classified as deserters because they didn't return to duty. Both documents were prepared by Merek Kahan and planted, with Polish approval, so as to hide the fact from the British that Begin received an honorable discharge. Begin first stepped foot in Palestine as a soldier in Anders' Army and would not desert as he felt the Irgun could not have a deserter as its leader.

# CHAPTER FIVE

# THE PAINFUL VICTORY[1]

## The Second Corps Goes to Italy

While the Polish Second Corps was preparing for battle on the training fields of Iraq and Palestine the tide of war turned decisively in favor of the Allies. In February, 1943, the German 6th Army surrendered at Stalingrad In May of the same year, German and Italian forces in North Africa capitulated before Anglo-American armies commanded by Field Marshal Harold Alexander. The Allied landing on Sicily in July led to the Italian surrender in September. The surrender made it possible for British and American troops to land on the southern part of the Appenine peninsula, thus gaining a foothold on the European mainland.

These developments had important implications for the Second Polish Corps. In November, 1943, Second Corps units had been transported by truck to Egypt, where they were stationed in a huge barrack camp in Quassassin. On December 7, 1943, during a meeting between General Anders and the Allied commander in Italy, General Henry

M. Wilson, a decision was reached for the Second Corps to be sent into battle on the Italian front.[2] From the middle of December, 1943, until May, 1944, Polish soldiers were sent by truck to ports in Alexandria, Port Said and Suez, where they boarded transport ships bound for the Southern Italian ports of Taranto, Bari, Brindisi and Naples.

The privilege of being the first unit to reach Italian soil was given to the 3rd Division of Carpathian Rifles, which included many veterans of the Independent Carpathian Brigade, who had fought at Tobruk. The Division landed at Taranto on December 21st, preceded only by a detachment of Polish Commandos. It was followed by the Corps Headquarters, the 5th Infantry Division and the newly formed 2nd Armored Brigade, which arrived successively between January and May. General Anders arrived on February 6, with the first detachment of the 5th Infantry Division.[3] The sea journey from Egypt to Italy was uneventful as the Allied navy and air forces had full control over the Eastern Mediterranean and the risk of a submarine or air attack was almost non-existent. The soldiers celebrated Christmas, even though many found it strange to do so aboard a ship. For those who were religious it was symbolic that they had arrived in Iran at Easter and left Palestine for Egypt and Italy at Christmas time.

Those soldiers who had come from the Soviet Union could not help comparing their trip across the Mediterranean with their crossing of the Caspian Sea, in 1942. They were now moving as an army and not as a group of refugees and there were no women and children aboard (apart from the nurses and ATS). All non-combatants had been left behind, in schools, hospitals and shelters in Palestine and Egypt. Leaving loved ones behind in Palestine was a lot different than leaving them in the Soviet Union. Family members left in Russia were likely to suffer great hardship or death while families left behind in the Middle East were safe and well provided for.

Veterans who had served in the Carpathian Brigade and had not been in Russia had a different experience in their earlier sea travel. The last time they boarded transport ships in Egypt their destination was Greece, but at sea the ships changed course and headed for Libya, as Greece had fallen to the Nazis. At that time the Allied forces were withdrawing from the continent while the invading Germans and Italians were surging forward. Now the roles were changed, the Allies were on the offensive, while the Germans were on the defensive and retreating on all fronts.

Everyone in Anders' Army knew their destination was Italy and that the Italians had surrendered. To those who had not fought in North Africa, the Italian surrender was unmitigated good news. The Carpathians on the other hand had an uncomfortable feeling that the Germans would be an even more formidable opponent now after getting rid of their undependable ally. Nevertheless everyone was pleased that they would not have to fight against the Italians, towards whom Poles bore no ill will; historically there had been good relations between the two countries and the two peoples. One of the most famous Polish queens – Bona Sforza came from Italy and in the days before World War II Italy had been a favorite vacation site for affluent Poles. Some of the Carpathians recalled, not without a trace of humor, that it was only after they had fought against the Italians in North Africa for some time, was it realized that officially there was no state of war between Poland and Italy.

There had been rumors that the Second Polish Corps would be sent to Burma to fight against the Japanese. Although rumors were a part of army life and any seasoned soldier knew better than to treat them seriously, everyone sighed with relief when the rumors turned out to be false. Their enemy was Germany! They had come to fight the Nazi beast.

The Second Polish Corps represented a well trained, well equipped force, led by dependable officers. It numbered over 52,000 officers and soldiers consisting of two infantry divisions (the 3rd Carpathian and the 5th Kresowa), an armored brigade, a reconnaissance regiment of armored cavalry and an artillery regiment. Each infantry division also had its own armored cavalry regiment. The Corps had at its disposal 156 medium and 33 light tanks, 245 armored cars, 84 medium and 418 light mortars, 250 anti-tank guns, 198 light and 32 heavy field guns, 132 anti-aircraft guns and over 3000 machine guns.

The organization and equipment of the Corps was not without weaknesses. The most serious was a lack of third brigades in the infantry divisions. The reason for that was a manpower shortage because the Polish Armed Forces in the west were cut off from their home base and had no manpower pool on which to draw. As we will see later, Anders found a very specifically Polish solution to the problem of finding replacements. From a tactical point of view the lack of third brigades meant that the Corps did not have sufficient infantry reserves to mount a sustained offensive or to exploit a breakthrough in the enemy lines. The Corps' artillery had weaknesses also. There were too few heavy long-range guns and, initially at least, no heavy mortars, a type of weapon particularly useful in mountainous terrain. Armored cars, which formed the main equipment of cavalry regiments, proved to be next to useless; they had difficulties moving on mountain roads, their armament was insufficient and their thin armor made them vulnerable to enemy fire.

However, these weaknesses should not obscure the fact that the Corps was a formidable fighting machine, fully motorized and equipped with modern weapons which provided it with considerable fire-power. The soldiers who wielded those weapons were unlike any other Allied soldiers in Italy, maybe with the exception of the Free French. They were, on the average, older than draftees or volunteer soldiers in the Anglo-American and Commonwealth armies. After their ordeal in Russia they were probably less fit physically than young American or British draftees, but on the other hand were more inured to the hardships of life in the combat zone. They were also exceptionally well motivated and eager to fight. Most of them had endured a string of trials and humiliations; the catastrophe of the September, 1939, campaign, the defeat of France in 1940 and the deportations, arrests and concentration camps in the Soviet Union. All these experiences tested their spiritual strength, and psychological and mental endurance to the outer limits of human capability. They had overcome these trials with unbroken spirits and a determination to repay the Germans for 1939 and all the cruelties of the occupation. Finally, what distinguished them from other Allied soldiers in Italy was the knowledge that they were fighting for the liberation of their families and their land. They believed and hoped, that with every inch of ground taken from the enemy, and with every dead German soldier, they were getting closer to their own homeland. As two British historians put it "The ardor of the Poles was not simply fueled by an understandable desire for revenge. An intensely political people, even the humblest soldier perceived that if they helped to gain an Allied victory the road to free and independent Poland might be opened once more."[4]

The dedication and skills of Anders' soldiers were recognized by one of the leading authorities on the military history of the War who wrote that, "in time II Corps (Second Polish Corps) would come to be recognized as one of the great fighting formations of the war."[5] In the words of Harold MacMillan "their spirits charged with a light hearted disdain for danger the likes of which he had met in no other." Another historian called the Polish forces at Cassino, "Exceptionally well led and highly motivated" and described them as "among the most effective members of the Allied contingent in Italy." British historians described the courage of the Polish troops as "unsurpassed" while praising the officers as "highly intelligent and thoughtful soldiers."[6] Soon their dedication and patriotism would be put to an ultimate test.

## The Italian Deadlock

The Polish troops arriving in Italy may not have been aware of the strategic deadlock in which the Allies found themselves on the peninsula, in the spring of 1944. The Poles would contribute decisively to breaking that deadlock.

The ultimate reason for the deadlock lay in differences between the American and British strategic visions which had emerged in 1942. The American military planners thought that the most efficient way of defeating Germany would be to land Allied forces in Northern France. The British, in particular Winston Churchill, favored an invasion in the Mediterranean, directed against, in a memorable Churchilian phrase, "Europe's soft underbelly." If the Americans were guided in their planning by military considerations, the British were thinking primarily in political terms. To Americans, with their large motorized and armored force, Northern France was attractive as it was the only area within close reach of the Allied bases in the United Kingdom, and with open and flat space offering favorable conditions for a fast offensive towards the German heartland. The British, with an eye towards postwar politics, hoped that by landing troops in Italy or the Balkans, the Allies would be able to prevent large parts of Southeastern Europe from falling under Soviet control.

Americans, being the dominant partner in the alliance, managed to persuade the British that landing in Northern France should be the primary strategic objective of the Western Allies. As a concession to British demands however, they reluctantly agreed that, if favorable circumstances arose, landing operations could also be launched in the Mediterranean. The Italian capitulation in September offered precisely such circumstances and the Allies landed troops on the Italian mainland. Unfortunately, the Germans reacted quickly to the Italian collapse and managed to send enough troops to the southern part of the Italian peninsula to contain the Allied advance. Instead of a quick push to the north, the Anglo-American troops got involved in bitter fighting with numerically inferior but skillfully led German units.

The Allies discovered very quickly that natural conditions of the Italian countryside favored the defending forces. Apart from a narrow coastal plain the terrain was mountainous and the roads were poor. Numerous rivers flowed on both sides of the mountain range, constituting the "spine" of the peninsula which formed perfect defensive positions which the Germans exploited expertly. The weather was cold, and frequent rains turned the roads into pools of mud, bringing the motorized Allied supply columns to a standstill. The clouded sky meant that the almost total air superiority of the Anglo-Americans could not be utilized. The advantages in numbers and material could not be exploited in the narrow mountain passes.

Theoretically, the Allies should have been able to "turn" the wings of the German defense by launching amphibious operations behind German lines. After all, the Germans could not possibly guard several hundred miles of the peninsula's coastline against such landings. The crunch was that the landing crafts necessary for such operations constituted one of the most carefully husbanded resources in the Allied war inventory and the Americans were extremely reluctant to use them for what they considered to be a secondary theater of operation. Because of this shortage only one such landing behind German lines was executed, and, as we will see,the Anzio beachhead did not bring the expected results.

While the German troops fought a delaying action, withdrawing slowly up the peninsula, their engineers hastily constructed a series of fortified lines, usually anchored on the river valleys. In December of 1943, after over three months of bitter and exhausting fighting, in the course of which they suffered tens of thousands of casualties, the Allies came against the main German fortification line south of Rome, the so-called Gustav line. Rome, the major prize of the campaign, was beckoning from the other side of the line, almost within a hand's reach of Allied troops.

The Gustav line ran from the sea, along the Garigliano, Gari and Rapido rivers, through the mountain massif of Monte Cairo and further along the Sangro river which flowed into the Adriatic. The key position of the line was centered on the medieval Benedictine monastery of Monte Cassino and a group of hills around it. The importance of this position was that it overlooked and effectively blocked the Liri River valley, which provided the only pass through the mountain range, and the only avenue of approach to Rome. Through the valley ran an ancient Roman road, Via Casilina, or Highway 6. The town of Monte Cassino, located at the base of the Monte Cassino hill, straddled this strategically important route.

The Germans had plenty of time to fortify this position by constructing hundreds of concrete bunkers, pillboxes and steel-turreted machine gun emplacements and by laying thousands of mines and barbed wire entanglements. They created unobstructed zones of fire by cleaning the ground of trees and brush and flooded the Rapido river valley by blowing up the dam. Their positions on the hills provided the Germans with an interlocking system of machine-gun, mortar and artillery fire. Advancing troops would be forced to storm uphill, in full view of German observers who had the advantage of higher ground. They would be exposed to a mutually supporting machine gun fire. The position was manned by crack German units of the 44th Hoch und Deutschmeister Infantry, the 90th Panzer Grenadier, the 5th Mountain Rifles and the 1st Parachute Divisions, renowned for their morale, tenacity and soldierly skills.

**The Battles for Monte Cassino**

Facing the Germans across the Rapido river was the American 5th Army, under the command of General Mark Clark, and the British 8th Army commanded by General Oliver Leese. Apart from the British and American troops these armies included Canadian, Indian, French, New Zealand and "Free Italian" units. Between January and May of 1944, the Allies launched three major attacks on the Monte Cassino position. The Germans repulsed all of them, inflicting terrible losses on the Allied troops.

The first to try were the Americans. Between the 20th and 22nd of January the 36th Texas Division was literally slaughtered as it made a heroic and valiant, but futile attempt to open the entry into the Liri valley by establishing a bridgehead on the western side of the Rapido river, immediately south of Monte Cassino. The Americans attacked alone, on a narrow front, trying to cross the river which, although narrow (2 yards), was 9 feet deep with an extremely strong current of 8 miles per hour. German artillery, guided by observers situated on hills dominating the valley, had a field-day. In three days the division lost over 2000 men.[7]

Simultaneous attacks launched north of the Monte Cairo massif by French Expeditionary Corps and on the southern flank of the Gustav line by the British X Corps also ended in failure. The aim of these attacks was to create a deep envelopment of the Cassino position, but they were launched too far from the spot of the American attack so the Americans did not benefit directly from the British and French pressure exerted on the German lines.

The American attack over the Rapido was also coordinated with an even more daring enterprise intended as a deep envelopment of the Gustav line. This was the amphibious landing at Anzio, some 60 miles behind the Gustav line, (about two thirds of the distance to Rome) the prized object of the Allied offensive. On January 22nd British and American Divisions successfully landed on the beaches, with almost no losses, and without encountering any serious German resistance. Unfortunately, their commander the American General, J. P. Lucas, failed to exploit this opportunity and began digging in at the bridgehead instead of continuing the attack. The German Commander-in-Chief of the Italian front, Field Marshal Kesselring managed to move enough units to launch a counter-attack which almost drove the hapless Allied soldiers into the sea. After that, the Allied units on the bridgehead were effectively blocked by the Germans and were not capable of any offensive action. Instead of rescuing the Allied armies from their debacle on the Gustav line, they now had to be rescued from their predicament.

British and American soldiers were fighting for their lives at Anzio, General Clark, who had learned a lesson from the defeat of the 36th Division, decided to shift the core of the attack to the north of the monastery. The 34th U.S. Infantry Division was ordered to cross the Rapido above the town of Monte Cassino. One regiment was to attack the town from the north while the two remaining regiments were given the task of bypassing the monastery position by capturing the hills north and northwest of it, and breaking through to the Via Casilina at the rear of the monastery. This attack came within an inch of success. After nine days of heavy fighting the Americans came within three miles of the Via Casilina, capturing Point 593 (Monte Calvario), the tactical center of the Monte Cassino massif. Four days later, on the 5th of February an American detachment reached the monastery walls. The Germans however managed to transfer their best troops to the Cassino sector. These were elements of the 1st Parachute Division which successfully counterattacked and recaptured Monte Calvario on the 10th of February. On February 11th the Americans gave up, with their infantry battalions down to 100 men. The surviving soldiers were so exhausted that some of them had to be carried away from their firing positions on stretchers.

The American II Corps (the 34th and 36th Divisions) now completely spent, were replaced by the 2nd New Zealand and the 4th Indian Divisions, both veteran units of the North African campaign and probably the best troops in the armies of the Commonwealth. The Nepalese Gurkhas in the Indian Division were considered the world's most adept soldiers for mountain combat.

It was at this point that the controversial decision to bomb the monastery was taken. The Germans declared the monastery and the area within 330 yards of its walls a neutral zone and pledged not to station troops there. The Allied commanders suspected, however, that the Germans had artillery spotters at least, if not actual firing positions inside the monastery. At the urging of the commander of the New Zealand Corps, General Freyberg, and over the opposition of the 5th Army Commander, General Clark, an order was given to bomb the monastery from the air. On February 15, two hundred heavy and medium bombers dropped 576 tons of bombs, totally destroying the basilica and monastery buildings.[8] Ironically, the bombing harmed the Allies more than the Germans who used the pretext of the bombing to occupy the monastery which they quickly turned into an impregnable fortress. Even 1000 lb bombs failed to destroy the solid stone external walls and the Germans converted the cellars into shelters and firing positions invulnerable to air and artillery bombardment. Astoundingly, the Commonwealth troops taking over the American positions around the monastery were not warned before the bombing and suffered casualties from the "friendly" bombs. What was worse, the lack of coordination and faulty flow of information did not allow them to follow up the bombardment with an immediate assault on the stunned Germans. General Fuller described the bombardment as "an act of sheer tactical stupidity."

On the evening of February 15th, the New Zealand Corps launched a second attack on the monastery. The Indian Division tried to storm Point 593 and the monastery hill, while the New Zealanders launched an attack across the Rapido river into the Monte Cassino town itself, trying to open a way directly into the Liri valley. In three nights of fighting the Indian Division lost over 600 men and withdrew. In its rifle companies the casualty rate was 40%.[9] The New Zealanders initially took a railway station in the town, but the Germans counterattacked with tanks which forced them to withdraw to the eastern bank of the Rapido. On the 18th, having lost half the men in their rifle companies, the New Zealanders had to break off the engagement and withdraw to take in replacements and to reorganize. A second attempt to take Monte Cassino met the same fate as the first.

Freyberg wanted to try once more, this time shifting the axis of the attack. The New Zealand Division was to attack the town from a bridgehead captured earlier by the Americans on the western bank of the Rapido north of the town. The Indian troops were to storm uphill along the hairpin road zig-zagging up the northeastern and eastern face of the monastery hill. The attack was delayed for two weeks because of heavy rain. The Germans used this break to advantage by replacing the exhausted soldiers of the 90th Panzer Grenadier Division with the creme de la creme, the 1st Parachute Division, elements of which had already been fighting against the American onslaught on the 10th of February.

The third attack on the Cassino was preceded by a heavy aerial and artillery bombardment of the town. Hundreds of bombers dropped about 4 tons of bombs per acre and 890 guns fired almost 200,000 shells during an eight hour artillery barrage. Again, some of the bombs fell on the Allied troops, causing casualties from "friendly" fire[10] This bombardment failed to annihilate or even to demoralize the German defenders while the town was turned into an impassable heap of rubble, dotted with huge craters. The rubble and craters hampered the attackers more than the defenders and made any tank support for the Allied infantry impossible. The attack lasted eight days and both the New Zealanders and the Indians made some progress, the former securing parts of the town while the latter captured the first three hairpin bends of the road to the monastery and Point 435, known as "Hangman's Hill" just below the monastery itself. Soon after that, the Germans counterattacked and the Indians were forced to abandon their conquests. In the towns, the Germans managed to hold on to the main defensive positions. On the 23rd of March Freyberg was forced to admit defeat. The New Zealand Corps was a spent force and had to be withdrawn to the rear.

Even before the New Zealanders gave up their assault, the commander of the Allied forces in Italy, Field Marshal Alexander, realized that isolated attacks on Cassino were hopeless and began to plan a much wider offensive that would decisively breach the Gustav line on a broader front. In that offensive, the task of capturing the central Monte Cassino position would be assigned to the Second Polish Corps command by General Anders.

## The Second Polish Corps at Monte Cassino

The first task given to the Polish Second Corps after its arrival in Italy in the winter and early spring of 1944 was relatively easy. At the beginning of March the Corps was entrusted with a passive defense of a sixty mile stretch along the Sangro river. Here, most of Anders' soldiers got their first taste of the front line. It was not too strenuous; in the still prevailing winter conditions the military action was limited to occasional artillery exchanges and skirmishes between patrols. This was about to change. On March 24th the commander of the 8th Army, General Leese paid a visit to Anders' headquarters. Speaking only to Anders and his Chief of Staff, Colonel Wisniowski, he revealed plans for the coming Allied offensive against the Gustav line and told them that he wanted to assign the most difficult part of the offensive,which was an assault on the Monte Cassino position, to the Second Polish Corps. He gave the Poles ten minutes to decide whether they were prepared to accept the task. If they were not, the Corps would be used at another attack axis.

Anders and Wisniowski needed less than ten minutes to accept the challenge even though Anders' had doubts about the viability of the offensive, as designed by Leese. He would have preferred a deep enveloping maneuver through the mountains rather than a head-on attack at the strongest point of the German fortifications. Such a plan had been proposed by the French General Juin, but was rejected by the Allied command. What was paramount to Anders was that Monte Cassino had already acquired world-wide notoriety as the main German position barring the Allies from the path to Rome. Anders realized that successfully storming Monte Cassino by the Corps would be the best way to counter Soviet propaganda claims that the Poles did not want to fight the Germans. He also calculated that an attack in a different sector would bring similar casualties, without bringing the same recognition to the Polish military effort. Finally, he hoped that a prominent victory would revive the spirit of the resistance movement in occupied Poland[11]

The task of the Corps was straight forward, to break through the Cassino massif to Highway 6 and then to attack and take the town of Piedemonte, which formed a hinge joining the Gustav line with an interlocking fortified line called the Hitler line. Anders, with his staff, pondered for some time about what plan they should adopt for the attack. In the end, they decided that it was useless to try to attack the monastery before securing the hills which formed an arc starting west of the monastery hill and turning gradually towards the northwest. The division commanders drew lots and the lot for storming Points 593 (Monte Calvario) and 569, as well as a subsequent attack on the monastery hill, fell to the 3rd Carpathian Division. The 5th Kresowa Division was to attack further west towards the so-called Phantom Ridge and then to take the key German positions at Colle San't Angeloo and Point 575. Taking these points would mean a break through to Highway 6 in the Liri valley, which would protect the right northern flank of the massive British attack which was to begin simultaneously with the 2nd Corps attack on the Cassino massif.

The positions facing the Corps were manned by two parachute regiments, a parachute machine gun battalion and a combat team of mountain rifles, supported by assault and anti-tank battalions (equipped with excellent self-propelled 88mm guns), 230 field artillery pieces and 70 six-barrelled heavy mortars (so-called Nebelwerfers). German heavy artillery had a longer range than the Allied guns and German mortars a larger caliber and longer range than those of the Allies.[12]

On April 17, the Corps began to take over the positions in the Cassino massif from the battle weary New Zealand and Indian troops. Anders' soldiers were entering a world completely different from their earlier experience at the front line on the Sangro river. Even the take over of positions on the front line was a complicated and difficult operation, since in some places the Allied and German soldiers were separated by no more than 30 yards and all approaches were within sight of German artillery observers perched on the hills. Consequently, the soldiers had to trek for more than seven miles through the pathless mountains under cover of night, bent in half under the weight of extra ammunition, rations, water and engineering equipment. The Poles learned quickly that one had to move especially fast in places marked by signs such as "Shell Trap-No Halting." It didn't take them long to understand that these were areas zeroed in by the German artillery.

Conditions at the front line were extremely harsh. Movement during the day was impossible. Soldiers had to spend daylight hours cramped in small and uncomfortable shelters built of stones, boulders and tins, or hollows in the rocks. Every move could draw the fire of German snipers, machine-guns or even mortars. The soldiers had to go for weeks on dry rations and were half-starved. Water was in short supply. Because the area was strewn with corpses of those fallen in previous assaults, a sickening smell of decomposing bodies hung like a cloud over the battlefield.

Logistical preparations for the forthcoming attack was a huge and complex operation. Hundreds of tons of ammunition, rations and water had to be brought to forward stores by jeeps, which were the only type of a vehicle that could travel over the rickety pontoon bridges across the Rapido and through the narrow mountain paths. All of this had to be done either at night or under the cover of smoke-screens, because of the danger of German artillery fire. From forward stores the supplies were carried on the backs of the 1,200 mules employed by the Corps.[13] That ancient form of transportation created another unanticipated problem. The mules were accustomed to working with Indian soldiers and responding to commands in Italian. The resulting trouble was that the Polish soldiers who tried to control them had difficulties that would have been comical if not for the fact that human lives were at stake.

On the eve of the assault, as the soldiers were bracing for the coming battle, General Anders issued the order of the day, in which he appealed to his soldiers thirst for revenge and retribution, their national pride and their sense of patriotism. It is worthwhile to quote it at length since it reflects so well the mentality of the army in exile and its commander. The order read:

> "Soldiers, the moment for battle has arrived. We have long awaited the moment for revenge and retribution over our long-time enemy. Shoulder to shoulder with us will fight the British, American, Canadian, and New Zealand Divisions, together with the French, Italian and Indian troops. The task assigned to us will cover with glory the name of the Polish soldier all over the world. Trusting in the Justice of the Divine Providence we go forward with the sacred slogan in our hearts: God, Honor, Country.[14]

As one British historian remarked "Leese and Alexander (the commanders of the 8th Army and of the 15th Army Group respectively) must have raised their eyebrows when they read the opening of Anders' Order of the Day..."[15] The Polish emotional hatred of the Germans, their "raw passion" seemed somewhat excessive. The touches of romanticism and self-sacrifice appeared out of place in the age of industrial warfare.

The reminiscences of Harold MacMillan, who visited the Second Polish Corps on the eve of the Monte Cassino battle, reflect the aura of romanticism and emotional patriotism that surrounded the Polish troops. What particularly struck him was that:

"The trumpeters played a curious and appealing call, which ends suddenly- broken off in the middle of a musical phrase. We were told that this is always played at noon. It commemorates a trumpeter who was calling the people of Cracow to muster against the Tartars. As he was playing an arrow pierced his throat. Ever since.his call is played at noon, in memory of the Poles' long struggle against barbarism and urging them still to fight in the same cause. It always ends in this broken note."[16]

On the eve of the attack the trumpeter was mustering the Polish soldiers to attack the fortified positions of the Gustav Line.

The beginning of the attack was set at 0100, May 12th. The Allied offensive was preceded by a two-hour artillery barrage of 1600 guns. Heavy artillery pieces were to fire 300 shells each, light artillery pieces 500 and mortars 250. Each identified target was to be covered by a thousand artillery shells. At 0100 the infantry began to move forward, trying to get to the German forward positions before the enemy managed to shake off the stunning effects of the artillery bombardment and come out of the shelters to man their firing positions.

The 1st Carpathian brigade launched its attack on two parallel axis. Its 2nd Battalion moved forward along the so-called Snakeshead Ridge towards Monte Calvario. The 1st Battalion advanced on the right flank of the 2nd, through the narrow "Gorge" valley toward the Albaneta plateau, located at the southern end of the valley. Its advance was supported by tanks and self-propelled guns. The attack of the 5th Kresowa Division up the "Phantom Ridge," was led by the 13th and 15th Infantry Battalions.

In spite of heavy casualties the beginning of the attack was promising. Following immediately after the artillery barrage, the leading company of the 2nd Battalion managed to capture Monte Calvario before most paratroopers, hiding in shelters on the reverse slope, returned to man their firing points. The troops continued their attack toward the second objective, Point 569 but were pinned down by enemy cross-fire on the saddle between Monte Calvario and Point 569. German paratroopers, sensing that the Polish attack was running out of steam, counterattacked under a cover of mortar fire. The Poles managed to hold them off, but the paratroopers did not give up easily. By night fall, after repeated counterattacks and hand to hand fighting, the Germans drove the bloodied remains of the 2nd Battalion back from Monte Calvario. Out of three companies that had participated in the attack only 34 soldiers returned unscathed.[17]

Initially, the attack of the 15th Battalion on the more remote, southern part of Phantom Ridge was also partially successful. Although two companies were almost totally destroyed, the other two managed to break through the crest of the ridge. As soon as they reached its reverse slope and descended into the valley, which separated the Ridge from the next object, Point 575, they were pinned to the ground by a rolling artillery and mortar barrage. Soon they were joined by the 18th Battalion which formed the second echelon of the attack. This only made matters worse, as the greater concentration of troops in a narrow valley caused even higher casualties. Similarly on the northern part of Phantom Ridge, the 13th Battalion managed to get two companies over the Ridge, at the cost of a total annihilation of the two other companies. The 2nd company was caught by the German artillery on the crest and within a couple of minutes lost 20 men and 51 were wounded. Due to the deadly German machine gun and artillery fire, the companies which entered the valley, dividing the Phantom ridge from Point 575, were unable to advance any further. At noon the brigade threw its reserve 16th Battalion into the fighting but it failed to turn the tide of battle. At dusk, Anders ordered the withdrawal of those units which were still holding out on the other side of Phantom Ridge. The two leading battalions of the 5th Brigade were almost annihilated: all were either killed or wounded. The attack on Phantom Ridge was a catastrophe: the 5th Division lost 20% of its soldiers and gained nothing.[18]

The 1st Carpathian Battalion attacking through the Gorge failed to achieve even the temporary success achieved by other battalions. The tanks which were supposed to support it, either got stuck on the rocks, or were destroyed by mines and artillery fire. The advancing infantry got into cross fire from the Phantom Ridge, Point 593 and the Albaneta Plateau and withdrew with heavy casualties.

Anders was not prepared to give up. He immediately ordered his staff to organize improvised infantry units from the anti-tank and anti-aircraft artillery, services, signals and other non-combatant units in the rear.

The General and his staff set down to analyze the reasons for the defeat. Certainly there was more than one cause for the failure of the attack. One of the major reasons was a lack of familiarity with the terrain and insufficient reconnaissance. This was largely a consequence of an unfortunate order by General Leese forbidding the Corps to send reconnaissance patrols into the no-man's land between the Allied and German positions. Leese wanted to prevent the Germans from learning that they were facing fresh Polish troops, but it is doubtful whether preserving that secret was worth the price the soldiers of the Corps paid in blood as a consequence of stumbling blindly into undetected German strongholds.

Romanowski, who was at the General's side throughout the attack, rejects the argument about insufficient reconnaissance. He claims the terrain was known since the staff had a detailed table model of the area. In addition, Anders flew over the future battlefield in a small plane to get the "feel" of the terrain. But the consensus was that even the detailed model, made on the basis of maps, could not provide accurate orientation to the very complicated mountainous landscape around Monte Cassino. What is more important, the German firing points could be detected and localized only by patrolling them. The excellent camouflage techniques used by the Germans meant that many positions were undetectable from the air or through binoculars.

Another reason for defeat was that communications between the units and its higher commanders was poor. Radios issued to the Poles didn't function properly in that terrain. The field telephones worked better but the cables were constantly damaged by German artillery fire, which also destroyed the Corps' communications center. As a result, movement of the units and their actions could not be synchronized. The commanders, lacking information about the location of subordinate units, quickly lost any real control of the developing battle.

There was also poor coordination between the artillery and the infantry. Romanowski attributes part of the failure of the May 11th attack to the "fear of artillery fire from our own side." Several times Polish units had been shelled by Polish artillery. This happened in particular on the crest of Phantom Ridge. Moreover, the Corps artillery received heavy mortars only in the last minute before the battle, and the crews had no time to be properly trained.[19]

There was another reason for the failure, which so far has not been explored by historians. The 18th Battalion of the 5th Division failed to carry out its assignment to stage a diversionary attack from Phantom Ridge in the direction of Point 575, to divert fire from the main attack of the 5th Division on Colle San't Angelo. Apparently the Battalion's commander lost his courage and failed to move his men when they were pinned down by German fire. He was relieved of command and was severely wounded in the next attack.

Soldiers who had been in the front blamed a lack of good communications for the defeat. Polish and Indian forces were supposedly coordinating their attacks but they had a language problem, because of an inability to understand the way the other spoke English. There was an allegation that the Indians were not as aggressive as they should have been. In comparison the Poles were very laudatory towards the French and the French Colonial troops.

Finally, the Poles simply had bad luck. As they learnt later from captured German prisoners, their attack coincided with the arrival of fresh German units to relieve the troops holding the position. Thus at the moment of the Polish assault the German positions were manned by double the number of defenders.

Almost immediately, the Corps set out to draw lessons from the first attack. Patrols were sent forward to reconnoiter German positions and provoke them to fire and reveal themselves. A coordinated and systematic program of artillery bombardment was carried out. It was decided that the new attack would follow behind the artillery barrage much closer than had the first. The engineers were to clear the entry of the gorge of mines and make it passable for tanks and new directions for the attack were assigned to the units. The battalions of the Kresowa Division were to concentrate their attack on the northern end of Phantom Ridge and then on Colle San't Angelo. Only after securing these objectives were they to push towards Point 575 and the Albaneta Plateau. It was decided that the Carpathians would still take Mount Calvario, but instead of attacking the Albaneta Plateau through the gorge, they would launch their attack through the eastern slopes of the Snakeshead Ridge. Only one battle group was to stage a diversionary attack through the Gorge to divert the fire from the Kresowa's attack on Phantom Ridge.

All preparations for the new attack were ready by May 15th but General Leese asked Anders to delay the attack until the 17th, in order to coordinate it with the 78th British Division attack in the Liri valley. General Kirkman, who commanded the division, told Leese, "Please don't let

Anders attack again until we are ready for him or there won't be any Poles left."[20]

However, on the 16th of May, a patrol of the 16th Battalion made a "fighting reconnaissance" of German positions on the northern edge of Phantom Ridge and discovered that the force there was extremely weak. The commander quickly seized the initiative and sent his battalion to occupy the crest. The 15th Battalion was able to use the area as a springboard for capturing the southern end of the Ridge. By the morning of May 17th the Kresowa Division was ready to launch an attack on Colle San't Angelo. It seized most of it but the Germans counterattacked and during the day, ferocious fighting followed, with both sides attacking and counter-attacking.[21]

By dusk, the Poles finally managed to wrest the hill from the Germans. They were not able to take advantage of their success by a follow up attack in the direction of Albaneta Plateau. It must be born in mind that Battalions of the Kresowa were badly mauled in the first attack and some were no larger then a company when they set out on the second attack. The 13th Battalion could muster only 140 men, and the 15th Battalion 180.[22] Similar situations developed on the section attacked by the Carpathians. They were able to capture Monte Calvario, but the Paratroops counterattacked repeatedly and both sides fought themselves to a standstill.[23] With its leading battalion (the 5th) loosing 40% of its soldiers, the Carpathian Division was unable to continue the attack toward the Albaneta Plateau. The offensive power of the Corps was exhausted, even though everyone had been sent to the front-line including clerks, cooks, drivers, etc.[24] Fortunately for the still surviving soldiers, by the evening of May 16th the German command decided that the Monte Cassino position was untenable and had to be abandoned. On the 17th the Germans began to withdraw from the monastery and ran into Polish and British patrols.

On May 18th, a sort of a race developed between the Poles and the British to see who would be the first to reach the monastery. A patrol of the 12th "Podolski" Lancers Regiment was the first to enter the ruins of the monastery. At 10:30 am the Lancers planted their regimental flag, which was soon replaced by the Polish flag. Following General Anders' instructions, they also hoisted a British flag next to the Polish one. Even before the first flag was hoisted, General Leese visited Anders, and they celebrated the victory by drinking champagne. At 1300 hours, General Anders had sent a formal report to the War Office, "The enemy on 2 Polcorps sector and in the Liri Valley has been defeated.[25] [26] The battle for Monte Cassino was over.

## Appendix "A"

### Battle Order of the Second Polish Corps on the Eve of the Battle of Monte Cassino

**3rd "Carpathian" Infantry Division**
Maj. Gen. Boleslaw Duch.
**1st Carpathian Rifle Brigade**
Col. Walenty Peszek.
**2nd Carpathian Rifle Brigade**
Col. Roman Szymanski.
**5th "Kresowa" Infantry Division**
Maj. Gen. Nikodem Sulik.
**5th "Wilenska" Infantry Brigade**
Col. Wincenty Kurek.
**6th "Lwowska" Infantry Brigade**
Col. Witold Nowina-Sawicki.
**2nd Polish Armored Brigade**
Maj. Gen. Bronislaw Rakowski.
**Artillery Group**
Maj. General Roman Odzierzynski.
**Engineers**
Col. Konstanty Skapski.
**Signals**
Col. Mieczyslaw Zaleski.
**Commando Company**
Maj. Wladyslaw Smrokowski.
**Medical Service**
Col. Marian Dietrich.
**Transport and Supply Service**
Col. Karol Wollen
**Fighter Reconnaissance Squadron**
Maj. Leszek Wielochowski.
**Artillery Observation Squadron**
British Commander Captain William Wright
**Polish Deputy Commander**
Captain Edward Pawlikowski

Footnotes

1. R. Trevelyan, Rome '44: The Battle for the Eternal City (New York, 1982), p. 266.
2. P. Zaron, ArmiaAndersa (Torun, 1996), p. 229.
3. The Independent Carpathian Brigade came under Anders' command in May, 1942.
4. D. Graham, Sh. Bidwell, Tug of War: the Battle for Italy, 1943-1945 (New York, 1986), p. 261.
5. P. Keegan Six Armies in Normandy, p 19.
6. Ibid., p. 286.
7. J. Piekalkiewicz, Monte Cassino: Anatomy of the Battle (London, 1980) p. 75.
8. Graham, Bidwell, p. 179-180, 192-194, 201, Ellis, p. 182, Piekalkiewicz, p. 104-105. Mark Clark wrote, many years later, "Not only was the bombing of the Abby an unnecessary psychological mistake in the propaganda field, but it was a tactical military error of the first magnitude."
9. Ellis, p. 194.
10. Ellis, p. 221-222.
11. Anders, p. 163-164. Graham, Bidwell, p. 259-260.
12. Zaron, p. 256 The controversy still lingers on the question of SS troops at Monte Cassino. Loftus claims the Belarus SS were part of the 29th Waffen Division which became the 30th Division in a reorganization.
13. Wankowicz, p. 90.
14. Anders, p. 175.
15. Ellis, p. 315.
16. Harold Macmillan cit. in Ellis, Cassino, the Hollow Victory: The Battle for Rome, January-June 1944 (London, 1984), p. 313.
17. Wankowicz, p. 178.
18. Piekkalkiewicz, p. 172, Ellis, p. 329, D.Kurzman, Race for Rome, p. 207
19. Graham, Bidwell, p. 286, Piekalkiewicz, p. 171-173.
20. R. Ryder, Oliver Leese (London, 1987), p. 166; Ellis, p. 309, 397.
21. Ellis, 333, Graham, Bidwell, 286-287, Piekalkiewicz, p. 177.
22. Wankowicz p. 322, 332.
23. Ellis, p. 334.

24. J. Lee Ready, Forgotten Allies, p. 231 Some military tactics experts said Anders should have held back some of his men in reserve, as Sikorski would have done.

25. Graham, Bidwell, p. 287; WO 204/10423.

26. Two generals, Anders and Juin (French)are usually spared criticism for the Monte Cassino battle. Juin's rejected battle plan could have saved thousands of lives. Anders is spared criticism because the major decisions had been made before his arrival and because he supported General Juin's battle plan. Race to Rome, p. 237.

# CHAPTER SIX

# ON TO BOLOGNA AND AN EMPTY VICTORY

## After Monte Cassino

There are many books on the subject of the battle for Monte Cassino and the consensus is that the lives of many allied servicemen were wasted, although some claim it was a military and political necessity. It has been argued that when faced with such an ill conceived battle plan Anders should have refused to commit the Polish forces. This was easier said than done. After the war Anders was asked if he agreed with Field Marshal Alexander that it was necessary to take Monte Cassino to open the road to Rome. He answered in the affirmative.

This battle has become a national legend in Poland because it had come to symbolize the ultimate sacrifice Polish soldiers were prepared to make for the cause of Polish independence. As the Americans have Valley Forge and the British have Trafalgar, so the Poles have Monte Cassino.

The victory at Monte Cassino was won at a heavy price. In a week of fighting the Corps lost 4199 men, including 923 killed, 2931 seriously wounded and 345 missing. The casualty rate in the infantry battalions was 50% among officers and 30% among enlisted men. In view of such heavy losses a question can be asked if Anders' decision to accept the task of storming the monastery was the right one. It can be argued that the battle was a sheer waste of human lives. On the other hand, the battle ended in a glorious victory for the Polish Army and an argument can be made that the casualties were a necessary price that had to be paid to demonstrate that the Poles were willing to fight for their freedom. Ambassador Raczynski,for example, thought that Anders made the right decision because it was a question of "Polish honor."

It is therefore particularly galling that some authors have been reluctant to give the Poles credit for the victory. Even Churchill denied that it was the Poles who reached the top of the Monte Cassino hill first. He wrote that the Poles were the first to plant the flag on the monastery "Although they were not the first to enter it." Churchill did not say who was first but we can assume he meant the British Army.[1]

Two American historians concluded that "Monte Cassino fell without a fight," since the Germans evacuated the monastery when threatened with encirclement by the Allied forces.[2] But to say there was no fight is to ignore the fact that Polish and other military cemeteries are around Monte Cassino to this day.

There was even an attempt to smear the name of Anders' soldiers by accusing them of atrocities. A German author, Wilhelm Bertold, alleged that the Poles murdered wounded German prisoners they had captured in the battle of Monte Cassino. A German television station repeated the accusation that the victorious Polish soldiers slaughtered the wounded.[3] In response, two veterans of the Second Polish Corps living in London brought a libel lawsuit against the television station. They conducted their own investigation in

Germany and found some German soldiers who had been at Monte Cassino who were willing to testify that the story of Poles killing wounded German soldiers was absolutely untrue. The station issued a correction after the author of the libel admitted that he had lied.

Today, the town of Cassino, as well as the monastery, has been rebuilt. The only reminders of the bloody battles are the cemeteries and small monuments scattered around the area. The inscription at the Polish cemetery states: "We Polish soldiers, for our freedom and yours, have given our souls to God, our bodies to the soil of Italy, and our hearts to Poland." In May, 1954, veterans of the battle, led by General Anders, commemorated the 10th anniversary of the battle with an "on site" ceremony. Similar ceremonies have taken place every five years since then. Anders attended every ceremony until his death, in 1970. As he directed, he is buried with his soldiers at Monte Cassino.

The graves in the cemetery are marked with the symbols of the dead soldier's religion, Roman Catholic graves with wooden crosses and rosaries, the 18 Jewish graves with small wooden Stars of David, the Orthodox with their characteristic cross, and a single Moslem grave with a crescent.

Each grave is decorated with a poppy, an early blooming flower that has become the symbol of the battle for Monte Cassino. The poppies were in full bloom when the Polish soldiers charged up those hills and they will continue to bloom each May even after the last Polish Veteran is gone.

## Breaking the Senger Line and the Adriatic Offensive: May 20th-September 2, 1944

The fighting didn't end with Allied flags flying over Monte Cassino. The Corps did not have time to celebrate the capture of the monastery. It was essential to exploit the success and try to break the next fortified line before the

Germans managed to recover after their retreat from Cassino. The Corps was ordered to continue the offensive and to take Villa Santa Lucia and the town of Piedimonte Piedimonte was strongly fortified with tank turrets embedded in concrete and stone pillboxes and with houses turned into infantry shelters and machine gun nests. It formed a key connecting point between the Gustav line and the next belt of German fortifications called the Senger line.

To attack Piedimonte, Anders formed an assault group called "Bob," commanded by Colonel W. Bobinski, consisting of the 6th Armored Regiment and the 18th Infantry Battalion, which after a week of fighting numbered only 180 men, self-propelled guns and artillery units. On May 20th, tanks from the 6th Regiment stormed the town with a horse cavalry-like effort but, without adequate infantry protection, suffered heavy losses from German anti-tank guns and had to withdraw. The assault group was reinforced by the 5th Carpathian Battalion and the 12th Lancer Regiment but it was only during the fourth attack that "Bob" managed to break the German defenses. On May 25th, Piedimonte was in Polish hands and the Senger line was decisively broken.

Simultaneously with the attacks on Piedimonte, the Carpathian and the Poznan Lancer Regiments set out to capture Passo Corno and Monte Cairo. These two peaks dominated the battle field and their control gave the Germans excellent observation points for directing their artillery fire. It was only on May 25th, after five days of heavy and bloody fighting, that the Lancers reached their objectives. The capture of Monte Cairo, the highest peak in the Senger line, meant that the last bastions of the Senger line were in Allied hands and that the road to Rome was finally open.[4]

It was only then that the Corps was given a short rest. It was allowed to withdraw to the rear and to fill the ranks of its badly mauled infantry battalions with replacements, drawn mainly from supply and service units. However, after only two weeks, before it was able to complete the necessary reorganization, the Corps was thrown into combat again.

On June 15, the Polish troops were moved to the Adriatic coast, where they took over a section of the front manned by the 5th British Corps. A British armored cavalry regiment, two British artillery regiments as well as several battalions of the Italian Liberation Corps were put under the command of the Second Polish Corps. The fact that the British allowed their units to be put under the command of a Polish general indicates how much their view of the Polish armed forces changed after the Cassino battle. When the Poles first arrived in Italy there was some distrust of the Polish Army and even talk that the Polish soldiers would have to be commanded by British officers. After Monte Cassino the distrust disappeared and the British acknowledged that Polish officers were equally, and perhaps sometimes even more competent, than their British counterparts.

Other Yugoslav and Italian partisans were fighting along side the Poles in separate units under Anders' command even though many were communists.

When the Corps took over its new sector from the British its tasks were defined as purely defensive. This was only appropriate in view of the losses which the Corps suffered during the Cassino battle and from which it did not have time to recover fully. Very soon, however, Anders received a new set of orders: the Corps was to engage in active pursuit of the enemy in the direction of the important Adriatic port of Ancona. In thirty days the Corps covered 75 miles, breaking heavy German resistance along the Chienti and Mussone rivers, and winning a seven-day battle near Loreto. After an enveloping operation, which was described as "brilliant" and a "master stroke" by the commander of the 8th Army, General Leese, the Polish forces liberated Ancona. The Corps inflicted heavy losses on the enemy, taking over 3,000 prisoners. Unfortunately, its own casualties were quite painful: 496 killed, 1,789 wounded and 139 missing.[5]

While Anders' soldiers were enjoying a few weeks of relative rest after capturing Ancona, the front reached the next German fortification line barring the way into Northern Italy, the so-called Gothic line. It was a formidable barrier, four miles in width, with mine fields, anti-tank obstacles and artillery positions. Originally, the main thrust of the Allied attack was directed against the middle section of the line, but a number of unsuccessful attacks there persuaded the Allied commanders to shift the axis of the main attack to the Adriatic coast. The 2nd Corps was given the task of breaching the outer defenses of the Gothic line, between the Cesano and Metauro rivers, reaching the town of Pescaro and preparing the ground for a decisive attack by the 1st Canadian Corps.

The subsequent fighting was, if not counting the battle of Monte Cassino, the heaviest and most difficult of the entire Italian campaign. The Germans were ensconced in well-prepared defensive positions, with considerable support from tanks, self-propelled guns, anti-tank and field artillery. Anders, again, conceived a plan which relied on a deep outflanking maneuver, intended to envelop and cut-off the main German defensive position from the rear. By August 22nd the Polish troops reached the Metauro valley. Four days later, after a three and a half hour artillery barrage, the Polish infantry successfully crossed the Metauro river and continued the offensive towards Pesaro. By September 2nd, the Carpathian Division, after three days of heavy street fighting, cleared the town of the enemy. In the meantime, the Polish armored units, accompanied by a battalion of infantry, penetrated deep behind the enemy line, joined the 1st Canadian Corps near the town of Cattolica and encirced a large enemy force. The victory could not be more complete. Between mid-June and September the Polish units covered a distance of 150 miles, liberated 3400 square miles of Italian territory and fought eight major battles. Sadly, however, the victory was marred by heavy losses suffered by the Corps. During the entire Adriatic campaign the Corps lost 288 officers and 3,403 NCOs and soldiers were killed or wounded.[6]

After Pesaro was captured the Corps was sent away for a well deserved rest. As the British Commander of the 8th Army put it in his farewell letter to the Corps: "After such great achievements, no formation has more fully earned a period of rest. I am very glad indeed that it is possible to give you three weeks out of the line."

**The Last Struggle. The liberation of Bologna and the End of the Italian Campaign**

With the coming of autumn the Allied offensive along the Adriatic coast began to fizzle out. Heavy rains turned roads into impassable pools of mud, and small rivers into rapid and dangerous torrents. The command of the 8th Army decided to shift the center of the offensive operations away from the Adriatic coast and into the Emilian Apennines, which formed the spine of the Italian peninsula. The Second Polish Corps was given the task of pushing through the trackless mountains to the north in order to outflank the German defenses on the Adriatic coast. This was probably the least enviable task the Corps had to perform. As Anders wrote later "There were no spectacular achievements; it was just a case of steady, relentless fighting, and duty well done." Between October 17th and December 17th, the soldiers of the Corps tenaciously and slowly fought their way north, until they reached the Senio river, where the front stabilized for several months. Again, the Corps paid a heavy toll: 669 killed, 2,814 wounded and 33 missing in action.[7]

After the winter break in military operations, the Allies braced for the final and decisive offensive, with the intention of destroying the German forces in Northern Italy and to break out from the peninsula into the North Italian plain. The Second Corps was assigned a sector in the middle of the peninsula, on the left wing of the British 8th Army. After crossing the Senio river it was scheduled to advance along Highway 9 toward Bologna. Anders divided his forces into two groups. The Carpathian Division, supported by the British 7th Armored Brigade, led the attack along the Highway. The 5th Kresowa Division, with the 2nd Armored Brigade and the 43rd Indian Brigade following behind in the second echelon. Their task was either to take over the attack in case the Carpathians faltered, or to exploit their success, if they managed to open a breach in the enemy front. The left flank of the attacking troops was covered by the "Rud" group, under General K. Rudnicki, consisting of the 3rd Carpathian and 4th "Wolynska" Brigade.

The last offensive of the Corps began with an ominous accident. On April 9, the leading battalion of the Carpathian Division was bombed by American planes minutes before it was about to begin the offensive by crossing the Senio river. The Carpathians lost 38 officers and soldiers killed and 188 wounded. Since there is nothing more demoralizing for troops than casualties caused by friendly fire, the unfortunate bombing accident threatened to disrupt the attack. Only a personal intervention by Anders, who immediately visited the site of the tragedy, ensured that the attack went ahead as scheduled.[8]

The unit which particularly distinguished itself in the crossing of the Senio river was the Commando Battalion, commanded by Major Smrokowski. The Commandos were an elite unit formed, in 1942, in Scotland from Polish volunteers. It served in the British Army in North Africa and was later transferred to the Second Polish Corps. The Polish Commandos arrived in Italy ahead of all the other Polish formations. When on a deep penetration raid behind German lines they immediately established an excellent reputation by managing to fight their way out of a German encirclement near the high mountain village of Caprocota.[9] Expanded from a company into a battalion, they had undergone five months of special training, learning how to cooperate with advancing tanks. The training paid off during the break through of the German positions on the Senio river. For that action, in which ten commandos, as well as their chaplain, were killed, the unit received the "Virtuti Militari" the highest Polish military decoration.[10]

After crossing the Senio river successfully, the Carpathians pushed forward and by April 11th had secured a bridgehead over another major water obstacle, the Santerno river. On the next day, all three Carpathian Brigades used the bridgehead to renew their offensive in the direction of Bologna. The Germans still defended every yard of ground viciously. The Corps had to spend three days (April 17-19) to break through another German defensive line on the Gaiano river and channel. This time it was the 5th Kresowa Division which broke through and finally opened the path to Bologna. On April 21 its 9th Battalion raised the Polish flag in the center of the town. During the last offensive the Corps defeated three German Divisions and took 2000 prisoners. Again, the price paid for success was heavy: 234 killed, 11,128 wounded and 7 missing in action.[11]

With the liberation of Bologna the Second Polish Corps ended its path of military glory. It was withdrawn to the army reserve and no longer took part in combat. A little over a week after its last fight the German command on the Italian front signed a document of unconditional surrender. The war in Italy was over. Anders' soldiers, however, had little to celebrate. One officer described the mood of the soldiers on the day of liberation of Bologna in the following terms:

> "Our soldiers look down from their vehicles on the enthusiastic crowd, returned smiles and greetings, but they do not share the general joy; they are rather serious and sad... In a few days the life in town will return to normal, while we will go further north. We will continue to liberate towns and villages, to carry on bloody battles, because all roads lead to Poland. And this Poland is closer and closer but so desperately distant."

As we will see the soldiers of the Second Polish Corps had good reasons to worry about the fate of their country as well their own.

## The Politics of War

When the Polish Armed Forces formed a "little Poland in exile" it was impossible to draw a line between professional soldierly duty and politics. Unfortunately for Anders and his soldiers the political future of Poland began to look increasingly uncertain as victories by the Red Army in the Eastern front gave the Soviets a powerful voice in the anti-Axis alliance, a voice the Polish Government in exile could not possibly match. When the Second Corps began its Italian campaign its soldiers had hoped and believed that every successful attack and each German soldier killed would contribute to the restoration of an independent Poland and bring them a step closer to their homes and families. It didn't take them long to realize there was no possibility of the Corps getting to Poland before the Soviets.

The intensely political nature of the Corps unsettled the British from the very beginning. Anders' initial misunderstandings with his immediate British superior, General Leese, reflected this well. Soon after the arrival of the Corps in Italy, Anders complained to Leese about some articles in the 8th Army's newspaper which, according to him, reflected a Soviet point of view and contained slander against the Corps and its soldiers. In response Leese rebuked him, saying that it was "superfluous" for him as the Corps Commander "to express in public any opinions concerning the political situation..." As a British historian commented aptly, Leese "found it positively irritating, regarding their concern with the future of Poland as an unsavory ulterior motive that had no place in the day-to-day business of war."[12]

As the Polish diplomatic and political situation continued to deteriorate, in the summer of 1944, there were two occasions when the question arose whether the Second Polish Corps should or should not be withdrawn from the Italian Front. From the Polish side the question was should they withdraw from battle in order to demonstrate their dissatisfaction with political decisions made by the British Government. From the British side the question was whether or not the Poles were a reliable ally and should they be removed from the front line, lest they decide to throw down their arms at a crucial moment. The British clearly underestimated the Polish soldier's desire to fight the Germans.

The first political crisis in relations between the Corps and the British was triggered by what the Poles perceived as the unwillingness of the Western Allies to aid Polish underground forces (the Home Army) which were being decimated in the ill timed Warsaw Uprising, in the summer of 1944. The crisis had been building for a long time. The first ominous sign for the Poles came in November of 1943, when Roosevelt, Churchill and Stalin gathered together in Teheran to talk about the conduct of war and about arrangements for postwar order. In Teheran, the Western leaders accepted Stalin's demand that the future border between Poland and the Soviet Union would run along the Ribbentrop-Molotov line (which Stalin deftly referred to as the Curzon line), i.e. to the incorporation of the eastern part of the prewar Polish state into the Soviet state. For the soldiers of the Second Corps, who came overwhelmingly from Eastern Poland, this was a bitter pill. The Polish Government in London refused to recognize and accept this agreement, as it deprived Poland of half its territory (even if promising to grant it large chunks of Germany, east of the Oder river), and did not provide any mechanism for ascertaining the wishes of the local population and was reached without even a pretense of consultation with Polish authorities. The fate of Poland and its citizens was being disposed of almost as if Poland was a defeated enemy rather than loyal Allies of the Western democracies.

The Teheran agreement was ominous not only because it deprived Poland of its eastern territories but also because it suggested that the Western leaders, convinced of the need to cultivate Stalin, would not defend Polish interests if they were threatened by the Soviets. In fact, after Teheran, the British began to apply pressure on the Polish

Government to accept the fait d'accompli. This created a lot of bad feelings between the Poles and the British. Churchill was particularly exasperated by what he thought was the obstinate refusal of the Poles to see the realities of power politics.[13] In June, 1944, he snapped to General Sosnkowski, then Commander-in-Chief of the Polish Armed forces, "You can take away your divisions now. We will manage without them."[14]

What was at stake was not only Poland's territorial shape but also its independence. In the spring of 1943, Stalin had already organized a body of non-entities called the Union of Polish Patriots and a "Polish Army" under Colonel Zygmunt Berling. Both were de facto controlled by a a small group of Polish Communists, and ultimately, by Stalin himself. Both would serve as tools for the Soviet domination of Poland. When, in July of 1944, the Red Army crossed the Ribbentrop-Molotov line, Stalin installed the so-called Polish Committee of National Liberation, which was dominated by Communists and claimed governmental authority over Polish territory liberated by the Soviets. In December, the Committee adopted the title, Provisional Government of the Polish Republic, and in January, 1945, it was recognized officially as the government of Poland by the Soviet Union.[15]

When in August, 1944, the Red Army began to close in on the Polish capital, the underground "Home Army," loyal to the government in exile launched an uprising against the retreating German troops. The Poles managed to liberate large parts of the city but soon found themselves fighting against an overwhelming German force. To their chagrin the Soviet-German front stabilized on the eastern bank of the Vistula. Since most of Warsaw lay on the western bank of the river, this meant that sooner or later the uprising was bound to fall under the German onslaught. There is no documentary evidence that Stalin stopped the Soviet offensive in order to permit the Germans to destroy the Polish underground in Warsaw but circumstantial evidence seems to indicate this. What is relevant is that the Soviets refused landing rights to the Allied bombers carrying supply drops for the insurgents. Since Warsaw was barely within range of Allied aircraft, this refusal made the supply operation impractical. The Americans and the British never tried to bring any pressure on Stalin to persuade him to change his mind. Claiming that the losses among the air crews were unacceptably high the Allies discontinued the supply drops.

The refusal of the Western Allies to use their clout against Stalin to obtain permission to land the Western supply missions, and their lack of enthusiasm in devising ways and means for helping the besieged city, obviously had a great impact on the Polish soldiers in Italy. According to Anders "We all felt very bitter about the inadequate support given to Warsaw..."[16] General Sosnkowski, Commander-in-Chief of all Polish Forces in the West, actually suggested that the Polish Government and the highest military commanders should resign because of the Allied refusal to aid the Home Army.[17] The Second Polish Corps had just had its days of glory at Monte Cassino and Ancona yet here was little support for Sosnkowski's suggestion. All that he accomplished was to bring about his own dismissal as commander of the Polish Forces. The rank and file of Anders' Army knew the British had arranged his dismissal but this did not lead to a wholesale rebellion. According to the testimony of Harold Macmillan, who discussed the whole issue with Anders, the latter regarded Sosnkowski's declaration as foolish and ill timed.[18]

The second crisis came in February of 1945, in the wake of decisions reached by the Big Three during their conference at the Crimean resort of Yalta. During that Conference the Western Allies not only confirmed the territorial arrangements made in Teheran but also adopted the Soviet proposal that the pro-Soviet and Communist-dominated Polish Provisional Government in Lublin should form the basis of a government, which would then be recognized by all Three Powers as the only legal and legitimate Polish Government. The government would be reorganized by incorporating the "democratic leaders from Poland itself and from Poles abroad." The process of reorganization would be put in the hands of the Soviet Foreign Minister, Molotov and of the British and American Ambassadors in Moscow. In other words, the Soviets would be able to veto any candidate put forward either in Poland or from abroad.[19]

According to Anders, "there was a violent reaction in the army as the men realized the great injustice that had been done to them. Each had trusted that at the end of his struggles, toil and suffering he would be able to return to his own country, his family, his cottage, his trade or his piece of land: now he knew that the reward for his efforts and his comrades' sacrifices was to be either further wandering in alien lands, or a return to a country under foreign rule. Only a sense of discipline and confidence in their officers prevented the men from taking precipitate and uncontrolled action."[20] Monte Cassino was captured, the road to Rome was opened, but the Western Allies preferred to assuage the Soviets and to forget the promises they had made to the Poles.

Anders' reaction clearly reflected the feeling of the soldiers he commanded. He immediately sent a letter to the commander of the 8th Army, General McCreery, asking for the withdrawal of his Corps from the front line, and a telegram to the President of Poland, Raczkiewicz, rejecting in the name of the Corps the decisions reached at Yalta and informing him of his letter to McCreery. Justifying his request to McCreery Anders wrote: "The soldier of the Second Polish Corps... feels this last decision of the Three Power Conference to be the gravest injustice and in complete contradiction to his sense of what is honorable...This soldier now asks me what is the object of his struggle? Today I am unable to answer this question."[21] Anders was obviously acting under the influence of very deep emotions. Harold Macmillan, who met him the next day, remembered him as being "in a mood of cruel disillusionment, almost despair."[22]

Very soon, however, calmer counsels prevailed and Anders, upon being told by McCreery that no troops were available to replace the Poles, and that this unilateral withdrawal could endanger the whole 8th Army, withdrew his ultimatum. In subsequent talks with the commander of the 5th U.S. Army, General Clark and with Field Marshal Alexander, he assured them that the Polish Corps would continue to fulfill its duty.[23]

Anders was later criticized by some of his generals who felt that after Yalta the Corps should have refused to fight, or at least should have limited itself to a passive defense of its positions. In the opinion of Romanowski, this was the only time the Poles seriously considered throwing down their arms. To the majority of them the provision relating to the Soviet-Polish border was not academic, it meant that their homes would be on the Soviet side of the border. For the people who had endured the Soviet prisons, camps and deportations, this was hardly an attractive prospect.

The fact that the Corps did not withdraw from fighting was due in part to some tactful persuasion by Clark and McCreery and to Anders' sense that the Corps must meet its moral obligations to other Allied soldiers even if its cause had been betrayed by the Allied leaders.[24] Macmillan later wrote, "I had underestimated the marvelous dignity and devotion of Anders and his comrades. They fought with distinction in the front of the attack in the last battles of April. They had lost their country, but they kept their honor."[25]

## Replacements From Behind the Enemy Lines

The Second Polish Corps had many unique features, due to the peculiar circumstances in which it was raised and the past history of its soldiers and officers. One of the most astonishing aspects of the history of the Corps during the Italian campaign was that in spite of heavy casualties (which totaled 17,924 killed, wounded, missing and psychologically disturbed)[26] the Corps was not only able to replace them but even to expand. When it set foot on Italian soil the Corps numbered 52,000 men, at the time of the German surrender it had grown to 56,000, despite heavy casualties sustained during the campaign. Anders organized two additional infantry brigades and reorganized the Armored Brigade into an Armored Division. How was this expansion possible, when Poland, the natural recruiting base of the Polish Armed Forces, was under German occupation and the reservoir of the Polish population in the Soviet Union was inaccessible.

In fact, one of the reasons the British staff officers doubted whether the Corps could be used in combat operation was that they could not see how the Corps would be able to find replacements.

When queried on this point by the British Commander of the Mediterranean Theater, General M. Wilson, Anders told him that "reinforcements would join us from the front line." He explained that he was counting on the Poles who had been forcibly conscripted into the German Army to desert or to surrender themselves to the Allies.[27] Wilson might have been a little surprised at such an unconventional method of recruiting. Yet, as we will see, Anders calculations turned out to be correct.

The Allies were well aware, at least since the time of the North African campaign, that there were Polish citizens in the German Army. A detachment of Poles in German uniforms were also spotted in Norway, and a commando who participated in the Dieppe Raid reported seeing Poles who "fought badly and unwillingly" in the German ranks.[28]

Why were there Poles in the German Army? The answer is relatively simple. After Hitler conquered Poland he incorporated the western third of the country directly into the German Reich. A large number of Polish citizens were deemed to be German by the occupying forces and were subsequently drafted into the Wehrmacht ranks. This violated international law, which barred military conscription of foreign citizens.

As the shortage of manpower in Germany increased, the criteria for "granting" German citizenship to former Polish citizens became more and more lax, enabling the Germans to draft them under the threat of being punished for evading the draft. Draftees were told that if they did not report for duty their families would be sent to concentration camps.[29] Altogether more than 300,000 Polish citizens were conscripted into the German Army during the war. Polish citizens living outside the territories incorporated into the Reich were drafted only into labor units until May, 1943, when German manpower needs required a change in policy. From that time onward they were drafted into military units.[30]

Polish authorities in London were understandably concerned with the plight of the conscripted Poles and quickly realized that they formed a pool of manpower that could be used for expanding the Polish Armed Forces in the West. In early 1943, the Polish Government expressed interest in the large number of Poles found among the Axis prisoners captured in North Africa and wanted to take over responsibility for the Polish prisoners. It asked the British for permission to send a Military Mission to the POW camps in order to screen the prisoners for possible recruits for the Polish forces and to transfer them to camps in Britain. The Joint Intelligence Subcommittee opposed this because it saw two potential political problems. It feared the possible Soviet reaction and was concerned that the Polish Mission, in violation of the Hague Convention, might put undue pressure on the prisoners to join the Polish Army. It was, however, overruled by the Foreign Office which allowed the Poles to proceed.[31]

The main problem faced by the Mission was how to separate those who were willfully serving in the German Army from those who were forced into a German uniform. The Polish press did acknowledge that some Polish citizens of various nationalities were in the German Army voluntarily.[32] Of course, those who had volunteered to serve with the Germans would not be accepted into the Polish Armed Forces.

A set of criteria was developed to screen the POWs. The criteria was not uniformly applied and was directed more at the individual's ability to prove Polish ethnicity then at determining his political attitudes. Thus, the first criteria was proficiency in Polish and those who passed that test were treated as potential candidates for the Polish Army. Another criteria was rank. Poles who had served in the German Army as officers were automatically disqualified. NCOs on the other hand were not excluded, as it was thought that NCO rank merely indicated good soldierly ability. Circumstances under which an individual had surrendered were also taken into consideration. Did he surrender or desert at the first opportunity? Finally, all those who had served in the SS were disqualified. The whole process of selection was very subjective and prone to error.

Obviously, the mere fact that the prisoner volunteered for service in the Polish Army was not sufficient proof he was a loyal Pole. The POWs were not only choosing between the safety of the prison camp and the risks of battle but between returning to postwar Poland in a Polish Army uniform or as a traitor. The risks of being in the Polish Army during the last months of the war were small compared to the risk of being punished for treason. There was a rumor that Poles who had served in the German Army, would be classified into three categories on their return to Poland: (a) those to be executed immediately, (b) those who would be sent to concentration camps, and (c) those who would be allowed to return to their homes. For most who had served in the German Army and intended to return to Poland, it would have been sheer folly to pass up the chance to return home in a Polish Army uniform. The Soviet presence in Poland increased the risks as the Soviets were known to execute their citizens who had served in the German armed forces, regardless of the circumstances.

Perhaps the biggest risk taken by those who volunteered to join the Polish Army was that the German authorities might take reprisals against their families left in occupied Poland. For example, on February 15, 1945, Berlin radio, broadcasting in English, reported that the entire Liess family was executed because one of the sons had deserted from the German Army.

A new recruit to the Polish Army was aware that if he were captured by the Germans he could be executed as a deserter. Each "new recruit" was required to sign a statement that he was aware that he was not under the protection of the Geneva Convention.[33]

According to Romanowski's estimate, between 12,000 to 15,000 Poles who had previously served in the German Army were recruited into the Second Polish Corps. The "new recruits" came from American and British POW camps and not directly from the front lines. There was never a situation where a soldier firing at the Polish soldiers, put his gun down and joined the Polish Army, although such a misperception might have been caused by The London Times article which stated that "other nations get their reinforcements from the rear, but General Anders will get his from the front."[34]

Only a small number of former German POWs defected back to the German Army. In general the policy of drafting former German soldiers turned out to be an unqualified success. Without the new replacements the Corps would not have been able to survive as a fighting front-line unit for the duration of the entire Italian campaign.

**The Lithuanians**

The following appeared in The Independent (London) dated 6 July, 1992:

> "The Lithuanians who have been traced in the United Kingdom come from a 160 strong company which defected to the Allies in Northern

Italy, probably in late 1944. The company was subsequently attached to the Second Polish Corps Commando Battalion."

The company in question was a SS unit. From discussions with commandos it appears that although the newspaper story refers to the defection of the entire company it was a battalion of only 40 soldiers (some say 90) and one officer, Lt. Giewich, who were inducted into Anders' Army. Giewich admitted that he was an officer in the Lithuanian SS 12th Police Battalion and that the unit was guilty of war crimes, but he denied having taken part. Giewich sued a Scottish Television station for calling him a war criminal. The television station was held by the court to be "not libel."

The acceptance of the Lithuanians violated basic policies of the Second Polish Corps. If the allegations are correct, accepting the Lithuanians violated Anders' stated policies, e.g. "non- acceptance of officers or SS, individual vetting, and not keeping a unit intact."

A Protestant chaplain in the Second Polish Corps said that acceptance of the Lithuanians who had served in the SS was ordered by General Anders. He quoted Anders as saying "the soldiers were very young and didn't appreciate that the SS was something other than an elite group." At the time Anders was recruiting tens of thousands of soldiers and its doubtful that he paid much attention to this small group.[35]

Footnotes

1. W.S. Churchill, The Second World War,v. 5 Closing the Ring (Boston, 1951), p. 600.
2. D. Hapgood, D. Richardson, Monte Cassino (New York, 1984), p. 230. Seventy percent of the American graves at nearby Anzio are empty the remains having been removed to the United States. In contrast there is no evidence of any remains being removed from the Polish military cemetery at Monte Cassino.
3.. Von Himmel zur Holle (Bayreuth, 1977); Kurzman, Race for Rome, p. 237. There were 30 wounded German soldiers captured at Monte Cassino.
4. Wankowicz, Monte Cassino, p. 479, 624-625.
5. HSWW,M &ME, vol.6, pt.111, p. 123n. A Polish Jew from Bielsk led a band of Italian partisans known as "Banda Izidore." When he met Polish forces in Italy, Izidore asked for a Polish eagle emblem to be attached to his cap next to his Italian badge. FO 371/394691/C153121.
6. W. Anders, An Army in Exile, p. 206-208, 214-217.
7. W. Anders, An Army in Exile, p. 233-235.
8. I.S.O. Playfair, History of the Second World War. United Kingdom Military Series; The Mediterranean and the Middle East (London, 1987), v. VI, pt. 3, p. 47.
9. Nowy Swiat (29 January, 1944); Evening Standard (London), (February 9, 1944); NA 6910 (Italy) (Poland). The first Polish soldier to die in battle in Italy was a commando, Cpl. F. Rogucki, a Polish-American from Pittsburgh. There was no shortage of volunteers when it was announced that a Polish commando unit was being formed. They came from the French Underground, escaped POWs, deserters who had been drafted into the German Army, the French Foreign Legion and escapees from forced labor camps in Greece. When the commando unit was expanded the manpower came mostly from the Second Polish Corps.
10. The killing of the chaplain infuriated the commandos. He was ministering to a dying German soldier when he was shot. In fairness it must be noticed that there is another version of the priest's death, i.e. he was on the field of battle taking photographs.The original commandos numbered less than 40, but by the time they arrived in Italy the unit had grown to 80 men, 10 officers and 17 cadet officers. An interview with Gasiwicz.
11. Zaron, p. 270-272.

12. W. Anders, An Army in Exile, p. 155; Ellis, Cassino, p. 318.
13. R. M. Watt, Bitter Glory: Poland and its Fate, 1918-1939 (New York, 1979), p. 446-449; N. Davies, Heart of Europe: A Short History of Poland (Oxford, 1984), p. 74-75, 103-104.
14. Cit. in Ellis, Cassino, p. 470. When he was no longer in the army General Sosnkowski said that if he commanded the British 8th Army he would break up the Second Polish Corps into small units and disburse them through the allied forces, something Anders would never have permitted. His point was that if left as a single unit they might cease fighting before the war ended. NA IG 108425X.
15. Davies, Heart of Europe, p. 76, 95-96.
16. W. Anders, An Army in Exile, p. 221.
17. NA IG 108425X.
18. Macmillan, War Diaries, p. 522.
19. The text of the declaration is in Anders, p. 249-250; N. Davies, Heart of Europe, p. 79.
20. Anders, p. 250-251.
21. Ibid.
22. Macmillan, War Diaries, p. 696-697.
23. W. Anders, An Army in Exile, p. 252-254.
24. Graham, Bidwell, p. 383.
25. H. Macmillan, The Blast of War, 1939-1945 (New York, 1967), p. 573.
26. This number included 2319 killed, 9352 wounded, 528 missing in action, 3182 killed in car accidents and 1560 rendered incapable of service by emotional and psychological problems.
27. W. Anders, An Army in Exile, p. 152-153.
28. NA 6940 and 6905.
29. NA 6240.
30. Federal Register (1943), p. 342.
31. The policy of the Polish Government in London included accepting enlistments from suitable German citizens of ethnic Polish background. The British Foreign Office didn't agree with this policy and stated in a memo, "Persons possessing the nationality of a country with which the U.K. is at war will in no circumstances be recruited." The Polish Government objected to this statement and in fact continued to accept German citizens, HI MSZ, box 100.
32. NA 6905.

33. Some allied generals were reluctant to use soldiers who had served in the German Army because oftentimes they brought with them habits and ideas gained from years of German indoctrination. The charges of anti-Semitism in the Polish Army in Scotland were, in part, traceable to recruits from the German Army, FO 371/56468.
34. Times (London) (May 19,1945). The Times article stated that the Polish Army at Monte Cassino had two Brigades of Polish citizens who had served previously in the German Army. It seems that the article, which appeared a year after Monte Cassino, and only two weeks after Bologna, confused the two battles.
35. Interview with Henryk Jedwab, Rev. Cimala, Gasiewicz and Chairman of the Polish commandos veterans organization. Why were the Lithuanians attached to the Commandos? The best answer is that the Lithuanians needed training at the same time.

# CHAPTER SEVEN

# IN POLITICAL LIMBO

## The Withdrawal of Diplomatic Recognition from the Polish Government in London

While the Second Corps fought bravely against the Nazis in Italy, the Polish Government in London was fighting a losing battle against Soviet efforts to win Western recognition for the Communist puppet government in Poland. During the Yalta Conference, in February of 1945, Great Britain and the United States conceded to their Soviet ally that a new Polish Government should be formed on the basis of the existing pro-Soviet Government in Lublin, by adding to it "democratic" politicians from the London Government and from Poland. The composition of the government was supposed to be decided by negotiations between Polish politicians, designated by the ambassadors of the three Great Powers. Of course, the prospective candidates had to accept the decisions of the Great Powers concerning the new Polish-Soviet borders (so-called Curzon line), which legitimized incorporating the eastern half of the prewar Polish state, including the two major centers of Lvov and Vilnius, into the Soviet Union.

The only major Polish political figure in London prepared to accept this condition was Stanislaw Mikolajczyk, leader of the Polish Peasant Party and Prime Minister of the Polish Government since the death of General Sikorski, in July of 1943. In 1939, Mikolajczyk was mobilized as a private in the Polish Army and fought in the defense of Warsaw. When Poland fell, he fled to France and was given an administrative position in the exile government. After the Polish Government moved to London, he held, in succession, the posts of President of the National Council (a Parliament in Exile representing all major Polish parties), Minister of the Interior and Deputy Prime Minister. The day after Sikorski's death, he was named Prime Minister. He enjoyed a good standing with the British Government as they regarded him as a realist ready to follow a conciliatory policy towards the Soviet Union. For the same reason he was well regarded by the press, especially the leftist press.[1]

Although Mikolajczyk argued before the British Government that the Polish people deserved, as a reward for their suffering and fighting, to emerge from the war with their territory intact, he was one of the few Poles willing to accept the Curzon line.[2] He believed it worthwhile to try to reach an accommodation with Stalin and calculated that border concessions would make it possible to preserve national sovereignty. After two visits to Moscow, in July/August and in November of 1944, and under intense British pressure, he finally accepted the fact that the Polish Government in London had no choice but to agree to the Curzon line as the future border between Poland and the USSR. In November, 1944, when his government colleagues refused to follow his lead on this issue, he resigned as Prime Minister and withdrew the Peasant Party from the London Government.[3] In April of 1945, Mikolajczyk publicly declared his acceptance of the Yalta agreements, and in the middle of June, went to Moscow to negotiate with Stalin and the Polish Communists about the formation of the new Polish Government. Pinning his hopes on the free elections promised by the Yalta agreements, Mikolajczyk agreed to join the government of

"National Unity," even though the Communists and their allies claimed 80% of the positions. He was given the posts of Deputy Prime Minister and Minister of Agriculture but little or no real power and authority. From the beginning he found himself a puppet, manipulated by the Soviets.

It was particularly distasteful that Mikolajczyk was negotiating his place in the new Polish Government at the same time the Soviets were staging a show trial of sixteen leaders of the Polish anti-Nazi underground. The leaders put on trial included the head of the Home Army, General Okulicki (formerly Anders' Chief of Staff), the deputy Prime Minister of the Polish London Government, along with leaders of all major Polish political parties. All those put on trial were eminently qualified to be included in the Moscow negotiations on formation of the new Polish Government, since the Yalta agreements included a provision for participation of democratic leaders from Poland. In March of 1945, these leaders were invited to a meeting at a town near Warsaw by Soviet secret police passing as Red Army officers. They were then flown to Moscow, imprisoned in the NKVD's Lubianka prison and charged with carrying out subversive activities behind the Red Army lines. The Western Allies protested, but shamefully, they did not exert any real pressure on the Soviets to force them to release the arrested Polish leaders. Thirteen of them received prison sentences ranging from 10 years to six months (three died in Soviet prisons and one in a Polish prison), and three were released.[4]

Anders was quite skeptical about Mikolajczyk and his political abilities. The appointment of Mikolajczyk as Prime Minister of the London Government, in 1943, had not inspired his confidence and he "felt uneasy" about it[5] and was alarmed by Mikolajczyk's first trip to Moscow, in July of 1944. In his view "all the circumstances showed that there was little chance of a negotiated settlement but a considerable danger of an imposed decision."[6] He was particularly critical of the fact that Mikolajczyk had spoken with members of the pro-Soviet Lublin Government whom he regarded as "traitors to their country."[7] Anders got a chance to present his views to Mikolajczyk before the latter's second trip to Moscow, in October of 1944, speaking to him at the express order of President Raczkiewicz. Anders was critical of Mikolajczyk's compromise proposal to draw a demarcation line between Poland and the Soviet Union west of the prewar Polish-Soviet border but east of the Curzon line (which would leave Vilnius and Lvov on the Polish side). Anders told Mikolajczyk that "such a suggestion should never have been made by the Polish side," and insisted that it was Mikolajczyk's absolute duty to defend the integrity of Poland's prewar borders. He also confronted Mikolajczyk about his direct negotiations with members of the pro-Soviet Government.[8]

Anders believed that Mikolajczyk was naive and inexperienced and and that he was handicapped by not having any first-hand knowledge of Russia and Communism. In Anders' view, the policy of looking for a compromise with Stalin only helped Stalin mask his aggressive and imperialistic plans toward Poland, and helped the Western Allies cover up their appeasement policy towards the Soviet Union. Anders was also critical of Mikolajczyk's November resignation from the Cabinet. He believed that by this act Mikolajczyk had split the unanimous front the Polish politicians in exile had so far presented by rejecting the Teheran agreement between Stalin and the Western Allies over Poland's borders. According to Anders, by resigning Mikolajczyk "opened a way by which Britain and the United States could betray the lawful government of Poland and so carry out the agreement they had concluded with Russia at Teheran."[9]

After Yalta, Mikolajczyk announced that he was preparing to go to Moscow to participate in talks about constructing a new Polish Government dominated by Lublin Poles. Anders tried to persuade him to give up this mission arguing that Mikolajczyk's participation in the new government would be tantamount to consenting to a new partition of Poland and it would give the impression that what had happened at Yalta was done with the agreement of the Poles. To count on free elections as promised by the Yalta agreements was an illusion or self-deception, since the Soviets were experts on conducting fake elections. Anders believed, too, that Mikolajczyk's presence would encourage many Poles to reveal their anti-Communist sympathies and thus expose themselves to persecution by the Communists. Finally, Anders predicted that within three months of the elections Mikolajczyk would find himself in a prison cell,[10] a prediction that turned out to be almost totally accurate. In 1947, with massive coercion and outright falsifications, the Communists "won" the elections and Mikolajczyk saved himself from arrest and trial by clandestinely fleeing the country.

After Mikolajczyk and his supporters joined the Government of National Unity a quick response by the British and Americans gave it diplomatic recognition on July 5, 1945. This did not come as a surprise to anyone. The worst nightmares of Anders and other Polish leaders in London were realized. The effect on army morale was shattering: soldiers felt betrayed and that they had lost control over their lives.

Not all governments immediately followed the major powers in the transfer of recognition. Five years later the exile government was still recognized by the Vatican, Spain, Ireland, Libya, Cuba and some Latin American republics. The last to withdraw recognition was the Vatican, in 1963.

The first practical problem raised by the transfer of recognition for the Polish Armed Forces in the West was that of command. Warsaw, of course, would not accept General Bor-Komorowski as Commander-in-Chief nor General Kukiel as Minister of National Defense, even on an interim basis. At the same time it was absolutely out of the question for the Polish Armed Forces in the West to accept General Rola-Zymierski, a communist, as their Commander-in-Chief.

In August of 1945, the British, after a month of discussions with the Polish Government-in-Exile, stopped recognizing the authority of President Raczkiewicz and the Commander-in-Chief, Bor-Komorowski over the Polish Armed Forces in the West and subordinated the Forces to British command. They preserved, however, the Polish General Staff under its Chief, General Kopanski, and left it in charge of daily activities of the Polish Forces. Generals Bor and Kukiel encouraged the unit commanders to continue functioning on the same day to day basis and stressed the fact that the Polish Forces outside of Poland were under no obligation to follow military orders coming from Warsaw.[11]

In October of 1945, Warsaw sent a military mission to London headed by General Modelski (a former deputy Minister of National Defense in the London Government who had resigned because of his differences with Sosnkowski) to negotiate the transfer of control over the Polish Armed Forces with the British. General Karol Swierczewski, a Soviet officer of Polish origin, was Warsaw's designated commander of the Polish Armed Forces in the West. The Warsaw delegation wanted the British to press the exiles to accept Swierczewski. The British refused to go along with this demand.[12]

From the time of the recognition of the Warsaw Government (July, 1945) until the disbanding of the Polish Army (October, 1946) the British showed good judgment and maintained the status quo for the Polish military. They also decided to continue training programs for Anders' soldiers in order to keep the men busy.

The continuing existence of the London Government and Polish Armed Forces was a great annoyance to Communist authorities in Warsaw, which launched a torrent of complaints and protests. They accused the London Government of recruiting soldiers and engaging in underground activities detrimental to the Warsaw Government. A protest sent to Washington claimed that the "unrecognized" government continued to exist and to exercise command of the Polish armed forces in Britain and Western Europe. The American Ambassador to Poland, Arthur Bliss Lane, responded that these matters were between the British and Warsaw Governments and outside the responsibility of the United States because it no longer recognized the London Government.[13]

In 1946, Warsaw complained that British officers were accepting medals and were being decorated in the name of the President of the exiled government. The British reacted by instructing British officers that they could accept only those medals which had been awarded prior to the transfer of recognition and that award ceremonies must be done without publicity. This ended the matter.[14]

Ambassador Raczynski presided over the changes and the turning of the embassy and its various operations over to Warsaw. It was a department by department transition which, under the circumstances, went smoothly.

## Smuggling

After Yalta the soldiers of the Polish Second Corps saw themselves as oppressed and deserted. Not surprisingly, this resulted in a deep morale crisis. In June 1945, a British liaison officer in a report, described the Polish Army as "inwardly distinctly perturbed." The officers were trying to hide their depression from the soldiers who still blindly believed that something good would occur, although they were desperate, depressed and fearful of the future.[15] Although the report doesn't mention smuggling, it is clear that such a psychological state provided fertile ground for all kinds of illegal activities and abandonment of ideological principles.

The most widespread form of illegal behavior was the smuggling of gold coins (called by the Poles "chestnuts" because they were decorated with an engraving of St. George's horse), which became something of a common practice among the Corps personnel. Sometimes hundreds of coins at a time were involved and brought big profits. One Polish officer was engaged in a transaction that involved 400 coins. In December of 1948, a Polish diplomat emigrating to Argentina with a group of Second Corps soldiers was found to have 750 sovereigns valued at 5,000 pounds sterling, an enormous amount of money at that time. Anders' aide-de-camp recalled that a Polish Colonel in Ancona claimed he was robbed of more than 400 coins by Polish soldiers. The Polish Military Police recovered 420 coins. The Colonel was not disciplined and if he had been criticized, it would have been for not giving a reward to the Military Policemen and not for dealing in coins.[16] General Rudnicki admitted freely in an interview that he had been engaged in the smuggling of gold coins and claimed his actions had not violated any law.[17]

According to an OSS report of April, 1945, the officers and women of the Second Polish Corps "have been engaged for some time in the smuggling of gold from Palestine and Egypt to Italy."[18] One veteran asserted that the smuggling began in Palestine and was virtually universal - "everyone was doing it."[19] It seems that it blossomed only after Yalta, when the Polish soldiers knew they weren't going home after the war. Since the bases and training centers of the Second Corps were in Palestine and Egypt there was a constant movement of Polish officers and soldiers between Italy and the Middle East, providing many opportunities to transport gold. Apparently the Polish Air Force was also involved in smuggling, and one interviewee remembered an incident in which gold coins had spilled out from a suitcase, inadvertently dropped by an air force officer.[20]

The principle of the operation was very simple. Gold was bought in Palestine or Egypt and sold in Italy. In Palestine or Egypt the price of a gold sovereign was about 5 pounds sterling, while in Italy it was about 9000 Italian lira, i.e. about 22 pounds. The Italians were eager to purchase gold coins for liras and the Soldiers were in a privileged position. Unlike the Italians, they could exchange liras for hard currency (pounds) by buying treasury notes or British postal money orders and they had access to transportation between Italy and the Middle East. When the British ultimately became aware that some members of the military were exchanging large amounts of foreign currency via British postal money orders they established a ceiling on the amount an individual could convert to pounds using postal money orders. This made the soldiers switch to selling Italian lira on the black market in the Middle East. Although the value of the lira was falling daily, there was a market for it in Palestine and Egypt. It was bought by Yugoslav refugees repatriated from the Middle East to Yugoslavia and by American and British soldiers bound for Italy. The British were clearly the losers in this operation as they were accepting Italian lira in return for British pounds.

There are conflicting reports about General Anders' role in the smuggling. One soldier, who admitted smuggling himself, asserted that "of course" Anders was involved in it. Another veteran said he had heard that Anders was behind the gold smuggling scheme and that he even had an airplane he used for this purpose. He admitted, however, that this was mere hearsay, although General Rudnicki claimed that Anders was involved.[21]

Nothing has ever been found to suggest that Anders was in any way involved in the smuggling, and after studying the man, whatever his failings, it is highly unlikely that he personally participated in or benefited from any smuggling operation. On the contrary, the evidence suggests that Anders was not involved and even tried to prevent it. First, there is testimony that he punished two officers who were very close to him, when he discovered that they were involved in petty smuggling. Lt. Stronski, a member of Anders' personal staff was confined to his quarters when his dealings became known to Anders and Romanowski was punished for a deal involving only four coins.[22] On October 14, 1945, Anders issued a direct order that all Poles coming to Italy were to be searched, regardless of rank, and that all gold found on them was to be confiscated. Anders said he understood the soldiers motives but the smuggling was violating British regulations and the Polish Army's situation with the British was very delicate. The next day a ship arriving at Taranto was searched and of the 346 Polish passengers, 103 were found to possess gold which was then confiscated.[23] In February 1946, the soldiers were given back the gold that had been confiscated from them and were encouraged to contribute it charity.[24]

Anders himself may not have been involved in the smuggling, but it is possible that a gold coin scheme was operating inside his headquarters. A doctor who had served with Anders claimed that Anders' Chief of Staff, "was behind the entire operation." Another interviewee reported that one of the General's aides, Captain Lubomirski, operated the scheme.[25]

The smuggling wasn't limited to gold. Some Poles were caught smuggling hashish and precious stones from the Middle East to Italy, but this was on a much smaller scale than the gold smuggling. Some less serious smuggling of items bought in army stores took place as well as black market dealings in cigarettes and nylon stockings. Poles also engaged in smuggling olive oil from the south to the North of Italy. Most of the olive oil was sold at a profit but a small quantity was kept by the soldiers to improve their meals. The smuggling of oil was illegal and some Poles were arrested for it by the British. There was also some smuggling of gasoline. Transportation between the north and the South of Italy was very poor but the Polish Army had trucks going both ways so some soldiers took advantage of the situation. Smuggling was not confined to the Polish Army, it was wide spread among all Allied forces.

Obviously not all Polish soldiers engaged in smuggling and some felt it disgraced the Polish Army. Alexander Blum wrote an article against smuggling, reminding everyone that the Polish Army was in the Mediterranean to deal in steel (bullets) and not gold. The article appeared in the monthly publication of the 5th

Division. He remembered being congratulated on the article by a high ranking officer. Ironically, he later found out that this officer was himself involved in serious smuggling.[26]

## Polish – Jewish Cooperation After the War

One of the most closely guarded secrets of Anders' Army was its cooperation with Zionist organizations after the war. The army helped the Zionists by smuggling Jews from the Italian-Austrian border to Italian ports. In return the Jewish organizations helped Anders by smuggling the families of his soldiers from Poland to Italy. The operation demanded strict secrecy because it ran directly contrary to the British policy of preventing the immigration of Jews into Palestine and contrary to the Warsaw Government's policy to control emigration of ethnic Poles from Poland. Even at this late date the officials of the Polish Government in Exile refused access to the relevant documents. The situation was discussed with Mr. Kazimierz Sabbat, President of the Polish Government in Exile, who promised to provide documentary proof with details from the archives of the Polish Government-in-Exile, but failed to do so. Apparently, the decision to reveal the records about Polish-Jewish cooperation was voted down by the National Council.[27] Nevertheless, it was possible to piece together parts of the story of this operation from interviews and available documents.

At a second meeting Mr.Sabbat did not discuss or produce any documents but asked his wife to join us and tell her story. Mrs. Sabbat was the daughter of general Sulik, who commanded the 5th Kresowa Division. She recalled being smuggled out of Poland with her sister and brother on a train carrying Jewish emigres, and to her knowledge, the three children were the only gentiles among the 800 passengers on the train. The children were taught some Yiddish phrases and told not to do or say anything that would identify them as non- Jews. At the Italian border everyone else got off the train and boarded canvas covered trucks driven by personnel in Polish uniforms. A car was waiting for the three Suilik children and one of the drivers was a Polish-Jewish sergeant whom she later recognized as being in the division commanded by her father.[28]

Mrs. Sabbat based her contention that the three children were the only gentiles on the train on the fact that they were the only ones who were separated from the group at the border. Mrs. Sabbat said the passengers on the train talked about going to Palestine and she recalled that there were no old people and few very young people, on the train. She didn't recall anything more except that the people on the train kept referring to "Operation Josef," which she assumed was the name of the Jewish leader.

No one interviewed claimed to have driven or had known anyone who had driven these or similar trucks under these circumstances. A Jewish officer from the Second Corps, when interviewed said he knew about the transport of Jewish refugees in Polish Army trucks across Italy, although he did not participate in the endeavor as the army did not involve Jewish soldiers in these operations.This is inconsistent with the statement by Mrs. Sabbat.

In separate interviews, three Jewish ex-soldiers said they had definitely seen canvas-covered trucks carrying people who were speaking Yiddish. This officer reported that he saw at least 20 lorries driven by Polish women taking Jews to Padua in Northern Italy.[29]

Apparently Mr.Sabbat under estimated the amount of opposition he would encounter in the National Council towards providing the promised documentation. At a chance meeting with Zbigniew Scholtz, a member of the National Council, he confided that he was one of the minority who supported Mr.Sabbat suggestion that these documents be given to me. Unfortunately Mr. Sabbat and Mr. Scholtz died before an additional meeting could be arranged. At a reception for the new President, another member of the National Council whispered that he was aware of Sabbat's promise and said there were others who wanted to give me the documents. No documents were ever received from this source.

In 1945, when tens of thousands of Jews were attempting to leave Poland (mostly for Palestine), the Warsaw Government allowed Zionist organizations to conduct Jewish emigration from Poland at the same time it barred ethnic Poles from leaving the country. The Polish Corps in Italy was trying desperately to get the families of its officers and soldiers out of Communist controlled Poland. Zionist groups which had organized the transport of Jews to Palestine were in a position to help the Corps by hiding Poles among Jewish refugees and bringing them by train to the Austro-Italian border. The Second Corps would then provide trucks to ferry Jewish refugees from the Austrian border to the Italian ports. When the Polish Military Mission in Pilzen was closed, in December of 1945, the Corps relied on "the Jewish Channels" to get the families out of Poland.[30]

The British Ambassador to Warsaw suggested to the Foreign Office that an agreement between Warsaw and the Jews may come in being. His suspicion was justified. A month before his report, on July 30, 2946, a secret agreement was signed between the Warsaw Government and a Jewish group, whereby, Warsaw would not interfere with Zionist efforts to get Jews from Poland to Palestine but the Jews had to provide assurances that no non-Jews would be included. The British were well aware of the cooperation between the Warsaw Government and the Zionists, if not of the agreement itself. The Western borders of Poland were open to the Zionists until February, 1947, when the secret agreement was revoked.[31]

Warsaw officially opposed allowing Polish families who wanted to join Anders to leave the country, but it is possible that they acquiesced at the time of their departure. This possibility is suggested by the large number of families who were able to get to Italy. The British Ambassador told the Foreign Office that the Jews are getting out of Poland and so are "the Polish nobility."

Communist agents undoubtedly were infiltrating the refugee trains and carrying on all kinds of intrigue. For example a name was given to me of a Polish officer known to be helping Jews, but in a letter from the British Embassy in Rome the individual is described as "working for us."[32]

The most important document in my possession on this subject is a copy of a duty memorandum by a Major Rudnicki, dated August 1, 1946, provided by a person insisting on anonymity. The duty memorandum states that there was an arrangement whereby Jewish organizations were to transport Poles from Poland. On the Polish side the operation was run by a man named Captain Orzechowski. Rudnicki complained to him that no Poles were brought out, although the necessary fees had been paid. In addition, eleven families were to be brought out of Poland free of charge, in exchange for transporting 80 Jews from Austria to Italy by the Corps. A truck with two NCOs and a reserve of gasoline was already waiting in Innsbruck. Rudnicki further reported that the Jews stopped smuggling Poles out of Poland as a reaction to the killing of Jews in an anti-Semitic demonstration (almost certainly a reference to the pogrom in Kielce,[33] which took place on July 6, 1946). He suggested that any further help to the Jewish refugees should be suspended at least until the arrival of the first group of Polish families.

Information in Rudnicki's duty memorandum is confirmed by a series of telegrams exchanged by a Polish Military Mission in Brenner (Austria) and the Social Division of the Second Polish Corps between June 24, and October 21, 1946. The telegrams confirmed the successful transport of the first group of Jewish refugees. They also make it clear that the head of Corps intelligence had followed Rudnicki's suggestion of ordering the suspension of further operations on August 6. However the telegrams sent between August 12 and September 31 referred to the arrival of Polish families in Jewish refugee transports, so it can be assumed that after a temporary hitch in the beginning of August, the operation was soon resumed. We know that the

Jews kept their part of the bargain. A list of names of the people to be brought out of Poland was attached to Rudnicki's report. Included on the list were the three Sulik children.[34]

Lubienski was the only Polish officer to state unequivocally that the Polish Army provided trucks to assist Jews in getting out of Europe. He said only a "handful" of Polish officers were involved, including officers from General Anders' headquarters and the Intelligence Bureau.

There are indications that the Second Polish Corps either turned a blind eye, or even facilitated the transportation of its Jewish soldiers to Palestine and Egypt. Again, this was a breach of British imposed regulations prohibiting the Second Corps from demobilizing Jews in Palestine. Jewish soldiers were transferred to Egypt where they could be demobilized and from there could easily make it to Palestine on their own. Every soldier in Anders' Army in Italy had access to transportation to return to Palestine. The Corps issued leaves to Jewish soldiers, probably knowing that they would not return. The Jewish soldiers who wanted to leave the army and go to Palestine had a choice, they could go to Palestine and desert or they could go to Egypt, be discharged and then make their way to Palestine. Moreover, Anders officially arranged for 300 Jewish soldiers to go to Palestine after the war.[35]

The reluctance of the Poles to produce documents showing Polish-Jewish cooperation, was probably caused by their unwillingness to admit that they had acted against the British in 1945 and 1946; the reluctance on the Jewish side is harder to explain. One reason could be an unwillingness to admit that there was cooperation with Poles at a time when Jews were murdered by Poles at Kielce and elsewhere. There could also be some reluctance to share the credit for what was a successful effort to get Jews to the ports from which they could board ships heading for Israel.

The respected historian Yehuda Bauer was consulted and he referred to the operation as being "low level and broken off quickly." Also consulted was Isser Herell, head of Israeli intelligence at that time who denied any knowledge of Polish-Jewish cooperation but commented that there were many rescue operations carried on at this time and it could have occurred without his knowledge.

There is another remote possibility. In Rudnicki's memorandum there is mention of money changing hands, which always offers the chance of profiteering. No evidence of this was found and its unlikely that this wouldn't have been disclosed by now if it existed.

## What to do with the Second Polish Corps?

The British considered various options of what to do with the Polish Forces. In February, 1945, Churchill told Anders that Polish troops had "an obvious place" in the occupation of Germany and in this situation would be willing to permit British weapon reserves to be used for an expansion of the Polish Army.[36]

In April, 1945, Churchill seemed responsive to the possibility of creating a British Foreign Legion but adopted a wait and see attitude towards the problem of what to do with Anders' Army and suggested waiting until the following month to see "how things develop."[37] Another possibility was to use the Poles as an occupation force in Germany. The Supreme Allied Headquarters wanted to utilize Polish manpower for so-called "Lines of Communications Battalions" and guard companies for German POWs.[38] Under the Protocols of the Occupation Agreement signed by Great Britain, the United States and France, it was possible for a party to the Agreement to use the army of another allied power to supply forces for their occupation zone. The sole criteria was that the other power must have been engaged in military operations against Germany. Of course Anders' forces easily met that test. In the spring of 1945, this possibility was still being seriously considered.

Similar suggestions came from the Polish side. Three months before the Allies recognized the new Government of National Unity in Warsaw, Anders, in anticipation of the transfer of recognition, prepared a lengthy memorandum in which he laid out principles for the treatment of the Polish Armed Forces by the Allies. First of all, the army was to remain loyal to the President of the Polish Government in London and was to be kept independent from the Warsaw Government and all Polish land forces would be combined together under one command. The size of the Polish Army would be augmented by recruitment from Displaced Persons and Prisoner of War camps. The troops would be used as an occupation force in Germany. Members of soldiers' families still in Poland were to be protected from persecution and allowed to leave the country. According to Anders' plan the British were to announce how they would deal with the problem of the Polish Army in the West, after its refusal to accept the authority of the Warsaw Government.

Anders' plan was supported by the British War Office which was eager to use Polish troops for internal security and administrative units on the continent. When conveying its opinion to the Foreign Office, the War Office stressed the immediate need for Polish soldiers as security guards, especially since the French Government refused to provide manpower for such duties.[39]

The War Office's motives were twofold. First, it wanted to get large numbers of British soldiers home as quickly as possible. The second reason, which was not put down on paper, was that the British Forces had sympathy for the Polish Forces which had fought at their side. The British soldiers were far more sympathetic to the Poles than were the British diplomats. Although Anders and the War Office were in agreement they turned out to be powerless in the face of the British Government's decision to transfer recognition to the Polish Government in Warsaw.

In the end, British reaction to Anders' proposals was negative. London feared that implementing them would only strengthen Anders' position which would make him more difficult for them and the Americans to deal with in the future. They commented that using Poles for the occupation of Germany would be tantamount to admitting that the Allies could not meet their obligations and had resorted to hiring foreign mercenaries.

The British rejected the idea of using Anders' troops for occupation duties because they became concerned that the Poles, with their "unrivaled talent for intrigue and propaganda against the Russians, could use their occupation position to get support for the rearmament of Germany against the Soviet Union." They also feared that using Anders' soldiers in Germany would antagonize the Soviets. Although they did not expect a major confrontation over the issue, they thought it might create problems with the Russians on day to day occupation matters. Anticipating a decision against using Poles for the occupation of Germany, the Foreign Office wanted to limit the growth of the Polish Army, and keep it as small as possible. Furthermore it planned to reduce Anders' influence, to withhold any supplies of additional arms and to refrain from concentrating Polish Forces in one area (as had been suggested by Anders).[40]

Strangely enough, we know that Foreign Office doubts were supported by Mikolajczyk as we know he wrote to the Foreign Office that he was opposed to the Polish Corps under Anders participating in the occupation of Germany. He argued that the Polish soldiers were so indoctrinated by Anders that they would provoke trouble between the British and the Soviets. Mikolajczyk was quoted as saying that "there was a possibility of the Poles and Germans forming some sort of bond against the Soviets." This notion was dismissed by Churchill as "silly."[41] Nevertheless, the possibility of employing the Corps in Germany was ruled out which meant the end of the Second Polish Corps.

In spite of the uncertain political prospects and the British refusal to employ Polish soldiers for occupation duties after the war, the Corps continued to recruit new soldiers even after hostilities in Europe had officially ended. With Poles having been liberated from POW and forced labor camps in Germany there was no shortage of recruits willing to enlist. Many officers were among the liberated military personnel so there were plenty of officers. In less than three months, taking advantage of the available manpower, Anders nearly doubled the size of his Corps, which grew from 56,000 in May to 111,000 at the end of July.[42]

The British delayed reacting to the expansion of the Corps. On July 13 Field Marshal Alexander had a meeting with Anders and warned him that "it would be most unwise to strengthen the establishment of the Corps" as this "would result in much friction and trouble." Alexander denied Anders' request to transfer 12,000 Poles from camps in France to Italy. He agreed, however, that some of them might be included in the Corps but only as replacements for soldiers of the Corps wanting to return to Poland immediately. On July 17th the British decided to impose a formal ban on any further expansion of the Second Corps and notified Anders of the decision on July 22nd.

Anders disregarded this order and continued the buildup. He expanded the 2nd Armored Brigade into an Armored Division and organized an additional armored brigade (the 14th). When, on September 17th, Alexander gave him a direct order to reduce the establishment of the Corps to 85,000, Anders resorted to subterfuge similar to that he had used while forming the Polish Army in the USSR. He cut the pay and food rations of the 85,000 soldiers, for whom he was getting supplies and funds from the British, in order to provide pay and rations to the "surplus" soldiers who officially did not exist.

In spite of constant British pressure and orders from Anders barring any further recruitment from Displaced

Persons Camps, in November of 1945, the Corps numbered 120,000 officers and soldiers.[43] Anders explained to Alexander that he thought soldiers choosing repatriation should not be counted against the ceiling set by the British and that he had continued to recruit on the assumption that the number of soldiers seeking repatriation would reach 15,000-20,000. The British told Anders that the "surplus" could be reduced only by discharging soldiers from service because the Poles choosing repatriation were merely reducing the quota. On January 19, 1946, the real strength of the Corps was still almost at 110,000 soldiers, well above the 85,000 allowed.[44]

Although Anders denied that he was increasing his army in violation of his agreement to accept the limits imposed by the British, at least one American was under the impression that the army was in fact being illegally expanded. A note to Anders from U.S. Headquarters in the Mediterranean stated: "Surely you know, dear friend, how we feel towards you and your gallant Corps, including those who belong although not enrolled."[45]

**Repatriation**

Recognition of the Warsaw Government by the Western Allies brought the issue of a possible repatriation of the Polish Armed Forces in the West to Poland to the fore. The basic policy of Great Britain and the United States was that displaced persons, former POWs, concentration camp survivors and demobilized soldiers should return to their country of origin.[46] Neither the British nor the Americans wanted their countries inundated with emigres. The Polish Armed Forces were under British jurisdiction and the British Government would have liked the Polish soldiers to return to Poland as postwar Britain was exhausted by the war and was suffering from serious economic difficulties. Polish soldiers who did not repatriate were viewed as an additional burden. Nevertheless, after meeting Anders on February 21, 1945, Churchill told his War Cabinet that "if in the last resort all else failed and Polish troops in Western Europe, or elements of them, felt that they could not return to Poland under the conditions, they should have the right to become the citizens of the British Empire and to receive the treatment accorded to the British soldiers who had rendered equal service." The War Cabinet approved this statement, and the postwar Labor Government of Clement Attlee kept the promise.[47] Still, it remained in the British interest to get rid of the Polish Army as quickly as possible at the lowest possible cost. The British looked in every direction for countries which could help to absorb the Poles. France, Belgium and the Netherlands were willing to take some Polish manpower, especially those willing to work in the coal mines. Canada accepted some, and efforts were made to influence other British Commonwealth countries to take a share, but the overwhelming majority stayed in the U.K.

While the British wanted to scatter the Poles all over the globe, Anders expressed the opposite view. He wanted to keep his Force intact, or at least in one area, so the army could be recalled rapidly should that become necessary. On July 9, 1946, Anders stated in an interview: "There is, of course, the danger of the Poles being dispersed. This would affect our work adversely, and we shall therefore do all we can in order to prevent it."[48]

The Warsaw Government pretended that it wanted an immediate repatriation of all soldiers who had served in the West and stated initially that it wanted the Polish Army to be repatriated as a military unit.[49] Marshal Rola-Zymierski, Commander-in Chief of the Armed Forces of the Warsaw Government, declared that he would welcome the return of the entire Second Corps with all its officers, including Anders. Rola-Zymierski claimed he needed officers because the Soviets had told him they were withdrawing all the officers they had "loaned" to the Warsaw Government.[50] On August 2, 1945, Warsaw issued a decree promising the veterans of the Polish Armed Forces in the West equal treatment with soldiers of the Polish Army organized by Berling in the USSR. It stipulated that returning soldiers would have their rank, length of service and decorations recognized and that allowances and pensions would be granted to soldiers crippled by the war. It also held out the promise of land grants, free travel to the place of their choosing and a possibility of employment in the army for career officers. Moreover, returning soldiers would be allowed to bring their personal belongings into the country duty free and to open hard currency accounts in Polish banks. Polish citizenship would be granted automatically to the soldiers of Polish and Jewish nationality who had come from the territories east of the Curzon line.[51]

During technical negotiations held with the British, in the fall of 1945, it turned out that Warsaw wanted to repatriate only a limited number of technical personal immediately and leave the repatriation of others for later discussions.[52] The assessment of Western diplomats and Mikolajczyjk was that the Warsaw Government was paying lip service to the idea of repatriation, but in fact did not want the Polish Army in the West to return. Mikolajczyk told the American Ambassador to Warsaw, Arthur Lane, that the government regarded the soldiers of the Polish military formations in the West as hostile and feared they might contribute to its defeat in the coming elections. Lane heard General Rola-Zymierski state that soldiers wishing to return to Poland from Italy would return on his, and not on Anders' terms. Lane reached a conclusion that the Warsaw Government didn't want these soldiers back, neither before nor after the election.[53]

In order to "encourage" repatriation the Warsaw Government set up, a "Military Information Bureau of the Polish Citizens Council" in London. The British approved of the Bureau's objectives, but were unhappy about some of its tactics. The Bureau told the soldiers not to accept orders from their officers and initially advised them not to sign any declaration of intent to return to Poland, except in the presence of a Polish officer from Warsaw. Later on, soldiers were advised to volunteer for repatriation by sending their names to the Polish Citizens Council with a statement that their officers had refused to add their names to the lists of those seeking repatriation.[54]

It wasn't long before a heated propaganda war between the Polish Governments in London and Warsaw began over the question of repatriation with each side complaining that its supporters were ill treated by the other side. Anders was accused of intimidating soldiers who were considering repatriation. For example, a Polish Army magazine published photos which supposedly showed returning soldiers being hung by Warsaw's executioner. The Warsaw Government News Agency called the photos a forgery saying they depicted collaborators who had worked for the Germans during the occupation.[55] The government, in turn, published claims by repatriated Poles that the command of the Second Polish Corps had persecuted them and threatened to charge them with breach of military discipline.[56]

In December, 1945, the British Ambassador in Warsaw reported, on the basis of testimonies received that the soldiers in Italy who had chosen to repatriate, had been abused and suffered at the hands of officers of the Second Polish Corps.[57]

In Italy, the Polish Embassy in Rome became the main center for pro-repatriation activities. These activities were orchestrated by the Polish military attache, Colonel Sidor, who proclaimed himself to be the head of the Polish Mission for Repatriation. The British authorities, however, refused to recognize the existence of the Mission. The War Office was advised that no reference was to be made to Colonel Sidor as head of any mission.[58] Sidor began a propaganda campaign against the Second Polish Corps, which the British Embassy described as replete with "definite falsehoods." He claimed, for example, that soldiers who had requested repatriation had immediately been sent to prison or "disappeared." Sidor's activities were so blatant that eventually the British Ambassador in Rome asked the Foreign Office to demand his withdrawal. The

Foreign Office demurred as some officials felt that Sidor's accusations were not necessarily false.[59] Indeed, the accusations were sometimes repeated by the British press. As an example the "Manchester Guardian" wrote that Anders was bullying his soldiers into refusing repatriation and argued that the British authorities should listen to Warsaw's version of the story.[60]

In Italy, by a paradoxical twist of fate, Anders had to face his old nemesis from Russia, Professor Stanislaw Kot. The old enemies met again in circumstances resembling those under which they had met for the first time, in 1942, in Russia. Anders was again commanding Polish troops on foreign soil, while Kot was the Polish Government's ambassador to the host country. This time though they represented two different governments hostile to each other. Kot, who was a member of Mikolajczyk's Peasant Party, recognized the new Communist-dominated government of "National Unity" and returned to Poland with Mikolajczyk. Kot believed that a compromise with the Communists was possible and that the "National Unity" government would gradually move towards democracy. He joined the diplomatic service of the Soviet dominated Warsaw regime, and was sent to Rome as ambassador to the Italian Government. Anders regarded Kot as a traitor to the national cause.

In Italy, Kot resumed his struggle against Anders, this time on behalf of the pro-Communist Polish Government. The conflict between Professor and General went beyond pure politics and became something of a personal struggle between two patriotic Poles. According to the British ambassador to Rome, Kot thought that Anders was "a poor mutt of a cavalry officer with two or three old politicians and newspapermen around him who lead him by the nose," while Anders regarded Kot to be "a crooked politician who changes his cloth to fit his circumstances." Anders also accused Kot "of having done his best NOT to save the Poles who were in Russia."[61]

Kot made no secret of his hatred of Anders and complained about him to anyone who would listen. In January, 1946, he circulated a document containing a direct attack on Anders which was intended to encourage Anders' soldiers to repatriate to Poland. In the document he accused Anders of disloyalty to Sikorski and the Sikorski-led government as well as inciting negativism towards the Soviet Union (as if the soldiers needed any encouragement on that score).[62] In March of 1946, Kot told the British ambassador to Poland that he was pursuing a personal vendetta against Anders and that the break up of the Second Polish Corps was the primary objective of his mission in Rome.[63] In February of 1946, the British ambassador reported from Rome that "M. Kot is untiring in his efforts to enlist sympathy for the anti-Anders campaign." The ambassador concluded that Kot "distills venom" and "misses no opportunity which might serve him to complain of the activities of the Second Polish Corps."[64]

In response, some members of Kot's staff in Rome were beaten up by Anders' soldiers. Reacting to Kot's complaint about this incident, the British Ambassador attached a censor to Anders' press office and also advised Kot not to provoke Anders and his soldiers by referring to them as "mercenaries."[65] He reported to London that if the lies coming from Kot's military attache Colonel Sidor didn't stop, "Kot will have himself to blame if soldiers of the Second Corps beat him up as well as members of his staff."[66] Trouble fomented by Kot in Italy won him few friends. When, in late 1946, he was recalled to Warsaw a British diplomatic report observed that "few of the Allied authorities here were sorry to see the professor out of Italy and many hoped he never would come back."[67] Ironically, Kot soon got disillusioned with the new regime in Poland and defected to the West where he denounced his former Warsaw employers in terms very similar to those used by Anders.[68] Kot's defection did not lead to reconciliation with Anders. The General continued to believe that Kot's defection did not cancel out his earlier treasonous collaboration with the Communist authorities.

Accusations against Anders also came directly from Warsaw. General Rola-Zymierski called Anders a dictator who would arrest anyone who disagreed with him and accused him of fomenting armed resistance against the Warsaw Government and of trying to undermine discipline in the Polish Army. Innocent people were being arrested by the Communist authorities in Poland on the suspicion that they had cooperated with Anders and he blamed Anders for their suffering. The Communist General also criticized the British for not relieving Anders of his command and falsely claimed that they were permitting him to send Polish troops to Palestine to fight against Jews.[69] Warsaw even accused the Second Corps' command of a systematic program of murdering the leaders who recommended repatriation. They alleged the death of General Kazimierz Radzwillowicz in a Polish Army hospital in Palestine was a case of murder, even though both a British medical doctor and a Warsaw representative concluded there was no foul play. There were deaths as well, which Warsaw claimed were due to murder, even after British medical experts had established that death was due to natural causes.[70]

British Foreign Secretary Ernest Bevin was also attacked for allegedly permitting Anders and other representatives of the London Government to intimidate soldiers opting for repatriation. Bevin defended himself by pointing to Anders' assurances that pressure would not be put on the soldiers to prevent them from going back to Poland.[71] At the Potsdam Conference, in July, 1945, Zygmunt Modzelewski, Deputy Minister of Foreign Affairs in the Warsaw Government, expressed to Bevin their dissatisfaction with the way General Anders was handling the repatriation issue and criticized his treatment of soldiers who had chosen to repatriate. He claimed that soldiers wanting to repatriate were being arrested and that this prevented others from openly declaring their wish to return, and thus forcing them to desert. He requested that the Warsaw Government be allowed to take control over all Polish Forces.[72] It is doubtful that anyone, including Modzelewski, expected the British to agree to that. One can easily imagine what the reaction of the Second Corps soldiers would be, had they been put under the authority of the Warsaw Government.

Anders was not against a small number of soldiers making a quick decision in favor of repatriation, figuring that the noisy and aggressive trouble makers would be the first to go and he was happy to get rid of them. Nevertheless he issued an order stating that any soldier who wanted to return to Poland would have to submit a written request and discuss his decision with an officer. Those who opted for repatriation were immediately separated and transferred to a special camp under British authority.

The British were worried about potential disciplinary problems in this sort of camp but eventually agreed to set one up in Cervinara which had the same amenities as the other Polish Army camps. Even though the representative from Warsaw was satisfied with conditions in the camp they did not stop complaining that the soldiers in the camp were subjected to severe discipline.

On September 21, 1945, at British request, a plebiscite was conducted in all units of the Second Corps. Soldiers wanting to return to Poland as soon as possible were instructed to tell their commanders of their decision and were assured that if they did not choose repatriation now, it would be possible to do so at a later date. By mid-January, 1946, 14,500 soldiers registered at the Cervinaria camp for immediate return to Poland. About 12,000 of them had been repatriated already, in 1945, due to an agreement signed on November 14, 1945, by the Inter-Allied Control Commission in Vienna and the Polish Repatriation Mission. Most of them had served in the German Army, before being inducted into the Second Corps.[73] For soldiers who had elected repatriation while stationed in the Middle East a special camp had been set up at Suez, Egypt. By the end of December, 1945, 500 Poles were in this camp.[74] Although Anders stated publicly that each soldier must make his own decision about repatriation, he became angry when whole groups would decide to return. He was particularly upset when 60% of a unit which had been part of the Independent Carpathian Brigade, chose repatriation. The high percentage may be explained by the fact that the soldiers in this unit had not been prisoners in the USSR and had never experienced the suffering that was common place for those who had come from the USSR with Anders. Among the 14,000 who opted for repatriation there were only 310 soldiers who had participated in the Italian campaign and very few who had come with Anders from the Soviet Union.[75]

Repatriation did not come about without problems. Seven soldiers (including one officer) who had been repatriated in November-December, 1945, showed up again at a repatriation camp in Italy, in January of 1946. No one was sure of their status since they didn't fall into any definable category. They were no longer soldiers and Anders refused to admit them back into the army. Colonel Sidor, the Polish military attache in Rome, accused the seven men of being collaborators and members of the Gestapo or the SS. The British authorities knew the allegations were false but nevertheless washed their hands of them, deciding that since they were civilian their fate should be decided by the Italian and Warsaw Governments.[76]

The British Ambassador to Poland recommended to the Foreign Office that Polish soldiers with Scottish or British wives should be encouraged against seeking repatriation. In his opinion, in three months or less of living in Poland the women would be seeking assistance in getting back to the U.K. His prediction proved accurate.[77]

## The End of the Second Polish Corps

After realizing the British would not allow the Polish Armed Forces in the West to be subordinated to its authority, the Warsaw Government declared on February 17, 1946, that it would not recognize these Forces as a part of the Polish Army of Poland. Warsaw demanded that the British Government dissolve all Polish units and forbade use of

Polish state symbols, military ranks and insignia. After that declaration repatriation of the Polish Armed Forces as military units was no longer possible. The British authorities now had no choice but to demobilize the Second Corps.

In March of 1946, Anders was suddenly summoned to London to meet with Prime Minister Clement Attlee at 10 Downing Street. The General could anticipate the reason for this invitation. Rumors of all kinds had been circulating for some time and Anders knew the news wouldn't be good. It had been 10 months since the war in Europe had ended and the Polish Army was still waiting for further orders. Inactivity wasn't healthy for Anders' soldiers as they were ridden with anxiety over their uncertain future. By now anxiety had reached such a point that the soldiers felt that bad news would be better than no news. From his five years of experience of meeting with British officials, Anders knew he had not been invited to discuss issues, but to be informed about British decisions.

Attlee informed Anders of two simple but crucial decisions. The Polish Army must leave Italy and it must be disbanded. One of the previously considered alternatives, transforming Anders Army into a British Foreign Legion, was now out of the question. Anders accepted the inevitable a asking only that Attlee delay announcing the decisions until he could get back to Italy and give advanced warning to his soldiers and officers. The "good news" was that Attlee promised that Anders' soldiers would not be forcibly repatriated to Poland. The British kept this promise. Anders was also relieved to learn that he would be left in command of the Corps until its end. Before coming to London he had been apprehensive of being deprived of his command and of not being allowed to return to Italy. He knew that such a scenario had been considered by the British and was pleased they had decided not to force him into retirement.[78]

On March 20, five days after the Anders-Attlee meeting in London, the British Foreign Secretary, Ernest Bevin, delivered a message to "All members of the Polish Forces under British command" informing them that the Polish Army was to be moved to Great Britain and disbanded. A Polish Resettlement Corps was to be created to take care of former Polish soldiers and help them in the transition to the civilian life.[79]

The announcement of the dissolution of the Second Polish Corps was met with sympathy by most of the press. The Daily Telegraph wrote about a "sad event" and exhorted civilians to help Polish exiles whenever possible. The Economist called Bevin's plan "fair and reasonable," and the News Chronicle agreed, saying it "sounds like a good practical compromise." The two leading newspaper in Scotland, The Scotsman and The Glasgow Herald, were sympathetic and complimented the Poles. Less sympathetic was The London Times, which stressed that by doing their quota of hard and useful work the Poles could "pass through the ambiguous period of the Resettlement Corps and eventually take their place as ordinary members of the community." The Times pointed out that Britain wasn't the only country the Poles "helped to victory," thus suggesting that other countries weren't sharing the burden of helping the exiled Poles. The Manchester Guardian complimented and criticized the Poles at the same time. It called Polish soldiers decent and brave but, "if some of them bear a grudge against the Soviet Union the fault is not necessarily on one side."[80]

On June 15, 1946, Anders acknowledged that the end of the Second Polish Corps was near. In his final order to his soldiers he did not hide his bitterness about the decision to dissolve the Corps and promised: "we shall continue our struggle for the liberty of Poland..." which, of course, did not sit well with the British Government. Anders was informed that if he continued to behave in this way he might be prematurely deprived of his command.[81]

The target date for dissolution of the Polish Armed Forces was set for October 1, 1946, by which time the entire Second Polish Corps was scheduled to be in Great Britain. But things didn't move as fast as anticipated and by that date a good portion of the Corps was still in Italy. The deadline was moved to October 31, when the last soldiers were supposed to be out of Italy. The Second Polish Corps was the first Polish unit to be demobilized. Five years after it had been created Anders' Army ceased to exist except in the hearts of the men who fought at Monte Cassino, Bologna and Ancona.

A tremendous outcry arose from some segments of the exile population who vilified Anders for agreeing to dissolve the Second Polish Corps and the remainder of the Polish forces loyal to the exiled government. Anders was accused of treason and of acting in violation of the 1935 Polish constitution by a small extremist group that believed it was still possible to maintain the army. Members of this small group could quote the paragraphs from the constitution that Anders may have violated but they couldn't propose any alternative solutions to the problems.They may have been right from a purely legal point of view, that Anders did not have the authority to disband the army, but when the British stopped paying salaries and providing maintenance, how could the army continue to exist? [82]

## Evacuation From Italy

The Italian Government in the immediate post war period acted more like the victor than the vanquished. In March, 1948, the Allies authorized the Italians to control the entry of foreigners into Italy with the exception of British and American nationals. The Italians promptly banned the entry and reentry of Polish soldiers into Italy, which infuriated Anders. It took two months of negotiations before the Italians agreed to grant entry to the Poles on the same basis as the British and Americans.[83]

The Italians wanted the Polish Army out of Italy for assorted reasons. First, some Poles meddled in Italian internal politics,and second, Italy's strong communist party was uneasy with the presence of an anti-communist Polish Army in their country. Lastly there was the economic consideration of not having enough jobs for Italians and new emigrants meant more competition for available jobs.

In 1946, it was costing the British Government two million pounds sterling per month to keep the Polish Army in Italy. The British were anxious to reduce these expenditures but initially they were in no rush to move the Poles to Great Britain as they were using the delay to find other countries that would take the Poles. Anders was in no rush as he wanted to keep his army intact as long as possible.

There were certain groups of people that the British refused to take and the Italians refused to have left behind. A deadlock was broken when the British agreed to take the criminals. According to a British report there were 1200 Polish soldiers with multiple bad conduct entries on their records.[84] These soldiers were taken to Britain, in the summer of 1946, and were segregated immediately upon arrival.

The British were not willing to accept the Italian wives of Polish soldiers for a number of reasons, not the least being prejudice.[85] The 1,400 Polish soldiers married to Italians were able to be demobilized in Italy with the warning that they would be subject to Italian law and that the British would not be able to help them. The British ban on Italian wives was taken very seriously and the few Italian wives who made it to Britain were ordered back to Italy.[86]

The soldiers and officers of the 5th Division did not want to go to Britain, they wanted to return to Poland and fight the Soviets. Anders met with 5th Division leaders to discuss the alternatives to going to Britain, and there were none. He pointed out that the Second Corps had 1,700 vehicles, including tanks but had only enough gas to get to the Austrian Alps.

The Second Polish Corps began leaving Italy for the U.K., on June 10, 1946, and the process continued until the end of October. Anders departed on October 31, after all but one small unit had been evacuated from Italy.[87]

Footnotes

1. NA Poland 5990. When the Poles complained about "fairness" Churchill was apt to remind them of Teschen where"Poland filched the Trans-Olza from the rachsack of the German soldier seizing the Sudetens." See, Memoirs of Anthony Eden v.III p.35
2. A. Eden, The Memoirs of Anthony Eden, (Boston: Houghton Mifflin, 1965), v. III, p. 344-345.
3. Federal Register IV (1944), p. 1023.
4. Mikolajczyk, Pattern of Soviet Domination, p. 129; W. Pobog-Malinowski, Najnowsza Historia Polski, III (London, 1960), p. 905.The 16 were invited to Poland by Colonel Pimenov of the NKVD who gave his "...word of honor of a Soviet officer guaranteeing the personal safety of the invited leaders." When the 16 presented themselves they were arrested.
5. W. Anders, An Army-in-Exile, p. 149.
6. Ibid., p. 197.
7. Ibid., p. 212-213.
8. Ibid., p. 228-229.
9. Ibid., p. 244-245.
10. Ibid., p. 258-260 The Jewish Agency was the source of a warning to Mikolajczyk that his life was in danger if he remained in Poland, in 1946. A "friend" passed the information in a letter to Shertok of the Jewish Agency who passed it on to Polish Intelligence in London. The letter stated that Mikolajczyk and "his gang" may soon be liquidated, when Osobka-Morawski gives the word. PISM 138/233
11. FO 371/47684/n14183; The Polish Army in the West refers to the Second Polish Corps plus all other units loyal to the exile government After General Sosnkowski's forced resignation the army was commanded by a committee. The committee was disbanded and General Bor was named Commander-in-Chief of Polish Forces in the West. Obviously the appointment of General Bor was a political move because he was a prisoner of the Germans at the time of his appointment and no one expected him to be released until the war ended. Anders was given the title, Acting Commander-in-Chief in February, 1945, over the objections of the British and kept that title until General Bor was released.
12. FO 371/47684;

13. Foreign Register of the United States, V (1945), p. 367; A. B. Lane, I saw Poland Betrayed (Boston, 1965), p. 369-370.All that Raczynski got to keep was the title of Ambassador. The passages in his book, In Allied London, of his giving up the embassy, his home, after 10 years are heart rendering. It was suggested that Raczynski continue as Warsaw's Ambassador to the Court of St.James, but the suggestion was rejected.See, FO 371/47750/8113. For more information see,FO 371/47750/N8063;FO 371/47670/N9646/FR 1945,vol.V p.367

14. FO 371/56464/n1867/86/55.

15. FO 371/47667.

16. Interview with Romanowski.

17. Interview with General K. Rudnicki. Attending this interview was K.Kosella, who witnessed the statements by General Rudnicki.

18. NA XL 8356.

19. Interview with Bau.

20. Interview with Czarnecki; NA, OSS file 127442.

21. Interviews with Rosengarten, Romanowski, Rudnicki.

22. Interviews with A. Stronski and J. Romanowski.

23. GSHI, Kol. 138/243, doc. #5971.

24. GSHI, Kol. 138/243, doc. #61/PFN/46.

25. Interview with Racieski.

26. Interview with Alexander Blum.

27. Interviews with Kazimierz Sabbat (August 15, 1988, and November 29, 1988) and short discussion with Zbigniew Scholtz, a member of the National Council (September, 1989). The meetings with Sabbat were attended by W.E. Szkoda.

28. Interview with Mrs. Sabbat (neé Sulik) in London (November 29, 1988)

29. Interviews with N.Rand and M. Buchweitz, said the Poles made it easy for Jews to get to Palestine after the war. A Polish soldier said he knew nothing about the Polish Army helping Jews, but he saw lorries traveling at night with canvas on top and he was sure there were people in the trucks. Rand said there were Polish lorries operating between Austria and Naples and he saw at least 20 driven by Polish women taking Jews to Padua, but he doesn't know where they went from there.

30. GSHI, Kol. 247. Help came from an unexpected source, Zoltan Toman, a Czech Jew who was Minister of Security affairs for the postwar Czech Government. The most common route was through Czechoslovakia where Toman opened the borders to Jews escaping from Europe. Toman was arrested but escaped to South America.
31. FO 371/56534/N10 See also, Soviet Jewish Affairs, Feb., 1980, Jews in Eastern Europe,p.62 & FO 371/55395
32. FO 371/41690
33. The incident at Kielce occurred just as the Jews were helping Polish families reach Italy. It would have been absurd for the Second Corps or Anders to be mixed up in a pogrom at this time
34. GSHI.Kol. 136/153 Rudnicki's document contains a great number of details e.g. the names and identification numbers of the drivers (Perelberg & Naajsbot) and the number of the truck.
35. Interviews with Lubienski, Romanowski and Dr.Dagoni.
36. M. Gilbert Winston S. Churchill Vol. VII Road to Victory (London, 1986) p.1229; PREM 45/153
37. FO 371/47663/N4518/G; PREM 45/153
38. FO 371/476601
39. FO 371/47633/N4696
40. FO 371/4766/2726/123G
41. FO 371/47663
42. FO 371/56366
43. Ibid
44. WO 204/10454 FO 371/56468/N3961
45. FO 371/56382/N6880
46. F.Morgan, Peace and War, A Soldier's Life. (London, 1961) p. 88.
47. M.Gilbert, Winston S. Churchill, vol.VII Road to Victory (London, 1986), p. 1229. According to the OSS there was a wide spread rumor that all Poles would be repatriated to Poland in September, 1945. NA 157193. Churchill promised that no Pole would be forcibly repatriated and that promise was kept. Nicholson quotes Churchill as having said, that British citizenship would be given to Poles, "Too frightened to return to Poland." The War Years. p.281. Soviet nationals were forcibly repatriated with disastrous results.
48. FO 371/66171.
49. FO 371/47676/N11415.
50. FO 371/41690/ ; FO 371/47666/N7446.
51. FO 371/47691; Foreign Relations v.V 1945 p.425.
52. 52. Ibid

53. A.B. Lane, I Saw Freedom Betrayed.
54. FO 371/47864/N11415
55. FO 371/566496// FO 371/56468/N11415
56. FO 371/56468/N5425
57. FO 371/41609/6372
58. FO 371/56393/N12194
59. FO 371/56366
60. Manchester Guardian July 14, 1945.
61. FO 371/When Kot arrived by airplane the pilot deserted on arrival and presented himself to General Anders to join the army. FO 371/56468
62. FO 371/56464/N1977
63. FO 371/56483/N1075
64. FO 371/56464/N The British Ambassador described Kot as "very sore about our apparent sympathy for the dissident Poles." FO 371/41690
65. FO 371/41690; London Times February 19, 1946
66. FO 371/56366
67. FO 371/56468. The Foreign Office was more supportive of Kot than the British Ambassador may have anticipated. The Foreign Office dismissed Kot's actions as part of Warsaw's propaganda campaign and commented on "the Polish aptitude for underground work and intrigue.FO 371/56464 Kot maintained that he went to communist Poland at the urging of the British Government.
68. FO 371/41690
69. FR V 1945 p.424
70. 371/47666/N7446
71. Polish Facts and Figures November 30,1946
72. FO 371/47670
73. FO 371/47686/N15207; FO 371/41609/6372; K.Kersten, Repatriacja ludnosci polskiej po II wojnic swiatowej (Studium historyczne) Wroclaw, Warsaw, Cracow, gdansk 1974, p. 238
74. FO 371/47691
75. W. Anders, An Army in Exile, p. 287
76. FO 371/56366/; FO 371/56372/N3943;FO 371/47691
77. FO 371/56372/N3943
78. FO 371/56467
79. Hansard vol.420 (March 28, 1946) no.106
80. May 23, 1946
81. W. Anders, An Army in Exile, p. 300-301

82. FO 371/71538/N2721

83. FO 371/ 56366 The same problem arose for families of soldiers who escaped from Poland. Initially the Italians turned back soldiers' families and they were sent to camps in Germany and Austria. There were 2,000 family members involved and the Italians reluctantly agreed to admit these families.

84. FO 371/56389/N9999

85. WO 204/1069

86. WO 204/11276

87. FO 371/39469/C12061

# CHAPTER EIGHT

# UNWANTED HEROES

## Arrival in Great Britain

When the Second Polish Corps began arriving in Great Britain during June and July of 1946, it wasn't received the way its veterans had expected. The first soldiers returning to Great Britain after the war were treated as heroes. The veterans marched in parades and received all the attention they deserved but by June, 1946, the war had been over for a year and welcoming troop ships and heroes had become routine and tiresome. The parades were over except for the Grand Victory Parade which was held on June 8, 1946, in London with almost all the countries that had fought against the Axis participating. Although the official program showed a Polish contingent to be included, Poland was not represented. Because the Second Polish Corps had not been invited the Polish airmen, who were invited, refused to march.[1]

While the other exile governments and refugees who had spent the war years in Britain were leaving for their home countries in a general exodus, the Polish Army was bringing 100,000 soldiers, many with families into Great Britain who, from the British point of view, were moving in the wrong direction. Now the wartime concerns had been replaced with the mundane problems of unemployment, housing and labor unrest. The popular perception of the Polish soldier changed dramatically. During the war the Poles were respected as fine soldiers and often seen as heroes. Now they were "refugees" and the British wanted them to go home. This feeling wasn't directed against Poles especially but against all refugees who competed with hundreds of thousands of British ex-soldiers for housing and jobs. War medals were everywhere but they didn't guarantee a job or a place to live.

In fact, the British popular attitude towards "the ungrateful Poles, for whom we went to war and who now refuse to go home" was almost hostile. The Scots especially, were upset at what they called the "Polish invasion" and resented, what they thought was the use of Scotland as a dumping ground for Poles, when the region was already suffering from housing and job shortages. The hostility met by the arriving Polish soldiers portended difficult times ahead.

The Polish soldiers tended to integrate into British life much more slowly than any other refugee group. For many, integration was impeded by their refusal to face reality -- namely that their emigration was permanent, that there was no hope for a quick return home. With that presence of mind people wasted years simply waiting for orders to mobilize instead of learning or improving their English,or acquiring job skills in order to become a part of English life. More than one veteran interviewed criticized Anders for unrealistically encouraging the exiles to believe they would return to Poland.

Other veterans realized immediately that they were in Britain for good and quickly tried to find a niche for themselves in British life. During the first two years the officers were very discreet about applying for British citizenship and those who did, hid it from Anders, fearing he would accuse them of disloyalty. Anders himself never applied for British citizenship.[2]

### The Polish Resettlement Corps

The Polish Resettlement Corps was a British scheme intended to give the ex-soldiers an opportunity to improve their proficiency in English and to provide education and training that would allow them to compete in the job market. It was organized along military lines, at least in the beginning, with units similar to military units. Members of the Corps wore uniforms and rank insignia but had no military duties, although they were subject to British military law. The plan was administered by Polish officers with British advisors. The length of service in the Polish Resettlement Corps was set at 2 years from time of entry. Entry terminated on April 1, 1948, and the Corps was dissolved on October 6, 1949.

There was much adverse reaction among the British population towards establishing the Polish Resettlement Corps and one has to admire the moral courage of the British politicians who supported the scheme in spite of its unpopularity. When members of Parliament objected to establishment of the Corps, they were asked what the alternative was. The government pointed out that if these soldiers were just turned loose in England they would flood the labor market.[3]

Anders was not appointed commander of the Resettlement Corps, even though Dr. Retinger recommended Anders as a strong and popular leader. The War Office rejected his candidacy choosing instead General Kopanski, another respected and honest officer. Upon taking the job Kopanski announced that he would resign if he felt that his duties conflicted with his conscience as a Pole. Kopanski suggested that Anders be appointed to head the Corps.

The British, although they did not want Anders to head the Corps, were nevertheless very anxious to secure his support for the scheme fearing the success or failure of the program could depend on Anders' attitude. General Kopanski sent a letter to Anders (for which he sought and got advance approval from the Foreign Office) stressing the need for cooperation and asking him to help the soldiers prepare for life in Britain. Anders reportedly was very calm about the British decision not to appoint him as head of the Corps. All British fears were groundless. Although the General complained that he and his soldiers had not been consulted about the scheme and had learned about it from newspapers, he was very cooperative and helpful.[4]

Anders did not join the Resettlement Corps but, at the request of Attlee and Bevin, he encouraged the Polish soldiers to do so. In special orders, dated May 29, and June 2, 1946, he announced his decision not to resist demobilization and gave his approval of the Polish Resettlement Corps. He implied that the Corps was a devious method of keeping the army together and exhorted the soldiers to give it their best effort and conduct.[5] Thus Anders was finally moderating his speeches to the satisfaction of the British, while at the same time pacifying his critics within the army, by implying the Resettlement Corps was really a continuation of the Polish Army. It is doubtful that the Polish soldiers would have accepted the Resettlement Corps without Anders' endorsement. Some of Anders' harshest critics agreed that once the Polish Resettlement Corps got underway it was helpful to those, and there were many, who chose to take advantage of the program.[6]

One of the most important functions of the Resettlement Corps was to enable Polish soldiers to find jobs in the civilian economy. The British Labor Exchange was obligated to assist the members of the Corps in finding jobs,but the Poles complained that the Exchange discriminated against them. This discrimination was due partly to prejudice and partly to poor knowledge of English. There was some resistance to Poles entering occupations where there was already a surplus of men seeking employment in those occupations. Demobilized British soldiers were, for example, given a preference over refugees in coal mining which led a Polish journal to conclude that the English did not like Catholic nations having esteem for Protestant Germans instead. "A true observation, I am afraid," commented a British Foreign Office official.[7]

In October, 1947, when the Polish Resettlement Corps had been operating for one year, Anders complained to Attlee and Bevin that they had not kept their side of the bargain and had not stopped various trade unions from creating obstacles for Poles seeking employment. He also asked Attlee to end rumors that the Polish Resettlement Corps was being prematurely terminated.[8]

Undoubtedly, there were many Poles who, perhaps because of the language difficulty, never rose above menial jobs. It was particularly difficult to find employment for senior career officers who were older and whose training could not easily be put to use in civilian occupations. Officers who rejected the Polish Resettlement Corps and wanted to seek employment on their own were allowed to do so. There are numerous stories, probably true, of generals cleaning lavatories, majors sweeping stables, and similar instances of high ranking officers assigned to menial jobs. But there were also those who fully utilized the available educational opportunities and entered the learned professions. The significant numbers of Polish architects, doctors and engineers living and working in the United Kingdom can not be ignored. It is probable that if accurate statistics were available we would find that the emphasis on education pushed so hard by General Anders and others, resulted in a disproportionately high number of Polish exiles in the professions.[9]

**Pensions and Bonuses**

The soldiers who were demobilized in Great Britain were entitled to bonuses which were intended to ease the transition into civilian life. The amount of a bonus was equal to eight weeks pay and varied from 25 pounds for privates to 3000 pounds for generals. At first the British wanted to exclude the soldiers who were returning to Poland (except for those who came from the part of Poland annexed by the Soviet Union, east of the Curzon line). They soon realized this might discourage repatriation so in May, 1946, Bevin declared publicly that repatriating soldiers would receive the same bonuses as those who choose to stay in Britain.[10]

However, the repatriating soldiers forfeited their pension rights. Since Warsaw also refused to count the time served under British command toward military pensions, General Kopanski tried to get the British Government to intercede but to no avail. The British also refused to pay pensions to families of soldiers who had died in combat, but paid small stipends to widows of veterans, regardless, of rank and disability pensions to those with combat wounds. Until 1948 they also paid pensions to widows of Polish officers who were killed in 1939, or murdered at Katyn.[11] Efforts were made to get the British Government to provide pensions for special groups, e.g. for former career officers or NCOs but none were successful.

Generals were invited to apply for loans from War Office funds. Twelve of them received grants and interest free loans amounting to 3000 pounds, of which only 2,000 was repayable.[12]

The Second Polish Corps, and some of its components had set up a series of welfare funds, e.g. "The Social Fund of the Second Corps," and "Third Carpathian Division's Widows and Orphans Fund" before the army left Italy. These funds were created by contributions taken out of the soldiers and officers pay.[13] By September of 1946, the Second Corps Welfare fund amounted to a half million pounds sterling. When the Polish Corps moved from Italy to Great Britain the money was deposited with the British for safe keeping. In Britain a conflict arose over the control of these funds. Claims were made both by the Warsaw Government and by Anders, who wanted to use the funds for welfare purposes and believed that the money should be administered only by Poles in London.[14] In 1947, the British transferred about a quarter of the Second Corps Social fund to the Warsaw Government, which corresponded roughly to the percentage of soldiers who elected repatriation. The British devised similar schemes for distribution of other funds, e.g. one third going to the Poles in London, one third for those who were repatriated and one third for those who had stayed in Italy. Anders and the Ex-Combatants Association filed lawsuits against the British Government asking the courts to prevent the transfer of funds to the Warsaw Government and to adjudicate the rights of the various individuals and organizations in London.

The British courts decided the lawsuits in favor of the plaintiffs and held that the British and Warsaw Governments had no legal rights to use or disburse the funds and ordered that the funds be turned over to the Ex-Combatants Association, the Third Carpathian Division Widows, Orphans and Invalids Relief Fund and other similar organizations. Warsaw protested that the money would be used for espionage and subversive activities but this had no effect.[15]

## U.S. Citizenship for Soldiers of the Second Polish Corps[16]

On April 13, 1946, a bill was introduced in the U.S. Congress (H.R. 6120) by Congressman John Lesinski to give special emigration rights to the soldiers of the Second Polish Corps, and their wives and children. The bill was endorsed by General Lee, the Commanding General of American forces in the Mediterranean, who, in a memo to General Eisenhower, requested that the personnel of the Second Polish Corps be admitted as emigrants to the United States on the basis of special legislation. The project, according to him, was backed by British officials and would grant American citizenship "to these gallant soldiers who can't return to Poland." General Lee added that he was personally convinced that General Anders could be relied upon to screen all the candidates for citizenship. It was clear to everyone that the American Army was sympathetic to the Second Polish Corps.

The project was killed by combined opposition coming from the Secretary of State, Dean Acheson, the Attorney General and the Bureau of the Budget. Although Acheson conceded that the Polish military personnel was suitable for immigration, the State Department did not want to depart from the existing emigration quota system. He was against admitting certain special groups and believed that a special bill exempting one group from the quota system might be used as a precedent in obtaining permission for other special groups to enter the United States. It is quite likely that the group he had in mind were the Jews. The horrors of the Holocaust had not swayed the State Department from its consistent anti-Semitic attitude. It is ironic that anti-Semitism might have played a role in keeping the Second Polish Corps from getting an open door to the United States.

**Anders' support for the Anti-Communist Underground in Poland.**

After the Soviet-backed Communists captured power in Poland, a large part of the anti-Nazi resistance movement remained in the underground to continue the struggle against what they considered to be a new occupation. The largest resistance organization, the Home Army, loyal to the Polish Government in London, had been dissolved by its commander, General Okulicki, on January 19, 1945. In its place a clandestine political-military structure was created, first called "NiE" and then "WiN" (Wolnosc i Niepodleglosc - Liberty and Independence). In addition there was a handful of ultra-right nationalistic underground organizations and military formations, such as NSZ and NZW.[17] The Communists often accused Anders of financing and directing the anti-Communist underground.

After arresting the first commander of the WiN in the autumn of 1945, the Warsaw Government announced it had evidence that Anders was in contact with the organization, Anders had appointed its commander, Colonel Jan Rzepecki, and ordered him to resist the "Sovietization of Poland" and to "liquidate dangerous individuals," according to Warsaw.[18] At the end of 1947, the Communist security service was able to penetrate the organization and to run it as a "sting" operation, successfully fooling British, Polish and American intelligence which continued to send gold, money and agents to Poland. In 1952, Warsaw authorities made the whole affair public by presenting two men who claimed to be leaders of WiN, who had defected to Poland. According to their story, WiN activities were encouraged by Anders' staff. Available evidence seems to suggest that Anders himself was not involved with the WiN, but, as leader of the emigre Poles, he was undoubtedly informed about its activities.[19]

During a trial of members of another anti-Communist underground group - a socialist group known as WRN (Liberty-Equality- Independence) - the government charged the accused of collaboration with the "Anders' spy network." One of the defendants admitted having casual and accidental meetings with W. Pilecki, "Chief of Anders' Intelligence Service" and with a certain Miss. Szelagowska, his secretary. The prosecution alleged that Pilecki and his secretary were sent to Poland by Anders with large sums of money for the purpose of organizing a spy network. It is inconceivable that Anders, or anyone else in a command position, would send his chief intelligence officer into "the enemy territory"[20]

The Warsaw Government also accused Anders of aiding the extreme-right group, NSZ. In August of 1946, during the trial of the NSZ's members, the prosecution charged the defendants of collaborating with "Polish organizations abroad, including members of General Anders' headquarters and Polish groups at Regensburg." One of the defendants confirmed the collaboration between

Anders and the NSZ. During another trial of the NSZ' members a prosecutor claimed the NSZ had received 40,000 marks from General Anders' Headquarters. A witness, who had been a NSZ member, testified that he had met with Anders and had received instructions from a Colonel Kijak whom he believed to be a member of General Anders' staff. All of this "evidence" is tenuous and not credible. The NSZ was a far right ultra-nationalistic group outside the main stream of Polish politics which refused to recognize the Polish London Government. It is probable that NSZ members served with Anders Army but everything seems to point to a definite dislike and distrust between Anders and that group.[21]

The Warsaw Government complained that the British were indirectly supporting anti-government forces in Poland. This complaint was logical. The British were maintaining and supplying the Polish Armed Forces, which in turn was giving financial aid to the anti-government forces. This logic appealed to certain members of the British parliament -- to those on the left because of ideological sympathy for the leftist government in Warsaw and to those on the right because it provided an opportunity to reduce government expenses. In February, 1946, the issue reached the floor of the House of Commons, when a Labor deputy called attention to the arrest of two Polish officers in Warsaw, whose papers identified them as belonging to Anders' Army. Supposedly they had $480,000 in their possession and Warsaw claimed that this money was part of the 2 million pounds allocated each month by the British Government for the upkeep of Anders' Army. The question was whether the funds supplied by the British Government to the exiles were being used to subvert the Polish Government, and if so, what action should be taken. Warsaw alleged that Kopanski and Pelczynski sent large amounts of money to Poland which had come from Second Polish Corps funds. Bevin denied this and explained that during the German occupation large sums of money had been sent to the Polish underground and there was no proof that this was not the source of the money carried by the Polish officers. He argued that the stories appearing in the Polish press about Anders funding the underground were just propaganda. He was supported by other members, one of whom reminded the House of Commons that Anders' Army had contributed to the defeat of Hitler. Another deputy stated that "General Anders has given the most firm and categorical denial of ever having sent any money and of ever having got into communication with the Poles in Poland and that we have no reason to doubt the word of this gallant officer."[22]

General Anders never denied that he opposed the Communist authorities in Poland and admitted giving financial and other non-military aid to anti-Communist organizations. His position was that until free elections were held, Poland was occupied by a foreign power. He publicly stated that if the Communists won in a free election he would accept their government as legitimate.

### What to do with General Anders

In January, 1946, British Foreign Minister Ernest Beven sought the cabinet's guidance on the question of removing Anders as commander of the Second Polish Corps. Beven's question was, "How to eliminate the pernicious influence of General Anders?" He wanted Anders removed even before the Polish Army was notified of the British intention to move them from Italy to the United Kingdom. No action was taken at that time, probably due to Retinger's warning that the sacking of Anders would result in a rebellion by the soldiers. He cautioned that some of Anders' generals were even more uncompromising and it would be difficult to find a successor. That discussion put the issue to rest for a year.

With the dissolution of the Second Polish Corps the British had to again face the dilemma of what to do with General Anders. Towards the end of the war Anders clearly became a liability for the Western Allies because of his continued verbal attacks on the Soviet Union and with the war over people were tired of hearing about old battles.

Complaints about Yalta and the Curzon line were old news. The current problems now were: housing, jobs,and coal mine and railroad strikes. Western leaders, aware of all the broken promises given to their Polish allies, were not eager to support those who reminded them of their own duplicity.

As 1946 ended, it was difficult to determine Anders' exact status. He was no longer commander of the Second Polish Corps (it had been dissolved), nor was he a member of the Polish Resettlement Corps or a member of the British Armed Forces. Yet he was drawing a general's salary.

The usual procedures for getting rid of surplus generals could not be applied to Anders, who at 53, was too young to retire and would not accept a meaningless desk job. Thus, Anders presented two distinct problems for the British. The first was how to employ him in a meaningful capacity, and second, how to find a way to stop him from making political statements against Warsaw and Moscow which were embarrassing to the British Government. The British authorities would not have been displeased if he were to migrate to the United States but thought it unlikely that the American Government would give him an entry visa.

Not every one saw Anders in same way. There were those who saw him as an able field commander and would have liked to see him utilized in a significant military position. There were others, who considered him a warmonger and didn't want to give him the opportunity of pulling Britain into a war against the Soviet Union. Anders had strong support from the British military establishment but in the final analysis this counted for very little with the politicians. Even War Office support for Anders eroded gradually, as personnel changes occurred and the memory of war service began to fade. At the end of 1946, the War Office advised the Foreign Office that "they would not much mind losing Anders now" and "would certainly like to get rid of him in due course."[23]

At the beginning of 1947, the British Cabinet created a Polish Forces Committee to decide what to do with Anders. The Committee considered various options: an offer of an "overseas appointment" with an annual salary of 1200 pounds sterling, the position of "traveling Ambassador" who would lobby foreign governments to accept members of the Polish Armed Forces as emigrants, or a pension large enough to allow Anders a comfortable existence in England or abroad. The pension would be granted on the condition that Anders withdraws from all "political activity," with the British being the interpreters of that term. The Foreign Office suggested the pension be granted by an open vote of the Parliament, to avoid charging it to secret funds. Similar pensions were recommended for other top generals of the Polish Armed Forces in the West. The Foreign Office was against the idea of appointing Anders a "traveling Ambassador" unless his activities were restricted to the British Dominions, but even this was vetoed by the Dominions' Office. A Foreign Office dignitary thought that employment of Anders in any official capacity could result in grave political difficulties, because the General lacked discretion and could not be controlled. As an example he pointed out a report in the London Times which quoted Anders as saying that Poles who had accepted repatriation were sent to Soviet concentration camps. The Committee felt very strongly about the need to prevent Anders from political activity and decided that even if Anders were to reject an offer of a pension with all the strings attached to it he would still be expected to refrain from political activity as a condition of his continued residence in Britain. The Chancellor of the Exchequer, Hugh Dalton suggested that if Anders were to be granted a pension, it should be on a year to year basis, with extension conditioned upon "good behavior."[24]

In the end, the authorities decided that for the time being things should be left as they were with a review to be made again in March of 1947. That meant that if Anders did not create any problems he would get a pension. In the meantime his salary was continued even though he had no duties. Finally, in February of 1948, it was announced in Parliament that Anders would be receiving a monthly pension of 88 pounds, 12 shillings.[25]

## Anders' Postwar Years

After the war Anders maintained an office in central London, which later was moved to the Sikorski Institute (an institution founded by former Polish soldiers to house the records of the Polish Armed Forces in the West and of the London Government). He went to his office every day, even when he was ill. In 1960, he finally agreed to buy a house in London and it was only then, according to his widow, that he accepted the fact that he would not be returning to Poland.[26]

Others dispute this and think that Anders realized much earlier that his stay in Britain would be permanent. He knew he would be able to return to Poland only if war broke out between the two superpowers and, in 1948, or thereabouts, he knew this was not to be. According to Jan Romanowski, the General stopped talking about returning to Poland a year after his army arrived in the U.K. In 1948, during the Berlin blockade he was so optimistic about the prospect of war between the Soviet Union and the United States that he sent some officers to France for advanced military training. As early as August, 1946, a British Foreign Office official reported that Anders had told him that he was no longer expecting a war between the West and the Soviet Union.[27]

General Anders came to the attention of the general public on two other occasions. The first was in 1953, when he published a book about the Eastern Front entitled, "Hitler's Defeat in Russia."and the second, when he was a plaintiff in a highly publicized libel suit which he filed in London against an obscure Polish emigre publication located in Paris.

When Anders published his book he had not yet given up hope that the Western Powers would confront the Soviet Union. He still believed that someday the Polish Army would march triumphantly into a free Poland. In the foreword, written by the American Colonel, Truman Smith, Anders was characterized as "as impartial writer on this controversial subject as it is possible to find anywhere in the troubled and divided world." This could only mean that Anders was consistent in equally opposing the Communist Soviet Union and Nazi Germany. He hated one as much as the other. If Colonel Smith meant that Anders wrote the book without an ulterior motive he was wrong. Anders' book argued, indirectly, that Russian invincibility was a myth created by their defeat of Napoleon's and Hitler's armies. Anders wanted to prove the myth false lest it discourage the West from going to war with Russia.

The book was an unemotional military analysis of the Nazi-Soviet war, the kind a high staff officer would write for a course taught at a military academy. It argues that it was not the Soviets who defeated Hitler, but that Hitler defeated himself by committing numerous military and political errors. His major error was his brutal treatment of the Russians, Ukrainians, Byelorussians and Balts who were eager to join him as allies against the Soviet Union. Hitler's racist ideology prevented the German Army from organizing and arming non-German recruits on a large scale. Hitler's plan for the fate of Eastern Europe had no room for allies, only for slaves.

Hitler also committed numerous strategic errors of a purely military nature, according to Anders' book. The major one was Hitler's taking over of the supreme command of the German Army. As a supreme commander Hitler constrained his generals from exercising their military skills and experience which led to disastrous military blunders for the German troops in Russia. Anders implied in the book that the democratic West could defeat Communist Russia by avoiding the repetition of these blunders.

## The Libel Lawsuits

General Anders was no stranger to the British courts. In 1951, he won a libel lawsuit in England's High Court of Justice against the publishers of the "Daily Worker" (the official publication of the British Communist Party), and its editor, Mr. J.R. Campbell. The "Worker" claimed General Anders was to lead a group of mercenaries, including some of Hitler's generals, in an army called "West Germany Security Troops" and accused him of conspiring with Hitler and German generals during the Second World War. The defendants had to admit they had knowingly printed a false statement about Anders. They maintained that an apology and admission of the falsity of the statement, which had been printed on page one, should give sufficient satisfaction to Anders. The jury returned a verdict in favor of Anders and, after an unsuccessful appeal by the defense, Anders was awarded 5,000 pound sterling in damages.[28]

No plaintiff in a libel lawsuit ever really wins, even when a favorable judgment is issued. Doubts linger on, and people remember the allegations and not the final verdict. There are always those who prefer to assume the worst. Even though Anders won the lawsuit against the "Daily Worker," many people still whispered that Anders conspired with the Nazis.

In 1960, Anders was back in court. This time he was suing a small Polish language newspaper "Narodowiec" which appeared in Paris and which, on January 28, 1956, published a letter from Mr. Adam Gas, Secretary of the Polish Peasants Party and a survivor of Auschwitz. In the letter Gas charged that during the First World War Anders did not consider himself a Pole; that, in 1920, Anders had refused to take part in the Battle of Warsaw against the Bolsheviks; that he was disloyal to the Sikorski Government; that he believed in Hitler's victory in the Second World War; that in the September Campaign of 1939 he failed to follow orders and retreated without the permission of his superiors; that he failed to cooperate with the Soviets, in 1941, and that he went over the heads of his superiors when he withdrew the Polish Army from Russia, in 1942.

Anders explained that he was born in Poland and considered himself a Polish patriot. At the start of the First World War he was called-up as an officer into the Russian Imperial Army and fought against the Germans. When the Russian Revolution broke out he considered himself released from his oath to the Czar and left the Russian Army in order to join the Polish Armed Forces. He didn't comment on the charge concerning the Battle for Warsaw because the defendants had earlier admitted that it was false and libelous and apologized for making it.

Anders was cross-examined about his role, in the 1939 campaign. He argued that on September 8, and 9, when he ordered his troops to blow up bridges on the Vistula then to withdrew to the southeast of Warsaw, he was acting in accordance with orders from General Rommel, the commander of the "Warsaw" Army. Similarly on September 13, when he broke off the battle with the Germans near Minsk and retreated towards Lublin, he did so only after receiving orders from Rommel's chief of staff.

As far as his alleged disloyalty towards the government of General Sikorski was concerned Anders pointed out that after the evacuations to Iran had begun, Sikorski awarded him Poland's highest military award. Anders conceded that a small group of junior officers in the Second Polish Corps agitated against Sikorski, and that this group included one of his aides, Captain Klimkowski. Anders explained that this aide had turned against him, and that he was subsequently dismissed and court-martialed.

In the witness box, Anders repeatedly denied that he had violated orders from Sikorski. He said he respected Sikorski, but thought he was inexperienced in dealing with Russians and as a result was too trusting.

At one point the judge intervened and asked Anders the following question: "You received an order from the chief of staff in London to stop the evacuation of women and children. You knew the situation in Russia. Because of that you decided not to obey? Is that right?" Anders answered in affirmative. Knowing the situation in Russia, where women and children were dying of hunger and disease, how could anyone disapprove of Anders' failure to obey an order to leave the women and children behind? Would the soldiers have obeyed orders to leave their families behind when they knew this would have meant a death sentence for most of them?

One of the witnesses called to testify for the defendants was Professor Kot, the former Polish Ambassador to the USSR. He said that the women, children and elderly should not have left prisons and work camps and should not have headed south towards Anders' Army, i.e. they were better off in the prison and labor camps. He accused Anders of keeping him in the dark about evacuation plans and criticized him for the breakdown of communications between the Polish Army and the Polish Embassy in Russia. Allegedly Anders withheld the lists of missing officers from the embassy. This last claim was subsequently contradicted by another witness.

On February 29, the jury reported its decision. It found the defendants guilty of libelous and malicious misrepresentation on all counts, except one. The jury found the statement that Anders was an opponent of Sikorski's Government true in substance and not defamatory. Anders was granted damages to the extent of 7,000 pounds. The judge, however, ordered Anders to pay one third of the court costs, which were estimated at 10,000 pounds.

After the verdict Anders made the following statement to the press: "What is important is that my military honor has been vindicated. I never brought this action for the sake of money; for years I would have accepted an apology. I'm very glad it's all over. The letter was published in 1956, and I asked my solicitor then to try and get an apology printed so I would not have to take the case to court. I fought for my name, my reputation, my military honor, my place in history. The one thing that was most important was my war career. I was not a 'yes man', and I had differences with General Sikorski and the government. But, when he gave me an order I carried it out."[29]

## The British Attitude Towards Anders

Attitudes towards Anders varied widely between the Foreign Office and the War Office. In a Foreign Office internal memo, Hankey wrote, "No Pole can be trusted to behave like a gent now towards any other sort of Pole. Its no good trying anymore." The attitude expressed in that memo was not inconsistent with his comments that he liked and respected Anders.

Roberts commented in a note that Anders would never accept a reduced Poland, so it may "be necessary to get rid of him and of his chief advisor, Czapski."[30] In an interview Roberts called Anders a "good soldier" and doubted that Anders was involved with right wing extremists.

"He didn't impress me", wrote Cadogan, of Anders, and when it became necessary to make a choice between Generals Sosnkowski and Anders he admitted "it depends on what the Russians think."[31] Roberts made it clear that even though Sosnkowski was the most disliked Polish General, he got the job as Commander-in-Chief. Anders never was in charge of all Polish forces, except for a short period in which he was "Acting" Commander-in-Chief. The British were so against this "Acting" appointment that Churchill immediately canceled his scheduled meeting with Anders after hearing of it.

Anders fared much better with the British Generals, although he got off to a poor start with General Leese when he complained that the 8th Army had published a Russian map of postwar Europe on which Poland did not appear.[32] In time, Leese and Anders liked and respected each other.

There is little mention of Anders in Field Marshal Harold Alexander's biography except to quote Alexander as saying of Anders, I had to "comfort him."[33] Alexander was sympathetic towards the Poles and Anders who he said "held together that superb formation when they considered themselves betrayed at Yalta." In the 1960 lawsuit, Field Marshal Alexander and General Beaumont Nesbitt, testified on Anders' behalf.

There was an excellent relation between Anders and future British Prime Minister, Harold MacMillan, who wrote the Foreword for Army in Exile. Anders is mentioned frequently in MacMillan's war diaries, and most of the comments are favorable. MacMillan wrote of Anders, "...I thought him very attractive, a keen soldier and a powerful political conversationalist."

**Churchill and Anders**

According to Mrs. Anders, her husband hated Churchill and never forgave him for betraying Poland. Her husband had told her that Churchill resented soldiers being involved in political decision making. Romanowski saw it differently, thinking that Churchill and Anders liked and respected each other in spite of their differences that Anders held Churchill in high regard but was also very critical of him.

To Anders it must have seemed as if Churchill always took the Russian viewpoint, yet in a Pravda interview on March 14, 1946, Stalin said "Mr.Churchill would like Poland to be ruled by Sosnkowski and Anders"

Always keeping the main objective in the forefront,which to Churchill was the defeat of Nazi Germany he was against anything or anybody that would endanger the Grand Alliance. He was against the Polish protests and criticisms of Stalin which served no purpose. He saw Anders' protest to Stalin over his refusal to let soldiers' families leave the USSR to be a weakening of the Alliance. Without military power far in excess of what they had, the Poles could not force Stalin to do anything he didn't want to do. Churchill criticized the Poles for standing up to the Russians when they had no power. He reminded Anders that it was not productive to make demands of Stalin at the same time you are criticizing him publicly on the same issue.

Churchill backed the Polish protest by sending Stalin a letter supporting Anders‘ request regarding the military families. Stalin did not respond.[34] The main issue between Churchill and Anders remained the Polish-Russian border. Churchill argued that Britain never guaranteed specific borders and Anders countered that there were to be no border changes until after the war, and then only with the consent of the nations involved.

The last Churchill-Anders meeting was the most important. Held on February 21,1945, the meeting took place after Yalta but before Anders was named Acting Commander-in-Chief of Polish forces. Churchill summarized the two and one half hour meeting by stating, "General Anders remained completely skeptical and refused to believe that the Soviet Government would allow any free expression of the will of the Polish people" Churchill noted on the staff report of the meeting,"When I asked him (Anders) finally what he would have had us do in the Crimea, he replied that we should have left matters alone; that would have been better from the point of view of Poland" It was at this meeting.that Churchill reportedly told Anders, "the Polish Army was no longer needed and can be removed." When the 5th Army Commander General, Mark Clark, heard about Churchill's statement, he responded, "To withdraw 100,000 Polish soldiers from the front lines would cripple the Allied forces."[35]

At the February 21 meeting Churchill asked Anders to stay in London for another week so they could meet again.[36] On February 25, the British learned of Anders' appointment as Acting Commander-in-Chief, something which they opposed. Churchill canceled the next scheduled meeting with Anders to demonstrate their disapproval of the appointment.

When Churchill canceled the meeting Anders attempted to meet with General Eisenhower and Field Marshal Montgomery. Following military protocol he made his request through Field Marshal Alexander who thought the request reasonable, but the War Office asked the Foreign Office to make the decision. Anders was advised that the supreme commanders were" too busy to see him."[37]

## Private Life

After the war the private life of General Anders began with family problems. His first wife his son Jerzy and daughter Hanna, had survived the war, by hiding in Poland under assumed names. But the long years of separation took their toll, and Anders and his wife divorced. He never enjoyed a close relationship with his children until the last years of his life.

On May 6, 1948, Anders married for the second time. His wife, Renata Bogdanska was of Ukrainian origin (her father was a Greek Catholic priest) but considered herself Polish. She was a well known stage singer with a strong "show business personality." Finding herself in the Soviet Union with millions of other Polish citizens she left "the inhuman land" with the first evacuation, with the army's entertainment band. Anders met her in Iraq, in 1942.

After the war the couple settled in London, at first, living in a modest rented house in a working class neighborhood. At the General's request, his wife did not give any performances during the first five years of their marriage. Anders liked to have guests and they frequently hosted evening parties. After the war the General became an avid bridge player. On weekends the couple attended the Polish theater and on Sundays attended Catholic Mass together. He was often seen in church, including Protestant churches, attending funerals, marriages, etc... of the soldiers and their families.

The General, a father at the age of sixty, spent long hours playing with his daughter, Anna -Maria. The family decided to buy a new house in a better section of London. Anders became so attached to the new house that he preferred to spend his vacations at home. After giving birth to their daughter, Mrs. Anders resumed her singing career. In 1968, she gave a concert in Tel Aviv before a full auditorium of mostly Polish-born Israelis. She was well known for singing ballads in Yiddish and was proud of the fact that she was the first person to sing in Yiddish on the BBC. At the time she was interviewed she was still giving performances.

The last years of General Anders were marred by deteriorating health. He suffered from terrible back pain - a consequence of the wound he had received during the 1939, September campaign. There were days when he could not get up from his bed. The General's illness had at least one beneficial side effect. It led to Anders' reconciliation with his children from the first marriage and friendly relations between Renata and his children. The family reconciliation was sealed when Anders visited his children in Montreal, where both children from the marriage resided.

Anders died in his London home in the early morning hours of May 12, 1970, the 26th anniversary of the Polish Army's first assault on Monte Cassino. At his request he was buried in the Polish Military Cemetery there. Until the end of his life he was considered the spiritual leader of the Polish emigre community in Great Britain.

Footnotes

1. FO 371/56635. It was 1988 before the London Poles were invited to participate in the annual victory march. One hundred fifty "London" Poles marched, in 1988, and they have marched in every subsequent parade.
2. In September, 1946, the Warsaw Government revoked the Polish citizenship of Anders and 70 other Poles who chose exile. Citizenship was restored in 1989. Actually the 1989 announcement was they had newly discovered that citizenship had been restored 20 years earlier.
3. WO 204/11276; FO 371/56393/N12337 and 371/56389/N6719 and 371/56389/N9827.
4. PREM 8/637.
5. FO 371/56387.
6. FO 371/71538/N2314 and 371/66144/N404.
7. PREM 8/637.
8. FO 371/71531/E4474.
9. FO 371/56389/9983; interviews with Romanowski and K. Rudnicki.
10. FO 371/66171 and 371/71617.
11. FO 371/100723/N1431/1.
12. FO 371/71554.
13. FO 371/56393/N12414.
14. FO 371/106415.
15. FO 371/5638.
16. A. Paczkowski, Pol wieku dziejow Polski, 1939-1989 (Warsaw, 1996), p. 123, 136, 141, 178.
17. London Times (December 20, 1946).
18. Edward J. Epstein, Deception, the Invisible War Between the KGB and the CIA (New York, 1989), p. 34-42; John Ranelagh, The Agency: the Rise and Decline of the CIA (New York, 1987), p. 227-18; see also NA 23032, NA 11705; T. Powers' claim, that it was Anders who put WiN emissaries in touch with British intelligence "a few years," after 1947 is not credible. In fact, in 1946, the representatives of WiN arrived in England and their first contacts were with British intelligence and with the Chief of Staff, General Kopanski. In September of 1947, one of them signed a cooperation agreement with British intelligence. They did however speak to Anders as well. S. J. Rostworowski, "Delegatura WiN za granica" Zeszyty Historyczne WiN-u III (1993), p. 9, 16, 20.

19. Polish Facts and Figures (November 27, 1948), p. 3.London Times (March 5, 1946).
20. Polish Facts and Figures (August 9, 1946) and (October 24, 1946).
21. London Times (February 21, 1946); FO 371/56464/N2218.
22. FO 371/56506.
23. FO 371/56635 and 371/71539.
24. FO 371/56636/N4765.
25. An interview with Anders' widow, Mrs. Renata Anders.
26. FO 371/56633/N1138
27. London Times (October 16, 1951)
28. London Times (February 10-March 1, 1960).
29. FO 371/56467/N49/
30. FO 371/56385/N7085
31. Cadogan, p.541
32. Oliver Leese, Richard Ryder 1987 Hamish Hamilton London p.158
33. Alex, Nigel Nicholson p.281
34. FO 371/34571
35. Martin Blumenson, Mark Clark, 1984, NY Congdon & Weed
36. Why did Churchill ask Anders to stay in London another week? Cadogan in his memoirs said the February 21 meeting should not have lasted more than thirty minutes. Did Churchill have a purpose in asking Anders to stay or was it an impulsive action?
37. FO 371/47662

# EPILOGUE

## Anders in the Eyes of Contemporaries

Different people appraised Anders differently. An OSS report of March, 1945, described him as "strong willed, somewhat head strong, quick of decision and devoid of sentiment."[1] Kamil Czarnecki characterized Anders as, "A Man; masculine, impulsive, strong character, short fuse, not a politician and loved by the soldiers." Most officers thought Anders was a good soldier but a bad politician. Others were very critical of him as a soldier. They thought he was not properly trained and called him a good politician but a poor general. General Rudnicki described him as being "the best man for the job. He was intelligent, the men loved him, an excellent soldier, clever, spoke Russian and knew how to deal with them. He liked his vodka." Romanowski remembered him as a demanding boss who gave hard assignments to his staff but never humiliated then and never raised his voice. Sharp reprimands to his subordinates were given but only in private. Anders was an excellent speaker and could talk at every level and was a good companion who liked to enjoy life. He was not egotistical, rarely carried cash and had absolutely no interest in finances. In Romanowski's view Anders' biggest fault was that he had an absolute trust in the people around him. He was extremely concerned with questions of honor, loyalty, etc., which were both his strength and his weakness.

Another of Anders' aides-de-camp, Lubienski, said Anders was "very human" but strict. He made great efforts to create schools for children and higher education courses for the soldiers. Lubienski called Anders a "good public speaker, loyal to his superiors, a good officer and a good General." Lidia Ciolkosz, a well known socialist and historian, who met Anders only after the war called Anders an excellent soldier who saved many lives, took responsibility for the Polish children and was loved by his soldiers. In her view he lacked a political mind and did not involve himself in party politics. She felt he was definitely "right wing" but was not a member of any political party. Anders' dentist, Slowes, did not hold Anders in high regard as a politician. He claimed that Anders lost control of affairs and reality.[2] Robin Hankey, a Foreign Office official, who, during the war, was responsible for contacts with the Polish Government in London, called Anders "marvelous and a genius". [AA] professed to having a great admiration for him. Macmillan thought him "very attractive, a keen soldier and a powerful political controversialist" with "equal hatred of Russians and Germans.never far removed from his thoughts."[3] The British officers who worked with Anders agreed that he was a most cooperative and efficient commander and regretted that his character had often been misrepresented. A writer and painter Joseph Czapski, who served under Anders as an officer for special assignments, gave one of the best descriptions of Anders when he said, "There was never a trace of triviality about his mental processes even when the question at issue might, at first sight, have appeared insignificant. Nor was he ever in a hurry. I cannot remember that I once heard him raise his voice when professional problems were the subject of argument, or offend against courtesy."[4]

As for the allegation that Anders was anti-Semitic, Mrs. Anders only laughed at the suggestion. She recalled a number of anti-Semitic incidents in the army and her husband's adamant reaction that there must be no anti-Semitism in the army. She said Anders shared Marshal Pilsudski's opinion that the anti-Semitism of some Poles was divisive and detrimental to Poland. Mrs. Anders cited several instances of officers being punished by the General for making anti-Semitic remarks. Hankey, while admitting that many high officers in the Polish Army were definitely anti-Semitic, was at the same time absolutely positive that Anders was not an anti-Semite.[5]

Anders certainly wasn't a philo-Semite. To suggest that would be to misunderstand the man. As his widow said, and as was repeated to this author by people who knew him well - including Hankey and numerous Jewish soldiers who served under him - "his mind didn't work that way." His primary concern was the Polish Army and the Polish nation. My interviews are replete with stories where Anders went to the side of Jews, not because they were Jews, but because they were Polish citizens. He was not concerned about Jewish issues except as they related to the army or Poland. When they arose the General looked upon them as a detraction from the issues that he considered to be the priorities.

The leniency Anders showed towards Jewish deserters in the Middle East, which included refusing to resort to penal measures as suggested by the British, along with his approval of Jewish migration to Palestine, implies a moderately favorable attitude towards the Jewish cause.

## Anders in Postwar Poland: From Villain to Hero

For over forty years Anders was venomously and viciously attacked by the Communist Government in Poland. He was by far the most vilified figure among the emigre Poles. To the Communist propaganda machine he became the symbol of an enemy. He was accused of being a reactionary, a fascist, an anti-Soviet war monger in the pay of the West, and even a servant of the so-called German revisionists. In 1946 he was publicly stripped of his Polish citizenship.[6]

As part of the anti-Anders campaign the authorities published, in 1959, the memoirs of his former aide-de-camp, Captain Jerzy Klimkowski.[7] Klimkowski endeared himself to Anders and became very close to him starting in Russia. According to Anders' wife, Klimkowski was, at least until his true role was discovered, "the best friend" of the general.[8] Now we know that in July of 1942 Klimkowski offered to stage a coup in the Polish Army by arresting Anders, thus preventing the army from leaving the USSR.[9] In the Middle East, Klimkowski headed an informal group of young officers that engaged in anti-Sikorski propaganda. This propaganda, emanating from circles close to Anders, considerably contributed to the worsening of relations between Anders and Sikorski.

Pretending to act on Anders' behalf, Klimkowski tried to incite young officers to organize a plot to kill Sikorski, while at the same time notifying British intelligence that Sikorski might be killed during his inspection trip to Anders' Army. The activities attributed to Klimkowski were so contradictory that they almost sounded unbelievable, and their effect was clear: they deepened the political divisions among the Poles and undermined their image with the Allies. It was the logic of a saboteur.[10]

In the end Klimkowski was caught in the possession of secret materials that had been missing from Anders' Headquarters. He was tried, stripped of his commission and sentenced to one year and seven days in jail. After the war he returned to Communist Poland.

His memoirs were published clearly to discredit Anders. They contained many unsubstantiated allegations. Klimkowski wrote that Anders was involved in prewar scandals and that the knowledge of these scandals enabled

General Michal Tokarzewski-Karaszewicz to blackmail Anders into giving him command of the 5th Division. Anders allegedly refused to fight the Germans in 1939 and attempted an escape to Hungary. Klimkowski claimed that Anders had disobeyed Sikorski by meeting with Churchill, by failing to send soldiers from the Middle East to Great Britain and by evacuating the entire army from the USSR and accused the General of buying a gold cigarette case with army funds. The accusations are endless and border on the absurd. Anders is, for example, said to have left 30,000 British uniforms in Russia so as to be able to blame it on Berling. Klimkowski also charged that Anders asked the Soviets not to send him recruits who were not ethnic Poles. According to Klimkowski, Anders wanted to have him killed but was unable to find anyone willing to do it. The most absurd of Klimkowski's claims, which totally undermines his credibility, was that General Anders collaborated with Churchill in arranging the airplane crash which killed Sikorski. Klimkowski's book illustrates the length to which the Communist authorities would go to smear Anders.

In spite of, or maybe even because of, the official propaganda campaign against him, General Anders remained to the majority of Poles the symbol of anti-Communist resistance and of an uncompromising commitment to the cause of Polish independence. With the fall of the Communist regime in 1989 the public persona of Wladyslaw Anders underwent a dramatic change from villain to hero. His books, for the publication of which during a Communist era a publisher could end up in jail, have been published and filmed in Poland. In newspapers, magazines and television programs Anders is now depicted as the hero of Monte Cassino. His portrait appears on Polish post stamps. His widow, one of his daughters and his son-in-law participated in a ceremony to name one of the main squares in Warsaw "Anders Square." It is symbolic that Anders' official recognition coincided with the restoration of Polish sovereignty, a cause to which the General devoted most of his adult life.

**Without the Last Chapter...**

The fate of Anders and his soldiers reflects the tragedy of Poland in World War II, the fate of a nation caught between the totalitarian powers that represented the two greatest threats to man kind in the twentieth century. It epitomizes the dramatic fate of many nations which fell prey to Nazi genocidal tyranny and brutal Soviet dictatorship.

For all these countries World War II was hell. Not all of them, however, experienced as many different hells as soldiers of the Second Polish Corps and their families. Uprooted by force from their homes, they saw their loved ones dying of hunger and physical exhaustion in the concentration camps of the GULAG Archipelago, which extended from the Arctic Circle to the deserts of Central Asia and from Kolyma to Workuta. Many of them were imprisoned, interrogated and tortured by the Soviet secret police. Others sat in POW camps, unsure of their future and tempted by the Soviets with offers of collaboration.

In all these horrible circumstances these people did not lose hope and remained loyal to their cause. The news about the formation of the Polish Army set off an unprecedented mass journey of hundreds of thousand of men, women and children, in search of a piece of Poland. Reaching the army did not mean the end of hardships. Lack of housing, shortages of fuel and food, as well as rampant epidemics took a heavy toll of the trekkers' lives. One could be sure how long the Soviets would tolerate an independent Polish Army on their soil. The mysterious disappearance of twelve thousand officers and the discovery of their bodies in the Katyn forest haunted Anders' soldiers for the rest of their lives.

On their way home, people who had just come out of the Arctic Circle and the ever-frozen Siberian tundra were thrown into the heat of the Middle Eastern desert. Here they found themselves between a British imperial policy and the Jewish-Arab conflict, which they could barely comprehended. At the same time, what they thought to be their final destination - an independent Poland - was becoming more distant. The shadow of the Soviet Union overcast the skies over Central Europe. The Western Allies were closing their eyes.

Despite their doubts, Anders' soldiers fought on for the Allied cause, shedding their blood in the battles of Monte Cassino, Ancona and Bologna. The fall of the Warsaw uprising and the Yalta conference ruined their hopes. When victory finally arrived, it had a bitter taste for the Poles. Unwelcome in the Soviet-controlled Poland and unwanted in the West they had to face grim realities of every day life on the margins of the nations for whose freedom they had fought. To add insult to injury Anders' soldiers were excluded from the great victory parade in London.

Back in civilian life, all of them went their own ways. Scattered all over the globe, from London to Argentina and from Toronto to California, veterans of the Second Polish Corps tried to adjust to the ways and rules of their newly adopted homelands. Many of them spent the rest of their lives in abject poverty in London, rejecting the reality and sustaining the dream of their return to independent Poland. Others chose to acquire new skills and went to seek better fortune in the Western hemisphere. During all that time the Polish veteran community was driven by increasingly deep and bitter political divisions and personal feuds. Sometimes the intensity of these conflicts dwarfed their hatred toward the Soviet-imposed regime in Poland. At the same time most former soldiers whom the author met during the ten years of research on this book, agreed on one thing. There was one unshakable pillar of their beliefs and their trust, which remained beyond any criticism. This was the figure of their beloved commander, General Wladyslaw Anders.

Footnotes

1. NA L53732.
2. S.W. Slowes, The Road to Katyn: a Soldier's Story (Oxford, UK; Cambridge, Mass.: Blackwell Publishers, 1992), p. 199.
3. H. Macmillan, War Diaries: Politics and War in the Mediterranean (New York, 1984), p. 390.
4. J. Czapski, The Inhuman Land (London, 1951), p. 174.
5. An Interview with Hankey.
6. Together with five other generals and 70 other staff officers, Zaron, Armia Andersa, p. 280.
7. J. Klimkowski, Bylem adiutantem generala Andersa (Warsaw, 1959). It was published by the Ministry of National Defense.
8. An interview with Mrs. Anders.
9. Beria to Stalin (July 24, 1942) in Armia Polska w ZSRR 1941-1942, p. 98.
10. Interviews with Racieski, Romanowski and Lubienski.

# BIBLIOGRAPHY

## I. ARCHIVES

American Joint Distribution Committee Archives, New York
Jerusalem [AJDC]

General Sikorski Historical Institute, London [GSHI]

Hoover Institute, Stanford, California [HI]
Ambasada USSR
Anders collection
Borkowski
Buzkowski
Mikolajczyk
MSZ
PSZ

Jewish Agency Archive, Jerusalem [JAA].

National Archive, Washington, D.C. [NA]
OSS files
Poland
Palestine
Middle East

Public Records Office, Kew (England),
Colonial Office [CO]
Foreign Office [FO]
Prime Minister [PREM]
War Office [WO]

Tsentral'nyi Arkhiv Ministerstva Oborony Rossiiskoi Federatsii (Central Archive of the Ministry of Defense of the Russian Federation), Moscow [TsAMO]
collection (fond) 280

## II. PUBLISHED PRIMARY SOURCES

Armia Polska w ZSRR 1941-1942 (ed.) W. Materski (Warsaw, 1992).

Correspondence between the Chairman of the Council of Ministers of the U.S.S.R. and the Presidents of the U.S.A. and the Prime Ministers of Great Britain during the Great Patriotic War of 1941-1945 (Moscow, 1957).

Documents on Polish-Soviet Relations, 1939-1945, v. I (London: Heinemann, 1961); v. II (London, 1967).

Dokumenty i materialy po istorii sovetsko-pol'skikh otnoshenii, (eds.) I.A. Khrenov, N. Gasiorowska-Grabowska, v. VII (Moscow, 1973).

Katy : Dokumenty ludobójstwa. Dokumenty i materia y archiwalne przekazane Polsce 14 pa dziernika 1992 r. (Warsaw, 1992).

Katyn: dokumenty zbrodni, v. I (Warsaw, 1995).

Konflikty polsko-sowieckie 1942-1944 (ed. W. Roszkowski) (Warsaw, 1993).

Perepiska Predsedatelia Soveta Ministrov SSSR s Prezidentami SShA i Premer Ministrami Velikobritanii vo Vremia Velikoi Otechestvennoi Voiny 1941-1945 gg. (Moscow, 1957), v. I-II.

Polskie Sily Zbrojne w II wojnie swiatowej v. II, pt. 2 (London, 1975).

Sovetsko-angliiskie otnosheniia vo vremia Velikoi Otechestvennoi voiny 1941-1945 (Moscow, 1983), v. I.

Vneshnaia politika Sovetskogo Soiuza v period Otechestvennoi voiny. Dokumenty i materialy (Moscow, 1944), v. I.
Anders, W., An Army in Exile (London: Macmillan, 1949).
Anders, W., Bez ostatniego rozdzialu (Newton, 1950).
Anders, W. Hitler's Defeat in Russia (Chicago: Henry Regnery, 1953)
Bohusz-Szyszko, Z., "General broni Wladyslaw Anders" in General Wladyslaw Anders: Zycie i chwala (London, 1970).
Casper, B., With the Jewish Brigade (London, 1947).
Cazalet, V.A. With Sikorski to Russia (London: Curwen Press, 1942)
Churchill, W., The Hinge of Fate (Cambridge, MA, 1950).
Churchill, W., The Second World War, v. V Closing the Ring (Boston, 1951).
Ciechanowski, J. Defeat in Victory (Garden City: Doubleday, 1947)
Ciechanowski, J., "Armia Polska w Rosji w Swietle dziennika Szefa Sztabu z 1942 r." Zeszyty Historyczne (Paris), v. LVII (1991).
Czapski, J., The Inhuman Land (London, 1951).
Czapski, J., Wspomnienia Starobielskie (n.p., 1945).
Eden, A., The Memoirs of Anthony Eden, v. III (Boston: Houghton Mifflin, 1965).
Harriman, A., Special Envoy (London: Hutchinson 1976)
Klimkowski, J. AAdjiutatem Gen. Andersa, Wydawnic Ministerstwa Obrny Narodowej 1959
Kot, S., Conversations wiith the Kremlin and Dispatches from Russia (New York: Oxford UP, 1963).
Kukiel, M.Six Years of Struggle for Independence (Newtown, 1947)
Lane, A.B., I Saw Poland Betrayed: an American Ambassador Report to American People (Boston, 1965).
Macmillan, H., The Blast of War (New York: Harper & Row, 1968).
Macmillan, H., War Diaries: Politics and War in the Mediterranean (New York, 1984).
Moats, A.-L., Blind Date with Mars (Garden City: Doubleday, 1943).

Mikolajczyk, S., The Rape of Poland: Pattern of Soviet Aggression (New York: Whittlesey House, 1948).
Raczynski, E. Allied Wartime Diplomacy (London, 1962)
Rawicz, S., The Long Walk (London: Constable, 1956).
Retinger, J., Memoirs of an Eminence Grise (Brighton: Susex UP, 1972).
Rozek, E. J., In Allied London Boulder, 1989
Rozen, L., Cry in the Wilderness, a short history of a chaplain, activities and struggles in Soviet Russia during the World War II (New York, 1966).
Rudnicki, K., Na polskim szlaku (Wspomnienia z lat 1939-1947) (London, 1983).
Rudnicki, K. Last of the War Horses (London, 1974)
Sagajllo, W. Man in the Middle (London: Leo Cooper, 1984)
Senger, Gen. F. Neither Fear Nor Hope (Presedio, 1989)
Slowes, S.W., The Road to Katyn: a Soldier's Story (Oxford, UK; Cambridge, Mass: Blackwell, 1992).
Virski, F., My Life in the Red Army (New York: Macmillan, 1949)
Zamorski, K., Telling the Truth in Secret (London: Poets and Painters Press, 1994).

## III. SECONDARY SOURCES

Abarinov, V., Katynskii Labirynt (Moscow, 1991).
Allon, Yigal, Making of Israel's Army (London: Vallentine, 1970)
Ascherson, N., The Struggles for Poland (New York: Random House, 1987).
Berberyusz, E., Anders Spieszony (London, 1992).
Bertold, W., Von Himmel zur Holle (Bayreuth, 1977).
Blumenson, Martin, Mark Clark (New York: Congdon & Weed, 1984)
Bond, Harold, Return to Cassino (Garden City, 1964)
Brenner, L., The Iron Wall: Zionist Revisionism from Jabotinsky to Shamir (London: Zed Books, 1984).
Bryk, A., "The Holocaust--Jews and Gentiles in memory of the Jews of Pacanow," Polin, v. II (1987).

Charlton, M., The Eagle and the Small Birds. Crisis in the Soviet Empire: From Yalta to Solidarity (Chicago, 1984).
Dallin, A., Soviet Russia's Foreign Policy 1939-42 (New Haven, 1942).
Davies, N., Heart of Europe: A Short History of Poland (Oxford, 1984).
Davies, N., God's Playground: a History of Poland, v. II (New York: Columbia UP, 1982).
Davies, N.. Polonsky Jews in Eastern Poland and the USSR, 1939-6, (eds.) (Houndmills, Basingstoke, Hampshire: Macmillan, 1991).
Ellis, J., Cassino, the Hollow Victory: The Battle for Rome, January-June 1944 (London, 1984).
Engel, D. Facing a Holocaust. U.of NC Press, Chapel Hill)
Engel, D., In the Shadow of Auschwitz: the Polish government-in-exile and the Jews, 1939-1942 (Chapel Hill: Univ. of North Carolina Press).
Feldman, J., Wojciechowski, Z., "Poland and Germany: The Last Ten Years," in Poland's Place in Europe (ed.) Z. Wojciechowski (Poznan, 1947).
Garlinski,J., Poland in the Second World War (New York: Hippocrene Books, 1985).
General Anders (eds.) J.L. Englert, K. Barbarski (London, Instytut Polski i Muzeum im. Gen. Sikorskiego, 1989).
Gefen, Abba., Unholy Alliance (Yuva Tal Tel Aviv 1973)
Gilbert, M., Winston S. Churchill, v. VII Road to Victory (London, 1986).
Graham, D., Bidwell, Sh., Tug of War: the Battle for Italy, 1943-1945 (New York, 1986).
Gross, J., Revolution From Abroad: the Soviet Conquest of Poland's Western Ukraine and Western Belorussia (Princeton, N.J., Princeton UP, 1988).
Gutman, I. & Krskowski, S. Unequal Victims (New York: Holocaust Library, 1986)
Hamzavi, A., Persia and the Powers, an account of diplomatic relations, 1941-1946 (London, New York: Hutchinson & Co., 1946).
Hapgood, D., Richardson, D., Monte Cassino (New York, 1984).

Irving, D. Accident, the Death of General Sikorski (London: Kimber, 1967)
James, R.R. Victor Cazalet, A Portrait (London: Hamish Hamilton, 1976)
Keegan, P., Six Armies in Normandy (London, 1982).
Kennedy, R.H., The German Campaign in Poland, 1939 (Washington: Dept. of the Army, 1956).
Kersten, K., Repatriacja ludnosci polskiej po II wojnie swiatowej (Studium historyczne) (Wroclaw, Warsaw, Cracow, Gdansk, 1974).
Kitchen, M., British Policy towards the Soviet Union during the Second World War (Houndmills, Basingstoke, 1986).
Kukiel, M., General Sikorski: Zolnierz i maz stanu Polski walczacej (London: Instytut Polski, 1970).
Kukiek,M. Six Years of Struggle for Independence (Newtown, 1947)
Kurzman, D., The Race for Rome (Garden City, 1975).
Lane, A. I saw Poland Betrayed (London: Regency, 1949)
Lebedeva, N., "Operatsiia po 'razgruzke' spetslagerei" in Katynskaia drama: Kozel'sk, Starobel'sk, Ostashkov: sud'ba internirovanykh pol'skikh voennosluzhashchikh (ed.) O. V. Iasnov (Moscow, 1991).
Lewin, R. Hitler's Mistakes (London: Leo Cooper, 1984)
Linklater, E. Campaign in Italy (London: HMSO, 1951)
Loftus,J. The Belarus Secret (New York: Knopf, 1982)
Lukus, R. Forgotten Holocaust (Kent: University Press, 1986).
Madeja, W. Polia Second Corps and Italian Campaign 1943-1945 (Allentown, 1984)
Maisky, I.Who Helped Hitler, (London: Hutcinson, 1964)
Maisky, I. Memoirs of a Soviet Ambassador, (London: Hutchinson, 1967)
Majdalany, F.Monastery (London: Bodley Head, 1945)
Meirtchak, B. Jewish Military Casualties in Polish Army in WW II (Tel Aviv, 1995)
Nicholson, N. Alex (London: W & N, 1973)
Parsadanova, V.S., "Deportatsiia naseleniia iz Zapadnoi Ukrainy i Zapadnoi Belorusii v 1939-1941 gg.)" Novaia i Noveishaia Istoriia, 2 (1989).
Parsadanova, V.S., "K istorii katynskogo dela" Novaia i

Noveishaia Istoriia 3 (1990).
Parsadanova, V.S., "Armiia Andersa na territorii SSSR (1941-1942 gg.)" Novaia i Noveishaia Istoriia, 5 (1988)
Parsadanova, V.S., Sovetsko-pol'skie otnosheniia v Gody Velikoi Otechestvennoi voiny, 1941-1945 (Moscow, 1982).
Piekalkiewicz, J., Monte Cassino: Anatomy if the Battle (London, 1980).
Playfair, I.S.O., History of the Second World War. United Kingdom Military Series; The Mediterranean and the Middle East, v. VI, Pt. 2 (London, 1987).
Pobog-Malinowski, W., Najnowsza Historia Polski, III (London, 1960).
Poland in the British Parliament 1939-1945, I (ed.) W. Jedrzejewicz (New York, 1946).
Polansky, A. Great Powers and the Polish Question (London School, 1976)
Powers, T., The Man Who Kept the Secrets: Richard Helms and the CIA (New York, 1979).
Prazmowska, A., "Polish Refugees as Military potential: objectives of the Polish Government in Exile," in Refugees in the Age of Total War, (ed.) A. Bramwell (London, Boston: Unwin Hyman, 1988).
Rawski, T., "Poland Did Not Cease Existence in September," Contemporary Poland, 6 (1989).
Ready, J. L., Forgotten Allies: the military contribution of the colonies, exiled governments, and lesser powers to the Allied victory in World War II (Jefferson, N.C., 1985).
Ready, J.L., The forgotten axis: Germany's partners and foreign volunteers in World War II (Jefferson, N.C.: McFarland & Co., 1987).
Rostworowski, S.J., "Delegatura WiN za granica" Zeszyty Historyczne WiN-u III (1993).
Rothwell, V., Britain and the Cold War, 1941-1947 (London: J. Cape, 1982).
Rothschild, J., Return to Diversity: a Political History of East Central Europe since World War II (New York: Oxford UP, 1993).
Ryder, R., Oliver Leese (London, 1987).
Schochet, S., An Attempt to Identify the Polish-Jewish Officers Who Were Prisoners in Katyn (New York, 1989)

Seago, E., With the Allied Armies in Italy (London: Collins, 1945)
Stewart, R., Sunrise at Abadan: The British and Soviet Invasion of Iran, 1941 (New York: Praeger, 1988).
Sword, K., "British Reactions to the Soviet Occupation of Eastern Poland in September of 1939," Slavonic and East European Review, v. LXIX/1 (January 1991).
Sword, K., "The Prospects will not be bright: British Response to the Problem of the Polish
Sword, K. Sikorski, Soldier and Statesman (London: Orbis, 1990)
Recalcitrants, 1946-50," Journal of Contemporary History, v. 21, no. 4 (1986).
Slusarczyk, J., Stosunki polsko-radzieckie 1939-1945 (Warsaw, 1991).
Stewart, R., Sunrise at Abadan: The British and Soviet Invasion of Iran, 1941 (New York: Praeger, 1988).
Terlecki, O. Poles in the Italian Campaign (Warsaw. 1972)
Terlecki, O., General Sikorski (Cracow, 1983).
Terlecki, R., "The Jewish Issue in the Polish Army in the USSR and the Near East, 1941-1944," in Jews in Eastern Poland and the USSR, 1939-46, N. Davies, A. Polonsky (eds.) (Houndmills, Basingstoke, Hampshire: Macmillan, 1991).
Thompson, C., The Assassination of Winston Churchill (Gerrards Cross: Smythe, 1969).
Trevelyan, R., Rome '44: The Battle for the Eternal City (New York, 1982).
Umiastowski, R., Poland, Russia and Great Britain 1941-45: a Study of Evidence (London: Hollis & Carter, 1946).
Wankowicz, M., Monte Cassino (Warsaw, 1978).
Wat, A. My Century (London: Norton, 1990)
Watt, R.M., Bitter Glory: Poland and its Fate, 1918-1939 (New York, 1979)
Werth, A. Russia at War 1941-1945 (New York, Dutton, 1964).
Wilmot, C., Struggle for Europe (London: Reprint Society, 1954)
Woodward, E.L., British Foreign Policy in the Second World War II v. II (London, 1970).

Zaloga, S., The Polish Campaign, 1939 (New York: Hippocrene Books, 1985).
Zaron, P., Armia Andersa (Torun, 1996).

## IV. NEWSPAPERS AND JOURNALS

Daily Telgraph, Daily Worker, Dziennik Polski, Evening Standard (London), Foreign Relations of the United States, Izvestia (Moscow), Jerusalem Post, Jewish Chronicle (London), Jewish Telegraph Agency Bulletin, London Times, New York Times, Novaia i Noveishaia Istoriia 2 (1993), Nowy Swiat, Voenno-Istoricheskii Zhurnal 6 (1990)

## V. INTERVIEWS

Renata Anders*, John Bartosz, Harry Bau, Yehuda Ben David, Oscar Bergman, Jack Bernier, Romuald Bilek, Alexander Blum* Leon Bonder, Rudolph Buchta, Menachem Buchweitz, Julian Bussgang#, Wladek Cichy#, Rev. E. Cimala#, Lidia Ciolkosz, Wanda Cioth, David Cynberg, Joseph Czapski, Kamil Czarnecki*, Zygmunt Czarnecki, K.T.J. Czelny, Stanley Damazar*, Saul Diagoni, J. Dowgiallo, Walter Drzewieniecki, Leon Feit, Rev. W. Fieria#, Richard Gabrielczyk, Zbigniew Gasiewicz, Abba Gefan, Jerzy Giertych, Helena Gladkowska, Zelig Goldberg, Stefan Grayek, Mieczyslaw Hampel, Robin Hankey, Emil Holzer, Patrick Howarth, Z.K. Jagodzinski, Henryk Jedwab#, Jan Jurewicz, Merek Kahan*, Maria Karpowicz, Percy Kaye, J. Kessler, Adam Kilian, Michael Kleinerer, Witold Kociejowski#, George Kolczynski, Mrs. Kossakowska, Stefan Kowalik, Charles Kraina, S. Krakowski, George Kulczycki, David Laor, Leopold Licht, Richard Liebeskind, Y. Litvak, Ludwik Lubienski*, Meir Lustgarten#, J. Magiera, Julia Maston-Kicinski, Ezra Mendelson, Yaccov Merridor, Aniela Mieczyslawska, Richard Mossin, Valentina Parsadanova, Frank Pawlak, Julian Piech, Zbigniew Racieski*, Edward Raczynski*,

Bernard Rand, Shimon Redlich*, Frank Roberts, Jan Romanowski*, Mr. Romberger, Rabbi Pincus Rosengarten*, Adam Rozel, Frank Rozycki*, Klemens Rudnicki*, Philip Rybeck, Kazimierz Sabbat*, Witold Sagajlo, M. Sas-Skowronski, Henryk Scigala, Ludwig Seidenman, Arnold Shay, Joseph Sheldon, Z. Siemaszko, J. Silberstein, Mr. Spector, Keith Sword*, Antoni Szachnowski, W.E. Szkoda*, Ely Tavin*, Janusz Trepka, Arie Weinberg, Edward Wojtczak*, S.W. Wydenfield, Kazimierz Zamorski#, Mr. and Mrs. Alexander Zvielli*.

* indicates more than one interview
# indicates telphone interview

## SHORT BIOGRAPHIES

***Baginski, Kazimierz.*** Followed Mikolajczyk to postwar Poland but broke with him after they escaped from Poland. Had been an active member of Polish Peasants Party.

***Bakiewicz, Lt. Col. Wincenty.*** Prisoner in USSR, head of intelligence for Second Polish Corps, loyal to London and Anders, Klimkowski said a conspirator. His wife and sons were smuggled to postwar Italy. Died in London late 1980s.

***Beaumont-Nesbitt, Maj. Gen. F.C.*** British general supportive of Anders but feared he would stop fighting. He was chief of the liaison section, AFHQ. Favored Anders being name commander of all Polish forces.

***Beck, Col. Joseph.*** Prewar Polish Foreign Minister. He was responsible for taking Teschen from the Czechs. In 1939 fled to Romania and died there in 1943. Failed in an attempt to get control of the Polish Government in Exile. Worked with Jabotinsky before the war to get Jews out of Poland.

***Beria, Lavrenty Pavlovich.*** 1899-1953, Soviet Minister of Internal Affairs, head of NKVD, reported directly to Stalin. Executed after the death of Stalin.

***Berling, K.*** He stayed behind after the evacuations; treated by Anders as a traitor. He was removed as military commander of Polish Units in the Soviet Army, in 1944, and was given an insignificant administrative assignment with an impressive title. In 1953, his role was further reduced as he was appointed Deputy Minister of state farms and agriculture. In 1962, Berling's name ceased to appear in the U.S. State Department list of important persons in Poland. He reached his pinnacle in 1944 and suffered a rapid career fall thereafter. In November 1943, he received the "Order of Lenin and eight months later he was relieved of his command. He died in 1980.

***Bielecki, Dr. Thadeuz.*** Leader of National Democrats and their Representative in the Sikorski government; far right of the far right.

***Boruta-Spiechowicz, General Mierczyskaw.*** Sympathetic to Jews. Friction with Anders and ultimately transferred to Scotland. Beria calls him an anglophile. First C.O. of 5th Division. Elected repatriation after war, one of three Second Corps general to do so. Claimed to dislike postwar Warsaw government but felt he must cooperate. Was said to be inclined to cooperate with the Russians.

***Boy-Zelenski, Tadeusz.*** Executed by the Germans. Journalist and academic, criticized for writing for a pro-Soviet newspaper.

***Buchweitz, Menachem.*** Jewish officer attached to the Documents Bureau. Worked with Poles on anti-Soviet propaganda. Became an officer when the Army was in the Soviet Union. He stayed in Palestine and didn't go to Italy. A retired judge living in Israel.

***Cazalet, Col. Victor.*** British liaison to Sikorski and died in same crash. Member of Parliament. Accompanied Sikorski to Moscow in 1941. Visited Polish forces in Middle East with Sikorski in 1943. Anti-Churchill. Was concerned for the plight of Jews, Poles and refugees. Christian fundamentalist and Zionist.

***Cichy, Wladek.*** He was a publicist for Polish Army with Czapski and Raciecki. One of a few protestants in an important position in Anders' Army. Was aide to commander of 6th Division when evacuated to Iran. Worked with Anders postwar, in propaganda campaign. Maintains Anders was very involved in postwar underground. He says Anders was predisposed to helping Jews.

***Czapski, Joseph.*** One of the founders of Kultura, author of *Inhumand Land*, he was strongly anti-Communist. Lived in France and Switzerland until his death in 1990. Famous as an artist. Well respected.

***Duch, Maj. Gen. Bronislaw.*** He replaced Kopanski as C.O. of 3rd Division in Italy. He commanded a division in France in 1940 and lost 45% of his men. Was not a prisoner of the Soviets. Buried at Monte Cassino. Very popular with the soldiers.

***Dagoni, Shaul.*** Born Shaul Lundfish, a physician who worked as hospital administrator in prewar Poland and same function in Italy with Anders and in Israel after the war. Very supportive of Anders.

***Dudzinski, Col. Kazimierz.*** Supported Berling, imprisoned at Latrun. Pro USSR. Parsadanova said he may have been an informer for USSR. With Berling he visited Anders the day he got out of prison.

***Rev. W. Fierla.*** First Protestant chaplain in Second Polish Corps. Implied discrimination against Protestants.

***Galadyk, Col. Jan.*** Known as a philo-Semite, headed group at Kultabanka. Before the war he was the commander of the Polish Military Academy. Previously attacked and then joined "Patriots".

***Gano, Lt. Col.*** Headed the Second Bureau for Sikorski and Sosnkowski. When the Second Bureau was dissolved after the war, became Deputy Chief of Staff. Replaced Col. Mayer.

***Gawlina, Bishop Jozef.*** Sikorski claimed he was a Pilsudskite and neither liked nor trusted him. Went to USSR after June 1941. Friendly to Jews and helped get them out of USSR. Klimkowski claimed he had Gawlina's support if Anders was to be arrested in the USSR. Member of National Council in 1941. General in army as were all Bishops.

***Hankey, Sir Robin.*** He was Anthony Eden's secretary in the 1930's. First Secretary in British Embassy in Warsaw, 1939. First Secretary in British Embassy in Iran when Anders' Army arrived from the USSR. Served in Romania during WW II as liaison with the Polish Government in Exile. After the war he headed the Northern Dept of the Foreign Office and was concerned with the Polish Resettlement Corps. Charge'd' Affairs in Warsaw 1945, returned to the foreign office to head the Northern Dept.

***Harriman, W. Averell.*** U.S. Ambassador to USSR, 1943- 1946. Author of *Special Envoy*. He was FDR's personal envoy to U.K..

***Harvey, Oliver*** 1893-1968. Worked in the Foreign Office from 1919 until 1954. Under secretary 1943-46.

***Hulls, Col. L.R.*** British Liaison officer attached to Anders, obviously an intelligence officer.

***Jabotinsky, Vladimer.*** A Russian Jew and leader of Irgun, planned an invasion of Palestine, but aborted because of the war. He was Begin's mentor. Died in 1940

***Januszajtis, General Marian.*** 1889-1971. Was a member of Pilsudski's legions. Was a prisoner of the Soviets. He was a National Democrat, but Retinger says he was fair and impartial. The NKVD objected to his being named head of the Polish Army in the Soviet Union.

***Kahan, Mier (Merek).*** A soldier in Anders' Army, he did not go to Italy with the Army. He "disappeared in Sept 1943". He claims he was ill in Iraq for one year. A strong advocate of a Jewish Legion in the Polish Army. Vague answers to question on working for Polish intelligence. Prewar he was editor of a Yiddish language newspaper in Poland. Says he was discharged from the Polish Army in 1943.

***Karski, Jan .*** Author of *Secret State,* was courier between Poland and the West. Postwar professor in Washington, DC.

***Klimecki, Gen. Tadeusz.*** Sikorski's Chief of staff. Died in same accident as Sikorski. Rumored to have conducted a purge in Anders' Army.

***Klimkowski, Jerzy.*** ADC to Anders, tried to revolt against Anders in USSR. Was known as opportunist. Reported to NKVD. Imprisoned in Middle East. Led conspiracy to oust Sikorski. After prison was leader and then anti-Patriots. Led "Future Poland" group.

***Koc, Col. Adam.*** Was a part of the conspiracy to replace Sikorski with General Tadeusz Klimecki. President of the Bank of Poland, Minister of finance. Alleged Anders sold out o the Soviets. He served with Pilsudski and was a friend of Smigly. He started the Fascist "Camp of National Unity". He was a threat to Sikorski's leadership.

***Kopanski, Gen. Stanslaw.*** 1895-1976. Was the first commanding officer of the Independent Carpathian Brigade. He is buried at Monte Cassino. Commanded the Polish

Resettlement Corps. In 1944 was appointed chief of the general staff under Sosnkowski, after the death of Klimecki. A very popular and capable commander.

***Kot, Amb. Stanislaw.*** A well known scholar and educator in prewar Poland, belonged to the same political party, the Peasants' Party, as his mentor and supporter, General Sikorski. Even the most ardent critics of Kot's roles as Ambassador and Minister acknowledge his excellent prewar reputation as professor of history at Cracow University.

***Kozlowski, Gen. Leon.*** Prewar Polish Prime Minister, fled from the USSR to Germany. Sentenced to death as a traitor, he was killed in a bombing of Berlin.

***Kukiel, Gen. Marian.*** 1895-1973. Associate of Kot and Sikorski. Foreign minister in Polish Government in Exile after Raczynski. Minister of Defense in Mikolajczyk government.

***Lange, Prof. Oscar.*** Born in Poland naturalized American, dropped American citizenship and became Warsaw's Ambassador to the U.S. Clearly a Communist, State department said he's not trust worthy.

***Lis, Major.*** Went to the Villa according to Slowes. Known to be very hostile towards Russians. Part of the group that wanted to replace Anders with General Tokarzewski-Karaszewicz.

***Lubienski, Captain Ludwig.*** Was a special duty officer assigned to Anders in June 1944. He was discharged from the Polish Resettlement Corp in 1947 and worked for Anders until March 1958. For the next 10 years he was European Director of the Polish American Immigration and Relief Committee based in Munich. He was production director for Radio Free Europe from 1968-1979.

***Lubomirski, Prince Stefan.*** Prewar counselor at Polish Embassy in Berlin. Worked for Polish Government in Exile.

***Lubomirsky, (Prince) Capt. Eugene.*** Aide to General Anders, interpreter and friend of Anders. Mrs. Anders calls him her husband's closest friend. Land owning family. Captured by Russians and sentenced to 7 years.

***Maisky, Ivan.*** Soviet Ambassador to United Kingdom, 1932-1943. Signed Sikorski-Maisky Agreement in 1941, which released Poles from Soviet prisons. Defected to United Kingdom after the war. Author of *Who Helped Hitler?*

***Mikolajczyk, Stanislaw.*** 1901-1966. Born in Germany, was named Prime Minister of the Polish Government in London on July 14, 1943. He resigned November 24, 1944. He was the head of the Peasant's Party. Enlisted in the Army as a private. Sikorski named him Minister of Interior. Became Vice-Primier of Warsaw government but fled from Poland in 1946.

***Odzierzynski, Gen. Roman.*** Commanded Polish artillery at Monte Cassino. In 1949 he was Prime Minister and Minister of Defense in London Exile Government. Retinger calls him an extremist with influence over Anders.

***Okulicki, Colonel.*** Romanowski said Okulicki was relieved as chief of staff in Russia because he was so anti-Russian he could not work with them. He said there was no hostility between Anders and Okulicki and Okulicki's nerves were possibly damaged in the Soviet Union. Okulicki was appointed commander of the 7th Division but resigned by mutual agreement with Anders. The 7th Division was never fully manned as a division and had never been operational, permitting Okulicki to take special assignments for Anders including working with the Irgun. He often argued with Anders and was put in charge of the training program in the Middle East and hated this assignment. He worked in training Polish Jews before the war and had been sympathetic to the Jews in the Polish Army.

***Panfilov, Gen. A.P.*** Russian, Associate Chief of Staff, and Intelligence Chief of Red Army. Chief Soviet liaison officer to the Polish Army.

***Parsadanova, Prof. Valentina S.*** Russian expert on Polish-Russians relations, retired in Moscow. Very opinionated, generally anti-Semitic. Interviewed in Moscow 7-17-93

***Pilsudski, Marshal Joseph.*** 1867-1935. See, biography by Joseph Rothschild, *Born in Wilno.*

***Pstrokonski, Col. Stanislaw.*** Anders placed him in second group in Middle East. Kot called him unfit and an anti-Semite. Kept Jews out of evacuation. Romanowski calls him a traitor.

***Racieski, Zbigiew.*** A prisoner in the USSR, he didn't go to Italy, instead was sent to England after staying for awhile in Palestine. Not an officer, he says the work he did in the Army would be usual for a middle rank officer. He was in PR with Czapski. Verified claim that he often had a private breakfast with Anders.

***Raczkiewicz, Wladyslaw.*** 1885-1947, President Polish Government in Exile 1939-1947. Prior to war was Minister of Interior and speaker of senate. Reluctantly named Sikorski as Prime Minister and Commander in Chief of Polish forces.

***Raczynski, Amb. (Count) Edward.*** Poland's Ambassador to United Kingdom, 1935-1945. Council of three with Anders and Arciszewski. Pilsudskite, after war Polish advisor to British Ministry of labor. Wartime Foreign Minister until replaced in July 1943.

***Radziwill, Prince Janusz.*** Former senator and chairman of Foreign Relations Committee, prewar. Refused to head a quisling government, suggestion he was on German "white list". Was prisoner of Soviets but sent abroad, prisoner exchange. Slowes says he received favorable treatment.

***Rakowski, Gen. Bronislaw.*** Had been Anders' chief of staff. Commander of second brigade in Italy.

***Retinger, Dr. Joseph.*** 1888-1960; Sikorski's secretary and advisor, no official role in Polish Government in Exile; was Charge'd'Affairs in USSR while waiting for Kot. He was anti-Kot.

***Roberts, Sir Frank K.*** 1907- ; British Foreign Service Officer 30 years, 1937-1945, 1945-47, Minister in Moscow.

***Romanowski, Jan.*** Before being released, he was interrogated by a Polish speaking Russian officer who later became the Russian liaison to the Polish Army. Although he didn't join the Army until September 1, he was only the 13th officer to join the newly formed army.

His first assignment was as an aide to Colonel Okulicki, who was Anders' Chief of Staff. Okulicki was transferred to the 7th Division, but Romanowski stayed behind to be aide to the new Chief of Staff, General Szyszko-Bohusz, in March 1942.

He left the USSR at the end of the second evacuation. An aide to General Anders died in Iran and Romanowski was named to replace him and he served as an aide to General Anders until he left the Army after the war.

***Romer, Tadeusz.*** 1894-1978. Succeeded Kot as Ambassador to the USSR and received the notice from Stalin that he was breaking off diplomatic relations. He was Foreign Minister in Mikolajczyk's government in London.

***Rosengarten, Rabbi Pincus.*** Chaplain at Kultabanka, He "buried" all Jewish casualties in the Second Corps, in Italy. Lives in Jerusalem.

***Rudnicki, Gen. Klemens,*** a/k/a Joseph Ruminski. Was at Villa and told Anders. In charge of last evacuation. Author of *Last of the War Horses, 1897-1993.* Commanded a division.

***Savery, Frank.*** 1883-1965, British Foreign Office, Consul to the British Ambassador Poland, 1939-1945.

***Schwartzbart, Dr. Ignacy.*** Was one of the two Jewish members of the Polish National Council. Postwar he conducted the Office of Polish-Jewish Affairs.

***Seideman.*** A Polish-Jewish lawyer and nephew of the well known Bundist leader Henrik Ehlich, was appointed as a legal advisor to the Polish Embassy in Kubyshev. He served in this capacity from the time of his release under the amnesty agreement.

***Seyda, Dr. Marjan.*** National Democrat/Rep. Endcja in Sikorski Cabinet, headed small group broke away from National Democrat, supported Sikorski unlike other National Democrats, anti-German.

***Slowes.*** Resident of Israel, author of *Road to Katyn.* Served as General Anders' dentist after having been a prisoner in the USSR. After successful service in the Second Polish Corps he emigrated to Israel where he currently lives.

***Sokolnicki, Henry.*** (or Henryk) Polish Government in Exile consul in Jerusalem 1944, was head of Polish Embassy in USSR between Kot & Romer. British respected and liked him.

***Sosnkowski***, K. Became the Commander-in-Chief of all Polish Forces after the death of General Sikorski. He was deemed to be the most anti-Communist of the London Poles. On two occasions, he resigned when he didn't agree with the decisions of the Polish Prime Minister. The first time was in 1941, when Sikorski signed a treaty with the USSR without settling the USSR-Poland border issue. He was removed from office in September of that year at the demand of the British.

***Strassburger, Dr. Henrik.*** Was postwar Poland's Ambassador to U.K. but resigned. Prewar he was Minister of Finance. Minister for Polish affairs in Middle East. No party but he supported Mikolajczyk on Middle East. Set up a Commission of Criminals in Middle East.

***Stronski, Prof. Stanislas.*** Rep. Endcja in Sikorski government his son was Captain worked in Anders' office. Former Minister of Propaganda, present at Sikorski-Maisky signing. Made pro-Jews statements, said he modified his anti-Semitism.

***Sulik, General Mikolaj.*** Commanded the 5th Division in Italy. Anders didn't like him, he was promoted to general by Sosnkowski. Daughter married Polish exile president Sabbat.

***Szyszko-Bohusz, General Zygmunt.*** Led Polish forces at Narvik. Popular among soldiers. Commanding officer of the 5th Division, later Anders' Chief of Staff. Chief of Polish military mission sent to Russia in 1941. Well liked by Anders, became acting commanding officer of the Second Corps when Anders was acting Commander in Chief.

***Shertok.*** Was head of the political department of the Jewish agency, and become the second Prime Minister of Israel. He advised Mikolajczyk to flee Poland as his life was threatened.

***Tavin, Ely.*** Chief of Irgun intelligence, 1945-46. Insider in the Irgun. He had been a prisoner of the Haganah for 6 months. At time of his death in 1994 he was director of the Jabotinsky institution in Tel Aviv.

***Tokarzewski-Karaszewicz, General Michal.*** Conspired to replace Anders with himself. In 1943 he was second in command. He commanded the Third Polish Corps. First commander of the Home Army. A known Pilsudskite.

***Tyszkiewicz, Count Stefen.*** Became Charge'd'Affairs in Iran for Poland. When prisoner of Soviets he was held in a separate compound for aristocrats. Was liaison to Italian King.

***Tyszynski, Col.*** Slowes calls him relative of Anders. He went to the Villa and accepted orders from Russians.

***Wasilewska, Wanda.*** 1905-1964. In 1944 President of the Union of Polish Patriots, born in Poland became a Soviet citizen and supported Soviet claim to eastern Poland. A colonel in the Red Army. In 1940 Stalin asked her to form a Polish Army.

## INDEX